To our families

Contents

Preface

A revolution is occurring in corporate America. Increased global competition and rapid technological change are prompting major organizational restructurings and producing fundamental industry realignments. Many firms are shifting from traditional organizational structures (manufacturing, marketing, and distribution) to flatter, more process-oriented designs. And the pace of change shows no signs of slowing.

In today's environment, managers are under increasing pressure to address organizational issues and manage organizational change. Narrow technical expertise in a single area—be it operations, accounting, finance, information systems, or marketing—is no longer sufficient. Firms now attack problems with focused, cross-functional teams. To be effective, managers must develop skills that bridge traditional functional areas. And because an inappropriate organizational design can torpedo even the most brilliant business strategy, managers must also know how to structure an organization that will enable the firm to reach its value potential.

Our objective in writing this book is to provide an approach to organizational structure that supports the firm's business strategy and maximizes shareholder value. We cover important management topics such as assigning decision-making authority among employees, developing an effective performance evaluation system, creating incentives through compensation plans, and resolving transfer pricing disputes among divisions. Our approach has at its foundation the most recent economic research and draws on numerous examples from the business press as well as from our own experience.

We are not, of course, the first to recognize the importance of corporate structure or to offer advice on how to improve it. The business section of any good bookstore displays a virtually endless array of prescriptions, such as benchmarking, empowerment, total quality management, reengineering, balanced scorecards, outsourcing, teaming, venturing, matrix organizations, just-in-time production, and downsizing. The authors of these books would strongly agree that the firm's organizational structure and the associated policies adopted by management have profound effects on performance and shareholder value. And they will buttress their recommendations with accounts of firms that followed their advice and achieved fabulous successes.

The problem with such approaches, however, is that they tend to focus on a particular facet of the organization—such as quality control, employee empowerment, or the compensation system—to the virtual exclusion of all others. Moreover, they offer little guidance as to which tools are most appropriate in which circumstances. In fact, their implicit assumption (if not their explicit assertion) is that a particular technique can be successfully adopted by any company. The reality, however, is that many of these prescriptions are internally inconsistent and will create more problems than they solve. The business literature to date has thus failed to provide managers with an integrated approach to identifying and resolving organizational problems.

Our book is designed to provide a systematic, comprehensive framework for analyzing organizational issues, one that can be consistently applied in addressing problems and in structuring more effective organizations. In particular, this book will help managers understand the following:

- How the elements of the business environment (technology, competition in both factor and product markets, and regulation) drive the firm's choice of strategy.
- How strategy and the business environment affect the firm's choice of organizational design—what we call *organizational architecture*.
- How the three key elements of organizational architecture—the assignment of decision-making authority, the performance mea-

surement system, and the compensation system—can be structured to allow managers to achieve their strategic objectives.

- How corporate policies in areas such as planning, finance, accounting, marketing, information systems, operations, compensation, and human resources are interrelated; why it is critically important that they be coordinated; and how to coordinate them.
- Why an organizational architecture that allows one firm to be wildly successful can cause another firm to fail; why one size doesn't fit all.

The framework presented in this book builds on decades of work by researchers from a variety of disciplines. Some of the key underlying concepts presented here were originally developed by other scholars. We are particularly indebted to our colleagues, present and former, at the University of Rochester's William E. Simon Graduate School of Business—especially Michael Jensen and the late William Meckling, whose pioneering work in organization theory kindled our own research. This book came about at Don Chew's suggestion that we rework our textbook (*Managerial Economics and Organizational Architecture*, 2d ed., New York: McGraw-Hill, 2001) for a management readership, and his editorial influence has improved both books.

We have used many real-world examples throughout the book. These examples come from our own consulting experience and research, as well as from the financial press and books written by other individuals. To make the book more readable, we have avoided extensive referencing and footnoting in the text. At the end of the book, we list key sources and references. We have tried to be comprehensive in these citations. However, given that we have literally spent years developing the analysis and compiling examples, it is difficult to recognize everyone who influenced our thinking and ultimately the material in this book (although omissions do not expunge the debt).

CHAPTER 1

Organizational Architecture: The Three-Legged Stool

*W*hy does the organization of the firm matter? Because a poor design can lead to lost profits and even result in the failure of the institution. History is replete with examples of firms—Enron and Barings Bank spring to mind—whose inadequate organizational designs had detrimental effects, sometimes spectacularly so. And what of the countless firms whose organizational structures are not crippling but whose value could be greatly enhanced by a revamping? In this chapter, we introduce the concept of organizational architecture, which comprises three elements that are major determinants of the success of a firm:

- *The assignment of decision-making authority*
- *The systems for evaluating the performance of both individuals and business units*
- *The methods of compensating individuals*

Like the legs of a stool, the three components of organizational architecture are highly interdependent. Changing one leg without careful attention to the others can topple the stool—and the firm. The

1

appropriate architecture for a firm depends on the business environ-
ment facing that firm and must be designed to complement the firm's
business strategy.

Design Flaws

Enron's $50 billion bankruptcy filing in December 2001 is the most
spectacular business failure to date. Enron's corporate history is well
known: The "sleepy, regulated natural gas company" of the 1980s
transformed itself in the 1990s by embracing a New Economy corporate culture with a flatter management structure, a dramatically
lower reliance on hard assets, and an entrepreneurial, risk-taking environment open to creative and unconventional products and practices.
Market cap reached a peak of nearly $70 billion in August 2000, and
the company was everybody's favorite glamour story. But then the
wheels came off, ending in the bankruptcy filing, a near-total evap-
oration of market cap, and the draining of $1 billion of assets from
employee retirement accounts.

What went wrong? According to *Business Week,*

> Enron didn't fail just because of improper accounting or alleged
> corruption at the top. . . . The unrelenting emphasis on earnings
> growth and individual initiative, coupled with a shocking absence
> of the usual corporate checks and balances, tipped the culture
> from one that rewarded aggressive strategy to one that increas-
> ingly relied on unethical cornercutting. In the end, too much lee-
> way was given to young, inexperienced managers without the
> necessary controls to minimize failures. This was a company that
> simply placed a lot of bad bets on businesses that weren't so
> promising to begin with.

In short, Enron's problems were rooted in a fundamentally flawed
organizational design. At fault were three key aspects of the com-

pany's corporate structure. First, in the course of flattening its management structure, Enron ended up delegating too much decision-making authority to lower-level employees without retaining the appropriate degree of decision control. Second, performance was evaluated largely on near-term earnings growth. Third, the company offered enormous compensation to its top performers, which encouraged excessive risk taking. The internal risk management group was charged with reviewing deals, but the performance appraisals of the 180 employees in the group were based in part on the recommendations of the very people generating the deals. And the legal staff was decentralized throughout the organization, where members were vulnerable to pressures to meet their individual business units' performance targets. It may be years before all the facts of the Enron case are available, and there is obviously the near certainty of breaches in ethical behavior. Yet these breaches were arguably a product of Enron's organizational design.

The abrupt failure of Barings Bank in the 1990s stemmed from similar organizational problems. Francis and John Baring established Barings Bank in London in 1762. The bank prospered by financing international trade, and its influence grew to such an extent that the Duc de Richelieu observed in 1818, "There are six great powers in Europe: England, France, Prussia, Austria, Russia, and Barings Brothers." Barings came close to failure in 1890 and never regained its former preeminence, but it retained its reputation as a gilt-edged institution run primarily by members of the Baring family and owned principally by a charitable foundation.

In the first half of the 1990s, Barings expanded considerably, and a significant part of this expansion was a substantial East Asian securities business. In early 1995, the board of directors met to review the 1994 results. The bank had experienced a small increase in profits—a good result in what had been a dreadful year for most of its competitors—largely on the strength of its extremely profitable securities operation in Singapore. But on the afternoon of the board meeting, things changed dramatically. The Singapore branch's trading star, Nick Leeson, unexpectedly walked out of the office and disappeared, and it became clear that something was seriously amiss.

In principle, Leeson was engaged in a simple operation: arbitraging security prices (specifically on futures contracts on the Nikkei 225) between the Osaka Stock Exchange and the Singapore International Monetary Exchange. He should have been able to lock in a virtually riskless profit by selling securities on the exchange with the higher price and simultaneously buying equivalent securities on the exchange with the lower price. Although these price differences are typically small, if the volume of transactions is large enough, this activity can produce a significant arbitrage profit. But the securities Barings bought and those it sold were supposed to balance. The bank should not have faced any net exposure to price changes.

Yet what management found as they reviewed the bank's records was that Leeson had *bought* securities in both markets. In effect, he had made an enormous bet that security prices would rise. Instead, prices had fallen, and the aggregate losses totaled nearly $1.4 billion. The very solvency of the bank was at stake.

Leeson was able to engage in unauthorized trading because he could circumvent the bank's internal controls. The Singapore branch was small, and Leeson had effective authority over both trading and the branch's back office systems (bookkeeping, clearing, and settlement). He used that power to conceal his losses and disguise the true nature of his activities. For example, he apparently told senior management that a number of his trades were on behalf of clients. The bank's internal control systems failed to uncover the deceit. Ultimately, Leeson was sentenced to three years in prison. And Barings, Britain's oldest merchant bank, was sold to ING (the large Dutch financial institution) for £1. Barings's owners had lost their entire investment.

What caused the Barings collapse? A poorly designed organization. As *The Wall Street Journal* noted:

> What is emerging from the documents and from interviews with current and former Barings executives is a fatally flawed organization: one that ignored at least several warning signs going back not just weeks and months, but years; one that so wanted to ensure the continuation of profits from Singapore—which boosted bonuses—that it was reluctant to impose tight controls; one that had a deeply split staff, which ultimately may have contributed to its downfall.

Three general aspects of the bank's organization contributed to the failure: the broad range of authority and responsibilities granted to Leeson; gaps in the bank's systems for evaluating, monitoring, and controlling its employees; and certain aspects of the firm's compensation system.

First, Leeson had responsibility for both proprietary and customer trading in addition to effective control over the settlement of trades in his unit. Having such a broad scope of decision-making authority gave him the opportunity to bypass the bank's internal controls. As the *Financial Times* observed:

> In Singapore, Mr. Leeson was in the process of settling transactions as well as initiating them. A watertight line between dealing and operational responsibility, crucial to internal control, was missing.

In response to the Barings collapse, the Singapore exchange changed its rules to require member firms to use different traders for proprietary trading and customer business. It also prohibited the head of the trading section from taking charge of the settlement process.

Second, Leeson found ways to hide his losses and misrepresent his trades as customer trades. As we describe later in this chapter, and in fact throughout the book, a better-designed and better-executed performance measurement system would have identified these problems long before the solvency of the institution was jeopardized.

Third, the bank's compensation system not only encouraged Leeson to speculate but also gave senior managers almost no incentive to exercise tighter control over their star trader. Barings had traditionally paid out approximately 50 percent of its gross earnings in annual bonuses. Yet a system in which managers participate in annual profits but not in losses can encourage excessive risk taking. This perverse incentive is most pronounced when a small bet loses and the employee tries to make it up by doubling the bet. If this second bet also loses, the employee has a strong incentive to double up again and "go for broke."

In hindsight, it seems easy to identify elements of both the Enron and Barings organizations that, if they had been different, might have prevented these debacles. But the critical managerial question is whether one could reasonably be expected to identify these and other potential problems *before the fact* and to structure a more productive organization. We believe that the answer to this fundamental question is a resounding *yes*. Examining these issues requires a rich framework that can be applied on a consistent basis. In this book, we offer a comprehensive approach that identifies the three critical aspects of corporate organization:

- The assignment of decision-making authority within the company
- The systems that measure the performance of both individuals and business units
- The method of compensating individuals

Not coincidentally, these are the same three aspects of the organization that we identified as being poorly designed in both the Enron and Barings cases.

Organizational Architecture

We use the term *organizational architecture* to refer specifically to these three key aspects of the firm. We choose not to simply use *organization* because, in common usage, that term generally refers only to the hierarchical structure—that is, decision-making authority and reporting relationships—and ignores performance measurement and compensation systems. Using *organizational architecture* allows us to focus attention on all three elements of the organization.

There are no automatic systems either for assigning decision-making authority to employees or for motivating employees to make decisions that promote corporate objectives. Successful firms assign decision-making authority in ways that effectively link that authority with the information employees need if they are to make good decisions. These firms then bolster the linkage by ensuring that their performance measurement and compensation systems provide decision makers with appropriate incentives to make decisions that increase shareholder value. Depending on its specific circumstances, a firm will assign decision-making authority in different ways (decentralizing certain decisions but centralizing others) and will tailor its performance measurement and compensation systems accordingly.

Although successful firms focus on all three critical aspects of organizational architecture, no two firms are likely to adopt precisely the same architecture. In fact, optimal architectures generally differ among companies. These differences are not random but vary in predictable ways according to differences in the underlying characteristics of the companies themselves. For example, companies operating

7

in the same industry tend to develop similar architectures. If an important aspect of an industry's operating environment changes, most companies in that industry will react by adjusting their architectures.

Figure 1.1 depicts the factors that are most important in designing the optimal architecture for a given firm. At the top of the figure are aspects of the firm's *external business environment: technology, markets,* and *regulation.* These three factors—the technologies that affect product demand, methods of production, or information systems; the structure of the markets in which the firm operates (i.e., its competitors, customers, suppliers, and employees); and the regulatory constraints on its activities—will influence the firm's business *strategy.* By strategy, we mean the firm's primary operating goals (nonfinancial as well as financial): its sources of competitive advantage; its choice of industry, products, and services; its target customers; and its pricing policies.

The operating goals of the firm, as reflected in its business strategy, in turn affect the optimal organizational architecture. As the celebrated architect Louis H. Sullivan, designer of the first skyscraper and founder of the American school of architecture, once observed, "Form ever follows function." Applying the same principle within organizations, we see that significant changes in the business environment and hence in a firm's strategy will typically call for major changes in decision authority, performance measurement systems, and compensation plans.

A Question of Balance

Managers and other employees are extremely resourceful in devising methods to exploit the opportunities they face. But it is important to keep in mind that individuals respond to incentives—and that when incentives are structured inappropriately, employees can act in ways that destroy value. In setting corporate policies, managers must antic-

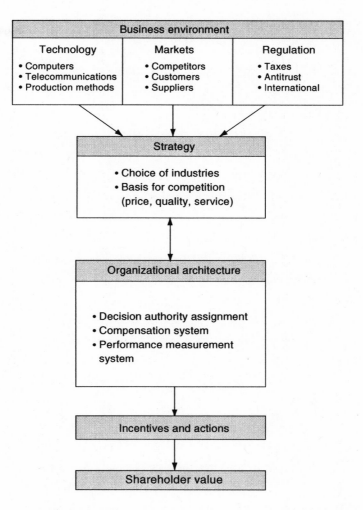

Figure 1.1 The determinants of strategy, organizational architecture, and firm value.

ipate undesirable outcomes. Changing a division from a cost center to a profit center will change employees' incentives, alter their decisions, and ultimately affect profitability. Neglecting to make the corresponding organizational adjustments can result in the utter failure of well-intentioned policies.

And no matter how change comes about, it is important to understand that the three components of organizational architecture are fundamentally interdependent. The performance evaluation systems and compensation plans determine the appropriate allocation of decision authority, and vice versa. For example, if decision authority is decentralized, it is important to have performance evaluation and compensation systems that can detect whether employees are making value-enhancing decisions and reward them for doing so. Similarly, if a firm adopts an incentive compensation plan, it is important that the employees have the decision authority to respond to the new incentives. In this sense, the components of organizational architecture are like the *three legs of a stool.* All three legs must be constructed in such a way that the stool is balanced and functional.

When the legs of the stool are not balanced, profitability can tumble. As an example, an airplane in the fleet of a major airline company was unexpectedly grounded for repairs. The nearest qualified mechanic was stationed at another airport. The decision authority to allow the mechanic to travel to make the necessary repairs lay with the mechanic's airport manager, whose compensation was tied to meeting his own budget rather than to the profits of the airline company. He refused to send the mechanic to fix the plane immediately because his budget would have been charged for the mechanic's overnight hotel bill. Instead, the mechanic was dispatched the next morning so that he would be able to return the same day. A multimillion-dollar aircraft was grounded overnight, costing the airline thousands of dollars. However, the mechanic's airport manager avoided a $100 hotel bill. Presumably, the mechanic would have been dispatched immediately if his manager had been rewarded on the overall profitability of the airline or, alternatively, if the decision authority had been granted to someone else who did have this objective.

The key is to design organizations that motivate employees to make value-increasing decisions. For example, suppose a firm links the CEO's bonus to earnings. A CEO who is retiring in two years might reduce R&D spending both this year and next in order to boost earnings and thereby increase his or her bonus. Five years hence, the firm's earnings will suffer because fewer new products will come on stream, but this CEO will be long gone. Recognizing these perverse incentives allows the firm to control them by basing part of the CEO's incentive compensation on the firm's stock price and by managing CEO succession so that decision authority is gradually transferred to the CEO's successor over the years prior to the CEO's final departure. A postretirement opportunity to serve on the board of directors can also lessen perverse incentives over the final years of a CEO's tenure.

Economic Darwinism: Survival of the Fittest

Charles Darwin might have seen the collapse of Barings Bank or Enron as an example of how competition tends to weed out the less fit. As described in *The Origin of Species,* natural history illustrates the principle of "survival of the fittest." In industry, we see *economic Darwinism* in operation as competition weeds out poorly designed organizations that fail to adapt. Competition in the marketplace creates strong pressures for efficient decisions—including efficient organizational decisions. If firms adopt inefficient, high-cost policies—including inappropriate organizational architectures—then competition will place strong pressures on these firms to either adapt or shut down. But while a well-crafted organizational architecture contributes to a firm's success, it does not guarantee success if the firm does not have a credible business strategy. The potential for value creation by a company that manufactures buggy whips is quite limited in today's world, no matter how well designed its organizational architecture may be.

Given a suitable business strategy, the choice of organizational architecture can have an important impact on profitability and value. An appropriate architecture lowers costs by promoting efficient production; it can also boost the prices customers are willing to pay by helping to ensure high-quality production, reliable delivery, and responsive service.

Benchmarking

In the biological systems that Darwin analyzed, the major forces at work are random mutations in organisms and shocks to the external environment (such as changes in weather). However, the changes that occur in economic systems are often purposeful and voluntary. In order to compete with Coca Cola, for example, Pepsi has copied many of Coke's practices. Pepsi spun off its fast-food chains (Taco Bell, KFC, and Pizza Hut) in order to focus on its core business—just as Coca Cola had done. Also, Pepsi is changing its network of bottlers. One analyst remarked, "Pepsi is starting to look a lot more like Coke." Similarly, General Motors eventually adopted Chrysler's cross-functional team approach to new model development.

This practice has been formalized as benchmarking. *Benchmarking* generally means observing companies that are doing something well and then emulating them. For example, a firm that is considering a change in its executive compensation plan will collect information on the compensation plans of other firms in its industry. This practice has obvious merit. Firms that survive in the marketplace tend to have strategies and architectures that fit their environment, and studying these firms has the potential to yield valuable insights—*Built to Last* by James Collins and Jerry Porras is based on this approach. But our analysis has at least two implications for effective benchmarking. First, different architectures are appropriate for different environments. When benchmarking, managers must look at firms that are facing similar environments, or they must take any differences into account when analyzing the benchmarked firms' policy choices. Second, it is important to view the architecture of another firm as a system of complements. Studying a single feature of another firm's architecture, such as its compensation system, without considering how that feature fits with the other elements of the firm's architecture, such as how it assigns decision authority, can lead to faulty conclusions.

Benchmarking occurs in less formal ways as well. If the cover article in *Fortune* describes an innovative inventory control system at Toyota, managers across the country—indeed, around the globe—will read it and ask, "Would that work in my company, too?" Undoubtedly, the managers with the strongest interest in adopting the new system will be those in firms that are currently suffering inventory problems. Some will adopt the new system successfully, but others may experience disastrous results because of unintended (though largely predictable) organizational side effects (such as Leeson's unchecked incentive for risk taking at Barings).

In some organizations, of course, changes do resemble Darwin's random mutations. Just for Feet operates more than ninety athletic footwear superstores. Its CEO, Harold Ruttenberg, says that he works by trial and error. Plenty of ideas have vanished like out-of-style sneakers. Gone are the in-store nursery and a $100,000 drive-through window. "Too busy for it," says Ruttenberg. "Things weren't well planned in the beginning. When I look back on it, it was just pure luck and a miracle that it worked." Firms sometimes adopt changes without a detailed understanding of their implications, but if the change is productive, it is likely to be exported to other locations. The more successful the company and its strategy, the more likely it is that its innovations will be copied by competitors.

Exporting Organizational Architecture around the Global Economy

In 1996, Tianjin Optical & Electrical Communication Group was a typical Chinese state-owned company. Although the electronics manufacturer boasted skilled technicians, mismanagement had left it on the brink of bankruptcy. Motorola, Inc., changed that. It offered to take on Tianjin Optical as a supplier, but only if Tianjin adopted Motorola's quality control and management practices. By 1999, Tianjin Optical was selling a third of its production to Motorola and reporting a small profit. "Now, we think we can survive," says Zhang Bingjun, Tianjin Optical's chairman.

Each Tianjin employee receives an average of two weeks a year of classroom instruction stressing modern management practices. That effort has paid off: The Tianjin assembly lines produce a slim cellular phone every $2\frac{1}{2}$ seconds with virtually the same defect rate as in Motorola's U.S. plants. Motorola also provides training for more than 100 outside suppliers to boost the quality of Tianjin's output. Motorola budgets about $2 million annually to "show [potential suppliers] Western management practices and create a mind-set where they understand what we're doing and why," says a training director, Ying Shea.

Since China opened up to foreign investment two decades ago, foreign companies have become an important conduit for economic reform. They have introduced not just modern production technology but also more efficient organizational architectures to the Chinese business community. Some estimates suggest that when these collateral benefits are included, foreign firms and their joint ventures account for as much as a fifth of China's trillion-dollar economy.

Yet uncritical experimentation with the organizational innovation *du jour* can expose a firm to an uncomfortably high risk of failure. Some organizational changes add value, but adopting the most recent business trend or fad can get a firm in trouble unless the change is warranted by the actual circumstances facing the firm. Unfortunately, many firms appear to adopt changes without careful analysis of the relevant costs and benefits. To quote *The Wall Street Journal,* "Many companies try management fads, only to see them flop." In fact, surveys indicate that a majority of companies are dissatisfied with the results of their organizational changes.

Before undertaking a major change, managers should understand how their firm arrived at its existing architecture and, more generally, develop a broader perspective on why specific types of organizations work well in particular settings. Outside consultants, of course, frequently argue that long-standing practices are inefficient and that companies would be better off if they followed the consultants' advice and changed their architectures. Popular management techniques in the 1990s included reengineering, total quality management (TQM), broadbanding, worker empowerment, the learning organization, and skill-based pay. Advocates of worker empowerment, for example, argued that profits would be improved if companies gave greater decision authority to lower-level employees. Although this advice clearly makes sense for some firms in some operating environments (especially if the environment has recently undergone a fundamental change that favors decentralization of decision authority), managers should resist jettisoning the prevailing organizational architecture without careful analysis—particularly if the business environment has been relatively stable.

Firms can even have problems when they try to export their own tried-and-true architectures to their operating subsidiaries. For example, managers from all over the world come to the Cleveland, Ohio, headquarters of Lincoln Electric, an arc-welding equipment manufacturer, to study Lincoln's unique reward system, which places a heavy emphasis on incentive compensation and is seen as a major factor in Lincoln's long history of solid profitability. But our analysis suggests that Lincoln's success should not be attributed to its reward system alone, but rather to how well this feature fits with its environment and overall architecture. Interestingly, at times Lincoln managers themselves have made the costly mistake of ignoring these considerations. During the 1980s, the management at Lincoln decided to implement the company's incentive system internationally through a series of mergers in Europe, Asia, and Latin America. Unfortunately, the system did not fit the business environments in many of the company's new locations. For instance, the influence of unions in Germany and labor laws in Venezuela made it impossible for Lincoln to introduce its compensation system successfully at those sites. Lincoln ended up losing millions of dollars on its international ventures.

Although competition tends to produce efficiently organized firms over the longer run, successful organizations are not just collections of good ideas. The elements of a successful organizational architecture must be carefully coordinated, and the different aspects of the firm's architecture must be structured so that they work together to achieve the firm's goals. For this reason, it is important to apply an integrated framework to analyze the likely consequences of a contemplated organizational change and to forecast its impact on the entire firm.

The concept of economic Darwinism thus has several important managerial implications:

- First, existing architectures are not random; there are sound explanations for the predominant organization of most firms in most industries.
- Second, surviving architectures at any point in time are optimal in a *relative* rather than an *absolute* sense; that is, they are the best among the competition, not necessarily the best possible.
- Third, if there are changes in the firm's operating environment—changes in technology, competition, or regulation—then the appropriate organizational architecture frequently changes as well.

Our Approach to Organizations

We base our analysis on two fundamental concepts: People tend to act in their own perceived self-interest, and people's knowledge bases differ. Successful organizations assign decision authority in a way that effectively links that authority with the relevant knowledge for good decision making. They then implement performance measurement systems and compensation programs that provide self-interested decision makers with the incentive to use their knowledge to make decisions that increase shareholder value.

A powerful feature of this framework is that it can be readily extended to incorporate a broad array of other managerial policies in areas such as finance, accounting, information systems, and marketing. In this sense, it can play an important integrating role within the organization. This type of integration is becoming increasingly important with the growing use of cross-functional teams.

The remaining chapters follow the road map set out in Figure 1.1. We begin with a discussion of how value is measured, how firms create and capture value, and how these considerations affect the strategy of the firm. We address the critical role of knowledge and its distribution within the organization as well as the management implications of self-interested behavior and conflicts of interest within the firm. We then discuss in detail the assignment of decision-making authority and the appropriate level of decentralization within the firm, before moving on to performance measurement systems and compensation policy. We conclude with discussions of organizational innovations and leadership.

CHAPTER 2

Maximizing Shareholder Value: Crafting a Strategy to Create and Capture Value

*M*anagers are under constant pressure to create value, and they are always on the lookout for new and better ways to increase their firm's profits and improve its competitive advantage. Yet many managers lack a clear idea of what it means to maximize value or how to do so. In the chapters that follow, we provide managers with a basic understanding of how to create value by appropriately linking the firm's strategy with its organizational architecture. This chapter focuses on important concepts that are building blocks for subsequent chapters. We begin by defining shareholder value and discussing why successful managers should focus on it. We then discuss how firms create value, the circumstances under which shareholders are able to capture this value, and how these and other considerations affect the optimal business strategy of a firm.

Changing Organizational Architecture
to Create Value

In 1984, ITT Corporation was the largest manufacturer of telecommunications equipment in the world. It was also broadly diversified, with a presence in more than eighty countries and operations in such varied areas as industrial and consumer products, insurance, automotive parts, telephone services, natural resources, food processing, and utilities. Yet ITT faced a variety of market pressures that made 1984 an especially difficult year. ITT's 1984 earnings were only $2.97 per share, compared to $4.50 a year earlier, and its stock had declined approximately 30 percent (in a moderately up stock market). The company cut its dividend by nearly $1.00 per share and was rumored to be a potential takeover target.

Part of ITT's problem was that it had become too large, too diversified, and too unfocused. Decision making within the organization was formalized and bureaucratic, making it difficult for the company to respond rapidly to either competitive pressures or changing customer demands. This inability to act quickly was especially troublesome given the dramatic changes that were taking place in both telecommunications and computers. ITT responded by announcing plans to sell over $2 billion in assets in order to refocus on its major lines of business and core strengths.

As part of this asset redeployment program, ITT sold off O. M. Scott & Sons Company, the largest producer of lawn care products in the United States. After the divestiture, the senior management of Scott made some significant organizational changes that were designed to enhance performance. These changes involved all three aspects of the firm's organizational architecture:

- The assignment of decision authority within the firm

- The systems for evaluating the performance of both individuals and business units
- The methods of motivating and rewarding individuals

In place of ITT's cumbersome, centralized approach to decision making, Scott gave its managers broad authority to make and implement decisions. The performance evaluation system was changed to place a heavy emphasis on financial measures, with specific targets for corporate, divisional, and individual performance. To motivate employees to make value-enhancing decisions, the bonus plan was expanded to include additional managers, and payouts for exceeding performance targets were raised materially: Average bonuses as a percentage of salary for the top ten managers increased from 13 percent in the two years before the divestiture to 52 percent in the two years after it. In addition, management stock ownership increased from a negligible amount to 17 percent of Scott's equity.

These organizational changes brought about a dramatic increase in Scott's profitability. In the two-year period following the divestiture, sales increased by 25 percent, and earnings before interest and taxes increased by 56 percent. These improvements did not result from reductions in either R&D expenditures or marketing and distribution expenses; in fact, expenditures in both categories increased, as did spending on capital projects. And there were no major layoffs of employees (although employment fell by approximately 10 percent over the period). Scott did an IPO in 1992, and its stock has performed well. The company continues to focus on lawn care products and maintains a high level of management ownership (the CEO owns more than 40 percent of the outstanding shares). The changes in Scott's organizational architecture gave experienced managers the authority to make and the incentives to implement value-increasing decisions. Organizational architecture provides managers with powerful tools for affecting a firm's performance and is an important determinant of a firm's success or failure.

Shareholder Value

Maximizing shareholder value has become the premier business mantra of the twenty-first century. Managers constantly profess to the media, to stock analysts, and to other constituencies a fundamental allegiance to shareholder value, as measured by the price of the stock. Compensation committees award stock options in the belief that options encourage managers to maximize shareholder wealth. Even companies whose traditional focus has been on a broader set of constituencies are paying more attention to shareholders. For example, the Keidanren, a national business association of more than 1000 major Japanese companies, recently concluded that it is "necessary for Japanese companies to place even more importance on shareholder value," and it recommended the increased use of stock options to compensate managers as well as the addition of outside directors to Japanese boards. A senior manager of a German beer company, reflecting on the current business environment in Germany, noted that "it used to be about beer, beer, beer—now it's about shareholders."

But what does it mean to maximize shareholder value? Shareholders invest in a firm's stock because they expect to earn returns on their investment that are at least comparable to the returns available on other, similar investments. Ultimately, these returns are determined by the cash payouts to shareholders (dividends and stock repurchases). Earnings per share is relevant only to the extent that it relates to what fundamentally matters to shareholders—the cash flows they receive from the firm. Investors' returns come from both cash payouts and the appreciation in the price of the stock, but price appreciation simply reflects expected future (after-tax) cash payouts. Individual investors may prefer capital gains to dividends for tax or other reasons, but an unrealized capital gain is simply an unliquidated cash payout. What ultimately matters to shareholders is cash flow. In fact, the stock price is merely a barometer of the firm's cash flow potential. And even though O. M. Scott's stock was not publicly traded in the initial period after the divestiture, management clearly enhanced shareholder value by improving profitability and increasing cash flows.

Since investors value cash payouts, managers increase shareholder value when they increase the present value of the firm's net cash flows, primarily by finding new ways to either increase revenues or reduce costs.[1] Generating more cash or receiving it earlier increases shareholder value. Manipulating the timing of sales or expenses to increase *reported* earnings, however, will actually *decrease* shareholder value if it reduces the cash that can ultimately be paid out to shareholders.

Of course, cash flows are not known for certain and must be forecast by investors in the marketplace. Given the uncertainty about future cash flows, investors look to earnings statements for information that is useful in developing these forecasts. Reported earnings can also affect cash flows directly, particularly through the covenants of bank loans and other agreements—low earnings may cause a company to default on a loan agreement, which might lead to bankruptcy. Nonetheless, reported earnings are not what investors fundamentally value. It is the actual cash flows that matter.

There is obviously a strong relationship in many companies between reported earnings and cash flows, so that if managers work to maximize future reported earnings, they also will be working to maximize future cash flows and share value. Too strong a focus on reported earnings, however, can decrease share value when there is a

---

[1] To be precise, the current value of a firm's shares is determined by the expected cash flows that ultimately will be paid out to shareholders, discounted at a rate that reflects the returns that investors could earn on alternative investments with similar risk, timing, liquidity, and tax consequences.

divergence between earnings and cash flows. Consider the choice between LIFO (last-in, first-out) and FIFO (first-in, first-out) inventory accounting. This choice does not affect pretax cash flows, but it generally will affect both reported earnings and after-tax cash flows, because the IRS requires that firms employ the same inventory accounting method for tax and reporting purposes. In an inflationary period, companies that switch from FIFO to LIFO report lower earnings, since their cost of goods sold is based on the more recent—and thus more expensive—items in inventory. Lower earnings, however, reduce the firm's tax liability and thus increase the after-tax cash that is available to shareholders. Studies have shown that firms that shift from FIFO to LIFO during inflationary periods typically experience an increase in their stock prices, even though their reported earnings decline. This evidence offers a particularly convincing illustration that investors value cash flows, not reported earnings.

Why Successful Managers Care about Shareholder Value

Shareholders are entitled to the residual cash flows of the firm—the cash that is left over after all other bills have been paid, including taxes and interest on debt. Boards of directors of U.S. companies have a legal responsibility to make decisions on behalf of shareholders and thus to concentrate on these residual cash flows, or the company's "bottom line." In contrast, most managers are motivated by their own compensation, their desire to operate a successful business, their reputation in the business community, and so on. However, if managers fail to maximize shareholder value, they are more likely to lose their jobs, either because the firm eventually goes out of business or because it becomes the target of a takeover bid, which frequently involves replacing the existing management team. Firms whose managers focus solely on such objectives as maximizing employee satisfaction will not be able to compete effectively against firms whose managers focus on the bottom line. Ultimately, inefficient firms have to change their focus to shareholder value or competition will force them out of existence.

In fact, many firms are now fighting for their very lives. In the past, the managers of these firms were free to concentrate on satisfying multiple constituencies, including local communities and employees. Companies such as IBM and Hershey, for example, paternalistically "guaranteed" lifetime employment and donated significant amounts of money to local arts and charities instead of striving for cost-efficient production. Of course, a certain level of employment security and charitable giving is consistent with maximizing shareholder value, but many firms arguably went too far. Moreover, the financing for takeovers was not always as readily available as it is today, and thus the managers of these firms were not overly concerned about the threat of a takeover—their market power and size protected them. With increased competition from both foreign and domestic producers, however, as well as changes in technology that have reduced the demand for their products, many of these firms have had to change their focus to the bottom line just to survive. When there are rumored to be possible takeover targets, they invariably respond by making it clear to employees, communities, the media, and stock analysts that increasing shareholder returns through value creation is their top priority.

Creating and Capturing Value

A company creates value whenever it sells something whose benefit to the customer is greater than the costs incurred by both the company in producing the product and the customer in owning it. These costs include all the company's production costs, whether or not they show up in the accounting statements. For instance, the typical accounting income statement does not include a charge for equity capital, even though it is clear that firms do not obtain equity capital for free. And the customer's costs include those for finding, researching, purchasing, and owning the product; we refer to these as *transaction costs.*

The price that the company charges determines how the total value is split between customers and the firm. Customers capture some of the value if the price they pay for the product is lower than the benefit they attach to it (net of their transaction costs). Shareholders capture the rest. In other words, shareholders capture value only if the selling price is greater than all the costs borne by the firm, including a "normal" rate of return on equity capital. Figure 2.1 illustrates this value-creation process.

Consider, for example, how value creation changed for the airline industry in the wake of the terrorist attacks of September 11, 2001. In the customers' eyes, the perceived value of flying fell, causing a dramatic drop in the number of airline seats sold and an immediate

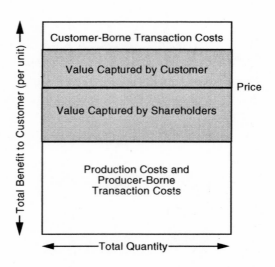

Figure 2.1 The distribution of value created among customers, shareholders, and producers.

decline in the potential for value creation. Moreover, because of the increased costs to the airlines of additional screening and tightened security procedures, as well as the additional transaction costs to passengers in the form of longer lines, longer airport waits, and limits on carry-on luggage, there was a decline in the value created on the seats that *were* being sold. Most airlines reported losses in the third quarter of 2001—their average costs exceeded the price they charged for tickets. Customers were willing to fly only if the value of their trip exceeded its total cost. Thus, the net value created by the airline industry in that quarter was considerably reduced and was arguably even negative (if the losses by the airlines exceeded the net value captured by their customers).

How to Create Value

Managers can create value by lowering costs (while holding customer benefits constant), by increasing the benefits customers obtain from the product (while holding costs constant), and/or by increasing the size of the market. Managers can also develop new products whose benefits to customers are greater than their costs. Whether shareholders capture any of this value depends on the product's price. Price is determined largely by competition in the marketplace, although the high salaries paid to successful pricing managers are testimony to the complexity of pricing decisions in some industries.

Reducing Company Production and Transaction Costs

One way in which firms can increase shareholder value is by discovering new technologies that reduce their production costs. For example, the first personal computers were relatively expensive to produce. Over time, companies learned to reduce these production costs. As a result, sales of personal computers increased substantially—as did the total value created within this industry. Firms can also create value by devising ways to lower the costs of doing business with customers and suppliers. For instance, large computer manufacturers have developed electronic connections with major software producers in order to lower the cost of ordering software. They have also developed computer links that reduce the costs of transactions with customers.

Dell Computers, for example, has created value through the development of a system that allows it to collect information from customers and assemble customized products quickly and inexpensively. This system allows Dell to bypass a dealer network with its required markups and enables it to offer computers at lower prices than the competition. Extending this strategy, Dell offers customized services to large corporate accounts. For example, Dell custom loads specialized software along with associated peripherals and network servers for First Union Capital Markets Group, which uses over 2500 PCs. Each package is then tagged and shipped directly to the specific First Union trader for whom the unit was designed. This process has reportedly saved First Union over $500,000 annually—and, presumably produced a tidy profit for Dell.

Another prominent example of a cost-reducing company is Wal-Mart, whose extremely efficient hub-and-spoke distribution system has greatly lowered the costs of stocking its stores. Direct computer links with major suppliers such as Procter & Gamble have cut the costs of restocking products and have streamlined vendor payments, which are now made electronically.

As a firm grows, economies of scale allow it to reduce its costs. Economies of scale also afford existing companies some protection against incursions by new market entrants who must produce at a high volume in order to be cost-effective. A firm may also be able to take advantage of *economies of scope* by leveraging its product development, distribution, and marketing systems. For example, Pepsi also produces a wide range of snack foods. Of course, as a firm becomes larger and its range of products becomes broader, coordination and control problems tend to become more severe, making its organizational architecture even more critical.

Reducing Consumer Transaction Costs

Reducing the cost to consumers of finding, researching, purchasing, and owning a product is another important way in which firms create value. For example, early Wal-Marts were established in small rural towns. These stores created value for local residents by reducing their travel time; Wal-Mart customers no longer had to drive to urban centers to do all their shopping. Wal-Mart also reduces consumer transaction costs through the layout of its stores. For example, the company captures "market-basket data" from customer receipts at all its stores. By analyzing these data, Wal-Mart can tell which products are likely to be purchased together. The company then places commonly purchased bundles of products together, reducing customers' costs in navigating the stores. Examples of such pairings include bananas with cereal, snack cakes with coffee, bug spray with hunting gear, tissues with cold medicine, measuring spoons with baking supplies, and flashlights with Halloween costumes.

Marketing via the Internet provides another example of reducing consumers' transaction costs (especially information and search costs). For instance, when prospective customers search the Internet for a particular book, they often see a list of related books, any of which can be ordered electronically at a discount through companies such as Amazon.com. This service reduces consumers' search costs by preidentifying books that are of potential interest and making it easier to place an order.

Increasing Consumer Benefits

Companies can also create value by increasing the total benefits customers obtain from their products. One way to do this is to enhance the perceived quality of the product. For instance, the introduction of titanium golf clubs increased the overall demand for golf equipment, and the development of parabolic skis increased the demand for ski equipment and skiing. Kraft Foods repackaged several standard products into Lunchables, a line of finger foods for kids. The Lunchables strategy tapped into the convenience trend while allowing children to have a hand in selecting their own lunches. With the help of flashy, colorful packaging and contests for trips to amusement parks, the product line has become a huge business for Kraft since its introduction in 1988. In fact, employment has tripled at Kraft's Avon, New York, plant, which was once on the verge of being shut down. The resulting increase in demand has been greater than the associated increase in production costs—thus, the total value created has increased.

For some products, demand will increase as the number of users increases. For example, fax machines and telephones are not particularly useful unless there is a network of users. This consideration is quite important for many of today's communication and information products. Compatibility with competing products reduces a new product's uniqueness, but the net effect can be to increase overall demand for the product because of network effects. When Microsoft Word was first introduced, compatibility with WordPerfect was a key factor, enabling the consumer who purchased Microsoft Word to network with WordPerfect users.

There are many other creative ways to enhance the benefits of a product. Consider McDonald's restaurants in Serbia. During the seventy-eight-day air war conducted by NATO against Yugoslavia in 1999, fifteen McDonald's restaurants in Belgrade had to be closed temporarily. Angry mobs—who saw McDonald's as a symbol of America and the West—vandalized the units. To increase the demand for their products and win back their local reputation, Yugoslavian McDonald's stores undertook a pro-Serbian marketing campaign. To evoke local pride and identity, they produced posters and lapel buttons showing the golden arches topped with a traditional Serbian cap called the sajkaka. They also distributed free cheeseburgers at rallies and allowed the basement of one of their restaurants to be used as a bomb shelter. They began promoting the McCountry, a domestic pork burger with paprika garnish. After the war was over, the demand for McDonald's products soared in Belgrade. Said sixteen-year-old Jovan Stojanovic, "I don't associate McDonald's with America. Mac is ours."

Cooperating to Increase Value

Firms sometimes increase value by cooperating with one another instead of competing. Although American antitrust law generally makes it illegal for rival firms to cooperate for the purpose of monopoly pricing, many forms of cooperation are legal and create value for both producers and consumers. Opportunities to increase value can arise through cooperation with customers, suppliers, producers of complementary products, and even competitors. For instance, cooperating with suppliers and customers in developing computer and information links can reduce supply costs and lead to the production of more valuable products that are tailored to the customer (recall the example of Dell Computers).

Competitors can also reduce costs by cooperating in development projects. For example, General Motors and Ford are investing jointly in research and development for electric car batteries, not necessarily because they will produce the batteries, but because better, longer-lived, less expensive batteries will increase the benefits that customers obtain from electric cars and thus enable the auto companies to market electric cars on a wider scale. If each company acted independently, development costs would almost certainly be higher. Another example is offshore oil drilling—prior to soliciting bids for offshore sites, the U.S. government allows oil firms to conduct a joint survey of the area; they then share the data and divide the survey costs.

Or consider the Advanced Photo System developed in the 1990s. This system has several advantages over traditional photo systems, including a convenient cartridge, special encoding features, formatting flexibility, and indexed prints. To maximize the consumer appeal of the new system, however, it was important for film and camera companies to adopt a standard set of system parameters. The mutual benefits from cooperating on the development of this photo system motivated traditional rivals such as Kodak and Fuji in film and Canon, Minolta, and Nikon in cameras to cooperate in a joint venture to develop the new system. Governments sanctioned this cooperative venture at the "precompetitive" stage. Now that the system exists and a set of standard parameters has been adopted, these companies are again competing in their respective markets.

Opportunities to Create Value

The discovery of better ways to use existing resources drives much of the value that firms create. Today's personal computers are far more powerful than the 1980s mainframes, yet they require significantly fewer resources to produce. The value created by improved computer technology has come not from the discovery of new raw materials or resources, but from using existing resources more efficiently. To quote Professor Paul Romer of Stanford,

> So it is not the raw materials or the mass of things on earth that really lies behind economic success and high standard of living, it is the process of rearrangement. And what underlies this process of rearrangement are *instructions, formulas, recipes, and methods of doing things* [emphasis ours].

The possibilities for new value creation are immense. Consider Romer's simple example of a production process that involves just twenty steps. The order of the steps can be varied in an extremely large number of ways (approximately 24 followed by seventeen zeros), and different orderings will affect the value created. In most production processes, of course, there is a natural ordering that precludes certain combinations of steps—it may not make sense to install car doors after the car is painted. But given all the ways in which the many resources on earth can be rearranged, the possibilities for continued value creation are enormous.

This discussion suggests that firms face an essentially unlimited set of opportunities to create better "instructions, formulas, recipes, and methods" for making improved products at lower cost. Still more opportunities are likely to emerge as technology continues to evolve. For instance, the latter part of the twentieth century saw a massive change in information, communication, and production technologies. This technological change has provided substantial opportunities for increasing value. The "business process reengineering" movement in the 1990s used computer and information technology to lower costs (for instance, by streamlining the systems used to process orders, shipments, payables, and receivables). Flexible production technologies have allowed firms to tailor the design of their products to fit specific customer demands. Computer and information technologies reduce the costs of transactions with suppliers. Using technology to increase value is likely to remain a significant focus well into the future.

Can Firms Capture the Value They Create?

Creating value is not sufficient for maximizing shareholder value. It is also important for firms to *capture* that value. The business world is full of firms that have created value but failed to capture it. A classic example is one of the most important inventions in American history—the cotton gin. In the southern United States in the eighteenth century, the laborious task of separating cotton from seed was done by hand. It took a worker an entire day to clean just one pound of cotton. On a visit to Georgia, Eli Whitney became intrigued by this problem. Within a few weeks, he had produced a machine that he called a cotton "gin" (short for cotton "engine"). It greatly increased the amount of cotton that could be cleaned in a day, and cotton soon became the chief crop in the South. Clearly, the invention of the cotton gin created significant value. Yet before Whitney's invention was completed and patented, his first model had been widely copied. Virtually all his profits went into lawsuits to protect and enforce his rights. (He did, however, make money in the financial markets speculating on the price of cotton.)

A more recent example involves Xerox. Researchers at Xerox's Palo Alto Research Center invented the first personal computer, the first graphics-oriented monitor, an early handheld computer mouse, the first word processing program for nonexpert users, the first local area communications network, the first object-oriented programming language, and the first laser printer. But Xerox failed to capitalize commercially on any of this innovative technology.

The most important constraint on capturing value is competition. If a firm finds a way to make a profit, other firms will strive to imitate or improve on that firm's innovation in order to profit for themselves. Competition tends to lower prices and reduce the value that is captured by the innovating firm. Much of this value ultimately goes to consumers, who receive highly valued products at competitive prices. Consider how competition in the electronics market has reduced the prices and increased the quality of products such as personal computers, televisions, camcorders, and DVD players.

Of course, firms can earn significant profits over a period of time if they can somehow limit competition through barriers to entry such as patents, government restrictions (for example, import quotas), and so on. For instance, the U.S. government provides relatively strong protection of intellectual property rights in order to ensure a profit incentive for new inventions. Nonetheless, barriers to entry are not always effective. Competing firms frequently devise ways to circumvent not only patents and other property right protections but also government regulations. In addition, intellectual property is protected for only a limited time period, and enforcement of these rights through the court system can be time consuming and expensive. Finally, even if effective barriers to entry exist, new technologies are likely to produce substitute products that reduce the market power of the producers of the original product. Consider, for example, the way new and improved drugs reduce the demand for existing drugs.

Some firms, however, are able to earn large profits over an extended period of time even in the face of significant competition. To do so, a firm must have a unique resource or capability that is immune to immediate imitation. It is also important that the unique resource not be a marketable asset, such as a talented manager, whose price can easily be bid up by other firms competing for the advantage. The original firm might retain the talented manager by offering him or her a higher salary. However, it is then the manager, rather than the firm's shareholders, who captures much of the new value that is created.

An example of a firm that captured value over a sustained time period in a competitive setting is Sharp Corporation. During the 1970s, Sharp began marketing electronic calculators with liquid crystal displays (LCDs). As the company gained expertise, it began to apply the LCD technology to other products, such as television sets. Sharp developed a set of resources and capabilities that other companies did not have. With the growth in consumer electronics and computers during the 1980s and 1990s, potential applications for LCDs expanded rapidly, and Sharp profited from this growth. Other companies could not immediately overcome Sharp's competitive advantage because of time constraints and their lack of accumulated assets and experience. Nor was Sharp's advantage due to a small set of employees that could be hired away by other firms that wanted to gain Sharp's advantage. Companies such as Matsushita, NEC, and

Canon entered the industry, yet Sharp was able to maintain its dominant position because of its special capabilities.

Strategy

The terms *corporate strategy* and *business strategy* refer to the big-picture issues facing the firm. What industries does the firm operate in? What products and services does it offer, and to which customers? In what basic ways does it compete or cooperate with other firms within the business environment?

As we have seen, the opportunities for continued value creation are almost unlimited. Competitors who succeed in developing new and better products and production processes will eventually overwhelm any firm that fails to innovate successfully. But while it is clearly important to *execute* an existing business recipe effectively, it is also important to *develop* new and better recipes. As an illustration, consider Polaroid. From 1948, when the company introduced its first instant camera, until 1972, when it unveiled its SX-70, Polaroid continually improved its almost magical product. The first Polaroid cameras produced sepia-toned prints, but over the years the company developed the ability to produce color photos that appeared right before one's eyes. In 1972, Polaroid's stock price was ninety times earnings, propelling the company into the Nifty Fifty (the top fifty companies in the *Fortune* 500). But the SX-70 was followed by a series of flops, including Polavision. Moreover, the development of digital imaging provided an alternative method of viewing shots immediately and precipitated Polaroid's Chapter 11 bankruptcy filing in October 2001.

The game of football offers a useful analogy. In the 1930s there was little passing in the game. The offense focused on running the ball up the middle of the field. Winning teams were good at executing the running game—their lines had sound basic blocking skills, their quarterbacks were careful not to fumble the ball, and so on. As the game evolved, teams developed better ways to advance the football. Today's teams employ explosive pass-oriented offenses that bear little resemblance to the run-oriented offenses of the 1930s. A team employing an old-style running game would lose badly today, even if it were exceptionally good at executing its game plan. On the other hand, a good offensive plan for today's game will not produce a winning team unless the plan is well executed.

In other words, both development and execution of value-creating formulas are important. However, their relative importance depends on the operating environment of the firm. In rapidly changing industries such as chip making or biotech, the development of new ways to create and capture value is likely to be more important than the solid execution of an existing formula. The reverse is likely to be true in more stable industries such as steel or tobacco. Nonetheless, even a producer of such a standard commodity as nails will lose out to the competition if it does not constantly strive to lower production and distribution costs and to enhance customer benefits.

Managers must continually develop new ways to create and capture value if their firms are to remain successful. In trying to achieve this objective, the focus should be on those areas where the firm has the best chance of success. A primary objective of strategic planning is to define the general areas and activities in which the firm's employees are most likely to create and capture value. The central message of the "core competency" literature is that managers need to identify what their firms are good at and devise ways to leverage those competencies. And the potential for value creation is not always limited to existing product lines. For example, Sony's skills in electronics might be leveraged in any number of areas, from office equipment to toys. At the same time, firms should avoid investing in activities where they are unlikely to create or capture value. The general lack of success of the unrelated diversifications of the 1970s (such as ITT's purchase of Sheraton Hotels and U.S. Steel's purchase of Marathon Oil) is a case in point. Similarly, Enron's demise is partly attributable to the mistaken belief that its considerable skills in the energy business would translate into such areas as creating markets for trading bandwidth.

It is also critical to consider competitors' responses when making major strategic decisions. Sound strategy formulation often requires putting yourself behind your rival's desk. For example, there is considerable cyclicality in the paper industry, much of which seems to be self-inflicted: When demand rises, all the companies in the industry invest in new capacity in order to gain market share, and then when demand falls, every company suffers from excess capacity and lower profits. A CFO in the industry acknowledged that although his firm made careful assumptions about worldwide growth rates, it never seemed to consider the response of its competitors. Similarly, Kodak decided to invest heavily in producing writable CD-ROMs, which had been a highly profitable business for the company, but failed to weigh the threat of potential competition and ultimately lost money in that business. According to CEO George Fisher, "I think we screwed up. We should have known that prices would fall as manufacturers worldwide ramped up production."

Architectural Considerations

We have indicated that strategy and organizational architecture are interrelated. If an important aspect of an industry's operating environment changes, most companies in the industry will react by reappraising their strategies and then adjusting their organizational architectures. In the early 1980s, for example, a regulated AT&T had been accustomed to little real competition and had thus felt little pressure about technological innovation. It operated within a reasonably stable environment—one in which the logical structure was a huge formal bureaucracy that made important decisions from the top down. Since the breakup of the company, however, the telecommunications industry has experienced almost continuous upheaval, with deregulation, increased competition, and rapid technological change. In 1992, after a nearly decade-long series of incremental moves toward decentralization, AT&T established a large number of fairly autonomous profit centers and began to compensate its managers based on pay-for-performance plans that were tied to the profitability of the managers' units. In 1995, AT&T broke itself into three separate publicly traded companies and laid off 40,000 employees. And by 1999, following a series of acquisitions, AT&T had expanded its scope and was serving more cable subscribers than any other cable company (including Time Warner Cable), which has led to increased value.

Strategy can in turn be influenced by organizational architecture. A company might decide to enter a new market in part because its decision and control systems are especially well suited to the new undertaking. Before the 1980s, Atlanta was widely acknowledged as the banking center of the South. Yet at the beginning of the twenty-first century, Charlotte, North Carolina, claims that title. Historically, bank branching was regulated by the individual states. Georgia limited its banks' ability to branch, whereas North Carolina permitted state-wide branching. As restrictions on interstate banking eased in the 1980s, the North Carolina banks—especially NCNB (now Bank of America) and Wachovia—exploited their experience in establishing and managing statewide systems to create regional and then national banks. These banks have been quite successful, in part because their organizational architectures were better suited to the new regulatory environment.

As another example of how changes in the operating environment can affect organizational architecture, consider the increased foreign competition that many firms faced in the 1980s and 1990s. For years, many large American companies, such as ITT, IBM, General Motors, Eastman Kodak, and Xerox, had encountered only limited competition in their product markets. Most of these companies had substantial market power and so had little external impetus to focus on rapid product development, high-quality production, or competitive pricing. Their organizations were highly bureaucratic, with centralized decision making and minimal incentive compensation. But many of these firms have experienced a dramatic increase in foreign competition over the past two decades—especially from Japanese firms. Competition has forced these firms to rethink their basic strategies and to increase their emphasis on quality, customer service, cost control, and competitive pricing. To accomplish these objectives, the firms have had to change their architectures. They have pushed decision authority lower into the organization, where employees have the relevant specific knowledge about customer demand (recall the O. M. Scott example). They have also increased their use of incentive compensation and developed performance evaluation systems that focus on quality and customer service.

Changes in technology can also precipitate changes in architecture. Purchasing decisions at JC Penney used to be relatively centralized, with buyers in New York City deciding on the company's clothing lines for the year. But this procedure failed to incorporate information about which items sold best in different parts of the country. In the 1980s, Penney invested in satellite communications that provided the company with closed-circuit television. This technology allowed central buyers in New York to display goods to local store managers, who could then stock their stores based on their knowledge of local fashions and tastes.

Can All Firms Create and Capture Value?

Some consultants argue that any firm can develop a strategy that will create value for shareholders, even firms that do not begin with a unique resource or capability. The only prerequisite is for management to be "visionary" and make sound investments in developing the internal skills and capabilities that will be needed to compete successfully in the future. (Of course, for a fee these gurus are quite happy to help the company try to accomplish this objective.)

But the logic of competition suggests that the consultants are wrong. Even if a manager is unusually good at predicting the future and recognizing which resources and capabilities are important, the firm will not systematically earn exceptional returns so long as there are managers in competing firms who adopt similar strategies. Competition will bid up the prices of the required resources in the input markets and bid down the prices in the product markets, thus eroding margins. As in any competitive market, the expected outcome is a normal rate of return rather than sustained above-normal performance. In fact, it can take significant managerial talent and effort (devoted to decisions like choosing products as well as producing and marketing them efficiently) just to earn a "normal" return in a competitive environment. And a normal return is quite acceptable to shareholders.

The business environment is constantly evolving, with new technological innovations, changes in consumer tastes, new business concepts, new firms, and other developments taking place, and it is unlikely that any strategic advantage will last forever. The list of today's top ten firms is quite different from the top ten firms of twenty years ago. Persistent competition tends to erode profits over time. Other firms have strong incentives to devise methods of wresting value from successful firms, and they will eventually find a method that works.

But even in relatively competitive industries, some firms perform exceptionally well over long periods of time. As they take different paths in their investment strategies, internal processes, hiring decisions, and so on, some firms find themselves with superior resources and capabilities, while others do not. In time, the lucky firms end up with a competitive advantage. These firms arrive at the enviable position of having developed team capabilities that are especially productive. Firms like GE and Microsoft, which enjoyed long periods of sustained success, seem to excel at creating and maintaining effective networks of employees and maximizing their potential. And if one looks carefully, a key factor that these firms have in common is an effective organizational architecture—a customized design that promotes the business strategy and rewards employees for making value-maximizing decisions.

CHAPTER 3

Knowledge and Incentives In Organizations

*D*evising a sound strategy for creating and capturing value is an important step in maximizing shareholder value, but it is not the only step. It is also necessary to design an organizational architecture that promotes the strategy's successful implementation. This chapter presents fundamental concepts about the role of knowledge and incentive problems in organizations. Subsequent chapters build on this material to provide a detailed analysis of the design and implementation of a firm's organizational architecture.

Unlocking Knowledge within Organizations

Kodak's Accumax is a film product that is used in the manufacture of circuit boards. Any dust on the film translates into a broken wire on a circuit board and makes the film worthless. Accumax is finished and slit into final products in a high-tech, ultraclean room. Unfortunately, the supply cart used to transport the film to storage was not dust-free, and thus much of the film was wasted.

Bob Cholach was a slitter operator with an idea about how the problem could be fixed—he envisioned an airtight transport cab.

Through his efforts, such a cab was designed and built, with significant benefits to the company. It came to be known as Cholach's Chariot. Kodak had recently reorganized its film manufacturing process, with decision authority now considerably decentralized. Comparing the new empowered work environment with the old system, Cholach noted:

> In the old days I'd have been told, "That's not your job—don't worry about it." But here I was given the power and finances to design and build something that would help my teammates. It wasn't like dropping a piece of paper into a suggestion box, either. They let me run with it from start to finish.

Kodak had succeeded in designing an organizational architecture that created incentives for Bob Cholach to use his specialized knowledge to reduce costs and thereby create shareholder value.

Converting Organizational Knowledge into Value

The resources within a firm can be divided into three general categories. The first category is tangible assets, which include property, plant, and equipment. The second category is intangible assets, such as patents, trademarks, and brand-name recognition. These assets are not typically shown on the firm's balance sheet, but they can be significant in creating and capturing value—the firm's methods of doing business, its formulas and recipes, are a particularly important type of intangible asset. The third category, and perhaps the most important, is its human resources.

Firms in Silicon Valley frequently refer to these three types of resources as *hardware*, *software*, and *wetware*. Hardware consists of physical assets. Software is broadly used to describe the firm's "soft" assets, such as its formulas and recipes for creating value. Wetware refers to employee brainpower, i.e., "wet computers."

A firm owns and can capture value from its hardware and its software, but it only rents its wetware. Wetware is the private property of individual employees, who can take it with them to another firm if they so choose. To generate shareholder value, managers must find ways to convert the knowledge contained in employee wetware (even knowledge that the employees may not realize they have) into software. The firm then owns the software and can use it to create and capture value for its shareholders, as with Cholach's Chariot.

The evolution of the McDonald's Corporation provides a good example of how this process takes place. The first McDonald's unit was established in 1956. The company's hardware consisted of property and equipment. However, its most important asset was its software. McDonald's major source of value was its new formula for selling hamburgers, fries, and drinks to customers. This formula translated into a business approach that McDonald's was able to duplicate in locations around the world. If McDonald's had stopped innovating in 1956, new companies that copied and improved on the original formula, such as Burger King, Wendy's, and Kentucky Fried Chicken, would have eventually forced McDonald's out of business. But McDonald's continually improved its formula for creating and capturing value by converting wetware into new software. Today McDonald's has a much wider product offering, more effective store designs, and better production processes than it had in 1956.

The development of the Filet-O-Fish sandwich at McDonald's illustrates the conversion from wetware to software. Originally, the only food products that McDonald's sold were hamburgers and fries. The product line was intentionally limited so that it could be produced efficiently and quickly, following McDonald's formula for value creation. A franchisee in a predominantly Catholic area, however, was unable to sell many hamburgers on Fridays because observant Catholics avoided meat on Fridays. The franchisee therefore worked hard to develop a tasty fish sandwich. At first, McDonald's would not let him sell the new sandwich because it was not consistent with Mc-Donald's image as a hamburger company. It would also lead to inconsistency across units—something that a franchise company generally wants to avoid. Eventually, however, McDonald's saw the value that could be created and captured by offering a fish sandwich. Specialists at the corporate level devised ways to improve the sandwich and to lower its production costs (for example, by using a different type of fish that could be precut into a standard size). Ultimately, the Filet-O-Fish sandwich was introduced across all McDonald's units, and it has been an important menu item ever since.

The idea of a fish sandwich was initially contained in the wetware of the franchisee, and the ways to improve the product were in the wetware of specialists at the corporate level. At this stage, the ideas and knowledge were not creating value. However, the wetware was eventually converted into software and is now part of the McDonald's formula for creating and capturing value. A similar story lies behind the Big Mac, which was the brainchild of a franchisee in Pittsburgh who wanted a heftier sandwich to sell to steelworkers.

Software is different from hardware in that it is not a scarce resource. While a given machine can be used at only one location, software can be replicated to create value at locations throughout the world. McDonald's currently has over ten thousand units operating under the same business format. (Of course, software can also be copied by competing firms, thus reducing its profit potential.)

General versus Specific Knowledge

The primary goal of any firm is to produce what customers want at the lowest possible cost. The likelihood that a particular employee will have the necessary wetware to develop the software for achieving this goal depends on that employee's knowledge base, as well as on the knowledge that the employee is likely to acquire through his or her position within the firm. For example, a scientist working in an

R&D lab is more likely to discover the next wonder drug than is a machine operator working at the production facility. On the other hand, the machine operator is more likely to discover better ways to use the machine.

In theory, all knowledge in the organization could be transferred to a central location, and a central planner could be charged with using that knowledge to devise new ways to create and capture value. This arrangement is characteristic of a sole proprietorship, but it is ineffective in larger organizations because of the difficulty of transferring and processing information. In fact, most firms centralize some decisions and decentralize others according to how readily the knowledge necessary to make each decision can be transferred.

At least three factors influence knowledge transferability:

- *The characteristics of the sender and the receiver.* Generally, it is easier for people with similar training, language, and culture to share knowledge.
- *The technology available for communication.* For example, the Internet has significantly reduced the cost of transferring information. In 1999, there were almost five million résumés on the Internet—two hundred times more than in 1994.
- *The nature of the information itself.* Some knowledge is difficult to comprehend or summarize or to transfer in a timely fashion. Knowledge of how recombinant DNA works is not easily transferred to nonscientists. Similarly, an accountant who has prepared a client's tax returns for several years is likely to have amassed important knowledge about the relevant parts of the tax code and the peculiarities of the individual's income and deductions. Finally, the employee at the warehouse is most likely to know whether a particular truck has room for additional cargo. If this information is not acted on in time, it becomes useless.

When decision makers rely on inadequate sources of information, costly mistakes can occur. In the late 1970s, for example, aggregate data indicated that houses and families were shrinking. Strategic planners at General Electric therefore concluded that smaller appliances were the wave of the future. But GE's planners had insufficient contact with home builders, retailers, or consumers, and as a result were not aware that working couples were actually installing larger refrigerators to reduce the number of trips to the supermarket, larger washers and dryers to reduce the amount of time spent doing laundry, and so on. Top management failed to catch the planners' error. As a result, General Electric wasted a lot of time and money designing smaller appliances.

The retailing industry provides an example of the impact of changes in the ease of knowledge transferability. Historically, economies of scale prompted retailers to concentrate on standardized distribution. In stocking individual stores, managers of large retail chains tended to ignore specific knowledge about the idiosyncratic demands of customers in various neighborhoods—it was simply too difficult to collect and process that information. The chain department stores were thus not always able to compete effectively with small local stores that catered to the demands of local customers. But the development of computers and electronic scanners has made information about local purchasing habits more available. As a result, retail companies have begun to engage in micromarketing to a greater degree. For instance, the Sears outlet in the North Hollywood section of Los Angeles is designed with an eye toward the neighborhood's Hispanic population. Signs are in Spanish, and the store is stocked with ethnic items, such as a broad selection of compact discs and tapes by Latin artists. A few hundred miles to the north, the Sears store in San Jose offers a wide selection of clothing items in extra-small sizes to appeal to the area's Asian population. Sears stores in Florida carry comfortable, roomy clothes geared to the population of elderly residents.

Converting wetware in the form of hunches, perceptions, mental models, beliefs, experiences, and other types of knowledge into a form of software that can be used to create value is a key aspect of successful new product innovation. Apple's first portable Mac had so many bells and whistles that it weighed a hefty 17 pounds. It did not do well in the market. In 1990, Apple completely reworked the design of the computer from the user's viewpoint. Software designers, industrial engineers, marketing people, and industrial designers were sent into the field to observe potential customers using other products. The team discovered that laptops were used on airplanes, in cars, and at home in bed. People wanted not just small computers but mobile computers. In response, Apple designed two distinctive features for its PowerBook computer—the TrackBall pointer and the palm rest in front of the keyboard. The new product was distinctive and easy to use. Sales improved dramatically.

The knowledge of what customers really wanted in a laptop computer was acquired by a team of workers who interacted closely with customers. The team members also had important scientific and design knowledge that allowed them to use the information that they gained to design a marketable product. Finally, they had the decision authority to modify the product based on their findings. A centralized design-engineering function is less likely to have access to such specific knowledge in its product design and will be less able to convert employee wetware to software.

Implications for the Assignment of Decision Authority

Effective use of knowledge within the organization is critical for value creation, both for the ongoing conversion of wetware into software and for the effective deployment of existing software. Thus, managers must consider the specific knowledge of employees when they assign decision-making authority within the organization. Linking decision authority and specific knowledge can be accomplished either by ensuring that employees with decision authority acquire the necessary knowledge or by granting decision authority to employees who have that knowledge. Given the costs of transferring information, however, it is often wiser to grant decision authority to the employees with the knowledge. (We discuss this further in the next chapter.)

But linking decision authority and knowledge is only half the battle. The other half is motivating employees to make productive use of their knowledge in their decision making—to convert their wetware into software that is implemented. For example, research personnel might want to complete a project out of scholarly interest even after it becomes obvious that the project is unprofitable. Managers at Iridium continued to invest in their global satellite communications system long after the spread of cell phone technology had severely limited the commercial feasibility of the system. Similarly, machine operators may have ideas about how to operate their machines more efficiently, but they may be reluctant to share those ideas if doing so means that their workloads will increase. In other words, there are incentive problems to overcome.

Incentives within Organizations

In June 1992, the state of California filed charges alleging that Sears Auto Centers were overcharging customers an average of $230 for unneeded or undone repairs; similar allegations by the state of New Jersey soon followed. Ultimately, Sears admitted that "some mistakes did occur" and agreed to a settlement of up to $20 million. Sears maintained that its senior management had been unaware of the problem and had neither condoned nor encouraged defrauding customers. This auto repair scandal was quite costly for Sears. As the complaints became public, the price of Sears's stock fell by about 6 percent, and revenues at the auto centers declined substantially.

To contain the damage, Sears's managers had to act quickly to address the problem. As a first step, they had to figure out what could have caused employees to recommend unneeded repairs. If the problem was a few dishonest employees, the appropriate response would be to try to identify and fire those employees. If the problem was disgruntled employees taking out their frustrations on customers, management's response might be to adopt a job enrichment program to increase employee satisfaction and, it would be hoped, customer service.

Managers are constantly seeking new and better ways to identify and respond to consumer demands. Much of this effort rests on an understanding of human behavior. But understanding behavior is important within the organization as well. In this section, we first present the *economic* view of behavior. We then contrast this view with other views of behavior and suggest that these views are typically less useful in managerial decision making.

Economic View of Behavior

The economic view of behavior holds that people make choices to enhance their personal happiness and well-being. Thus, managers must examine an individual's personal incentives in order to understand or affect that individual's behavior. As it turns out, the salespeople at Sears Auto Centers received commissions based on total sales. In addition, they were assigned sales quotas for particular products and services. If they missed these quotas, they would receive lower pay and could even lose their jobs. By being dishonest—for example, by telling customers that they needed new shock absorbers when in fact the shocks were fine—employees could increase sales and meet their quotas. Management realized that the compensation scheme was creating the wrong incentives and responded by moving from commission to straight salary. Sears also eliminated the sales quotas and introduced a program to reward employees for high levels of customer satisfaction. The Sears example illustrates a general point: Managers' understanding of what motivates behavior is likely to affect their decisions and policies. In this example, Sears's managers employed the economic view of behavior and responded by changing employee incentives.

In general, of course, people value greater wealth, faster service, larger houses, more luxurious cars, additional personal material items, and more time for leisure activities. They are concerned about vitality, integrity, and gaining the respect and affection of others. But most people are not selfish in the sense that they care only about their own personal well-being—they also care about such things as charity, family, religion, and society. Many people want to improve the plight of others—starving children, the homeless, disaster victims—because they obtain satisfaction from doing so. Much of the work of the Red Cross is undertaken by unpaid volunteers. An individual will donate time or money so long as the donation provides greater satisfaction than alternative uses of that time or money.

In contrast to wants, resources are limited. Households have fixed incomes that preclude their making every purchase or expenditure that members of the household would like to make. Individuals assign priorities to their wants and choose among the available alternatives as dictated by their resources. In other words, they make *trade-offs.*

In making trade-offs, people do not make infallible decisions—they are not endowed with perfect knowledge and foresight, nor is additional information costless to acquire and process. People simply do the best they can in the face of imperfect knowledge. Still, they learn from experience and tend not to repeat the same mistakes in judgment time after time.

Another consideration is that most people are *risk-averse*—for example, they are willing to accept a lower level of compensation if that level is guaranteed, rather than a higher but less certain level of compensation. A salesperson might prefer a package with a $90,000 base salary and a potential bonus of $20,000 to a package with a $50,000 base salary and a potential bonus of $75,000. Moreover, few employees have formal training in decision making that involves risky outcomes, and most find such decisions difficult. Understanding risk has important managerial implications. The CEO of Trilogy Software believes that taking risks and suffering the consequences are critical to the firm's success, and wants to develop people who are willing to take chances. Trilogy's three-month training program educates all new recruits about, among other things, how to evaluate risky projects and not to just immediately accept or reject a project because it is risky. The program also advises employees that they will not be rewarded at Trilogy unless they are open to taking risks. Thus, although most employees do not inherently like taking risks, they have economic incentives to do so at Trilogy. The company recognizes that risk is unavoidable; it thus tries to train employees to make reasoned decisions about risky alternatives. Of course, this approach is more appropriate at some companies than at others.

Fundamentally, the economic view argues that individuals will try to maximize their personal well-being given the constraints they face. Indeed, people are quite creative and resourceful in minimizing the effects of constraints. When the government passes a new tax law, accountants and financial planners almost immediately begin to develop clever ways to reduce its impact. Hackers and corporate spies continue to develop more sophisticated schemes to steal information from Web sites or networks, although software tools that detect break-ins have also grown in popularity and sophistication—this intrusion-detection software was a $100 million industry in 1999 and is expected to grow to $1 billion within a few years. Constraints will change whenever prices, income, regulations, or technology change, and individuals will make different choices as a result.

The fact that individuals try to maximize their well-being given the constraints they face implies that behavior can be altered either by changing people's opportunities to improve their well-being or by changing their constraints. In general, rewarding a particular course of action makes it more likely that an individual will follow that course. Similarly, an individual is less likely to engage in activities for which they are unrewarded or penalized. Analyzing the impact of changes in rewards or constraints yields important insights that can be applied to a broad array of problems. Understanding the creative, self-interested nature of individuals thus has important managerial implications.

Managerial Implications

Because managers are interested in affecting the behavior of employees, understanding what motivates individuals is key. In our framework, individuals' actions are the outcomes of efforts to maximize their personal well-being. People are willing to make trade-offs (for example, less leisure time for more income) if it is to their advantage to do so. Employees at Sears were pushed to trade personal integrity for increased income and job security because Sears's strict quota plan made integrity more expensive. Managers can promote desired behavior by appropriately designing rewards and constraints that affect the trade-offs that individuals face and hence their choices. In the same way that pricing policies will alter consumer behavior, compensation policies will alter employee behavior.

The fact that individuals are creative in minimizing the effects of constraints complicates managers' problems. A change in incentives will sometimes affect employee behavior in a perverse and unintended manner. Consider two of the former Soviet Union's early attempts at adopting incentive compensation plans. To discourage taxi drivers from simply parking their cabs, the government rewarded drivers based on total miles traveled. In response, the taxi drivers would drive empty cabs at high speeds on highways outside Moscow in order to accumulate mileage. Similarly, to encourage chandelier production, the government established rewards based on the total volume of production—measured in kilograms. Chandelier manufacturers started producing fixtures so massive that they literally would collapse ceilings. (It is less costly to make one 100-kilogram chandelier than five 20-kilogram chandeliers. Manufacturers also substituted lead for lighter-weight inputs.)

Closer to home, Lincoln Electric decided to extend its well-known incentive compensation program to its clerical workers. Counters were installed on all typewriters, and secretaries were paid based on the number of characters typed. Predictably, this new plan resulted in an increase in the number of pages typed. The plan was terminated, however, when the company discovered that a secretary spent her lunch hour typing reams of worthless pages (by depressing the repeat key) in order to increase her compensation. Similarly, a manager at a software company devised an incentive plan that paid $20 for each software bug found by the quality assurance staff and $20 for each bug that the programmers fixed. The programmers responded by creating bugs that they could then find and fix. The plan was canceled within a week after one employee netted $1,700. Sears initially adopted its commission plan and sales quotas to motivate its salespeople to work harder. The dishonest behavior was a side effect that undoubtedly was not anticipated when the plan was adopted.

Alternative Models of Behavior

We have described in general terms how the economic view of behavior can be used in managerial decision making. Yet there are many other models that are popularly used by managers (either explicitly or implicitly) to explain behavior and set policies, and we would be remiss if we did not address them. Our discussion of each of these models is simplified. The intent, however, is to capture the essence of a few of the more prominent views of behavior and to illustrate how managerial decision making can be affected by a particular view.

Only-money-matters model. Some people believe that the only important component of the job is the level of monetary compensation. As we have already suggested, however, people have a very broad range of interests and concerns, extending well beyond money. And people frequently choose early retirement, walking away from a regular paycheck in order to enjoy additional leisure time. Money is merely a convenient unit of value—it represents general purchasing power. Its use as a unit of value does not suggest that only money matters. In fact, Sears employees undoubtedly placed a high value on integrity, but Sears's compensation plan was structured in such a way that the employees were encouraged to sacrifice their integrity in order to keep their jobs.

People respond to various incentives, both monetary and nonmonetary. Promotions, public recognition of a job well done, and increased responsibility within the organization are all examples of nonmonetary incentives. In fact, the incentive effect of money declines dramatically at higher levels of compensation. Financial compensation is a universally accepted motivator and is regularly the first tool selected from the incentive kit, but it should not be the only tool.

Happy-is-productive model. Managers frequently assert, and not incorrectly, that happy employees are more productive than unhappy employees. Managers who follow this happy-is-productive model see as their goal the creation of a work environment that makes the employees happy. Psychological theories such as Maslow's and Herzberg's frequently serve as guides in efforts to increase employee job satisfaction.

The Hawthorne Experiments

Seven productivity studies were conducted at Western Electric's Hawthorne plant over the period 1924 to 1932. All seven studies focused on the effect on assembly-line workers' productivity of manipulating different aspects of the work environment (for example, length of break times and workday). Surprisingly, productivity rose virtually regardless of the particular manipulation. For example, productivity increased whenever the illumination of the work area was changed, regardless of whether the lights were turned up or down. This result is known as the Hawthorne effect, and it is among the most-discussed findings in psychology; it is often taken as support for the happy-is-productive model. The workers in the experiments were given special attention and nonauthoritarian supervision relative to other workers at the plant. Also, the affected workers' views on the experiments were solicited by management, and the workers were given more responsibility. These actions, it has been argued, increased job satisfaction and performance.

Parsons argues that the findings of the Hawthorne experiments can also be explained by accompanying changes in the compensation system. Prior to the experiments, all workers were paid based on the output of a group of about a hundred workers. During the experiments, the compensation plan was changed to base pay on the output of only five workers. As a result, a given worker's output more directly affected his or her own pay, and economic theory predicts increased output. Interestingly, the last of the original Hawthorne experiments observed workers whose compensation system was not changed. In that seventh experiment, there was no change in output.

The Hawthorne experiments are often cited as evidence that showing employees that managers care about them leads to higher productivity. Yet the experiments convincingly document that changes in pay-for-performance systems cause output to change.

In this view, productivity can be increased by promoting employee satisfaction—by designing less tedious jobs, redecorating the cafeteria, permitting longer coffee breaks, holding meetings at which employees can vent their grievances, and generally improving the work environment. In Sears's case, happier employees would be expected to provide customers with better, more honest service. But consider an employee who has been guaranteed lifetime employment with a large salary regardless of performance. The happy-is-productive model suggests that this employee will be extremely productive because the additional job security and high salary will increase his or her job satisfaction. In our view, however, productivity is more likely to go down, since the employee will receive no additional reward for working harder and will not be fired for slacking off (some would cite government jobs as examples). Several decades of research have demonstrated no clear relation between worker satisfaction and productivity.

Even if improving the work environment increased productivity, it would not necessarily motivate the employees to take specific actions. If top management adopts a strategy of emphasizing customer satisfaction and simultaneously institutes various policies to increase employee happiness, there may be a general increase in productivity but no detectable increase in customer satisfaction per se. As a motivating tool, improving the work environment falls short.

Good-citizen model. Some managers subscribe to the good-citizen model, which posits (again, not incorrectly) that employees have a strong personal desire to do a good job—that they take pride in their work and want to excel. Under this view, managers have three primary roles. First, they need to communicate the goals and objectives of the organization to employees. Second, they need to help employees discover how they can achieve these goals and objectives. Finally, managers should provide feedback on performance so that employees can continually improve their efforts. There is no need for incentive pay, since individuals are intrinsically interested in doing a good job. In the good-citizen model, there is never a conflict between an employee's personal interest and the interests of the company because employees place the interests of the company first.

This view suggests that the problems at Sears occurred because employees misunderstood what was good for the company—they thought that it was in the company's interest to increase sales at any cost, even if doing so required treating the customers dishonestly. Under the good-citizen view, Sears's management could motivate employee honesty by clearly communicating that Sears would be better off in the long run if employees refrained from deceiving the customers. Managers of each automotive center might be asked to hold a series of employee meetings to stress the value of honesty in customer service. In our framework, however, pleas from Sears managers for more honesty would have little effect on behavior without changes in the associated rewards and constraints.

In the former Soviet Union—the ultimate proponent of the good-citizen model—attracting workers to Siberia was always difficult. Now, however, despite the inhospitable climate and other privations, companies have no trouble drawing workers to the giant oil, gold, and diamond deposits. With the rest of the economy faltering and people sometimes paid in tires and brassieres, Siberia is a highly enticing environment, with workers receiving cash wages of about seven times the median Russian salary.

Which Model Should Managers Use?

Behavior is a complex topic, and no behavioral model is likely to be useful in all situations. However, our focus is on managerial decision making. In this context, there are at least two reasons to believe that our framework is particularly useful.

First, managers are typically interested in developing an organizational architecture that will work well regardless of the specific individuals filling particular jobs. People come and go, and the manager wants the organization to continue to thrive as these changes occur. Our framework is likely to be particularly useful in this context because it is based on very general assumptions about human behavior. (Of course, when the characteristics of a specific individual are important, other frameworks may be more valuable. For example, since a CEO's personal traits are perhaps the single most important determinant of his or her success, the board of directors might request a detailed psychological assessment for insight into a prospective CEO's behavior.)

Second, managers might be particularly interested in fostering *changes* in behavior. In contrast to other models, our framework provides managers with concrete guidance on how to alter behavior by changing the relevant costs and benefits facing the decision maker. Our characterization of people as creative maximizers of their own well-being subject to the constraints they face is a workable premise for designing effective performance evaluation and reward systems.

The principal challenge in designing the firm's organizational architecture, then, is to ensure that decision makers have both the relevant information to make good decisions and the incentives to use their information productively. There are no automatic systems for achieving this. Decision authority must be granted to employees through formal and informal job descriptions, and performance evaluations and rewards must be specified in formal and informal compensation contracts. In large corporations, the board of directors makes major policy decisions, such as naming the CEO. The CEO, in turn, retains certain areas of accountability but delegates many operating decisions (for instance, pricing, production, and financing decisions) to lower-level managers. Even the lowest-paid employee in the firm usually has some decision-making authority. These relationships are governed by formal and informal agreements and procedures. But even within a relationship that has been formalized with an explicit agreement such as an employment contract, there are many aspects of the relationship that will not be spelled out in the written agreement. And because employees are creative maximizers of their own well-being, their goals will not necessarily dovetail with the goals of their managers (or of the shareholders).

One of the significant benefits of a large corporation, of course, is that capital is provided by many investors who share in the risk of the company. Individual shareholders invest only a small amount of their wealth in any given company, and thus avoid "putting all their eggs in one basket." This diversification permits risk-averse investors to supply capital to corporations at a reasonable cost. The downside, of course, is that the rights to any residual profits are held by thousands of shareholders who take little direct interest in managing the company, and decision authority is delegated to professionals who often have limited (if any) ownership in the firm. As a result, incentive conflicts often arise between managers and shareholders. Decision makers within the firm will not inherently feel that their primary objective is to maximize shareholder value. For example, managers are not likely to care a great deal about cash flows that extend beyond their tenure. Or they may retain unprofitable divisions if the alternative involves laying off colleagues and friends.

Incentive conflicts can produce some excessive behavior. In 1994, CEO Eugene Lockhardt moved MasterCard's operations out of Manhattan to the suburbs near Greenwich, Connecticut. Relocation expenses of $26 million were 24 percent higher than expected, and operating costs were also 12 percent higher than expected. One-fifth of the workforce quit. Direct savings were only $8 to $10 million per year, not $11 to $15 million as had been projected. So why did MasterCard move? Three years after the move and after Mr. Lockhardt had left MasterCard for a new job in California, some conceded that the move was motivated by his desire to be "an eight-iron shot from Greenwich," where he was an avid golfer.

Excessive use of perquisites is another manifestation of incentive conflicts. In *Barbarians at the Gate*, Bryan Burrough and John Helyar vividly describe lavish expenditures and decisions of questionable merit by executives at RJR-Nabisco in the 1980s:

> It was no lie. RJR executives lived like kings. The top 31 executives were paid a total of $14.2 million, or an average of $458,000. Some of them became legends at the Waverly for dispensing $100 tips to the shoeshine girl. [CEO Ross] Johnson's two maids were on the company payroll. No expense was spared decorating the new headquarters, highlighted by the top-floor digs of the top executives. It was, literally, the sweet life. A candy cart came around twice a day dropping off bowls of bonbons at each floor's reception areas. Not Baby Ruths but fine French confections. The minimum perks for even lowly middle managers were one club membership and one company car, worth $28,000. The maximum, as nearly as anyone could tell, was Johnson's two dozen club memberships and John Martin's $105,000 Mercedes.

Certainly, some level of perquisites is desirable from the standpoint of both the managers and the shareholders, not only to increase productivity but for tax reasons. But excessive perks are symptomatic of an organizational architecture that is out of balance. And evidence from the stock market suggests that the level of perks at RJR was not consistent with the shareholders' objective of value maximization. RJR's stock price went from about $55 per share in October 1988, when a takeover offer was received from Kohlberg, Kravis, and Roberts, to about $110 per share when the company was actually taken over and the management team was replaced, reflecting the market's expectations of improved operating performance. Thus, it does not appear that the old RJR management team was maximizing value.

Naturally, there are various mechanisms for controlling incentive conflicts. Concerns about reputation act as a powerful force to bring disparate objectives into alignment, and the penalties on organizations and individuals for unscrupulous behavior can be quite severe. Managers who encourage welshing on product guarantees in order to save on repair expenses will find that sales take a nosedive. In an unusual case, the Bank of Credit & Commerce International (BCCI), based in Pakistan, collapsed in 1991 in a fraud and money-laundering scandal. Because of adverse publicity surrounding the firm, many of its former employees were unable to find new jobs and ultimately brought suit against the bank for the stigma on their careers. Britain's House of Lords allowed the case to go to trial, saying that a business could be forced to pay damages for breaking its implicit agreement with its employees to operate honestly.

Concerns about reputation will also motivate individuals to act in the best interests of the firm, at least to some degree. Employees with good reputations for being hard-working team players are more likely to be promoted or given pay increases. But it is primarily the firm's organizational architecture—its decision authority, performance evaluation, and reward systems—that serves to control incentives. This architecture provides an important set of constraints and incentives that can help resolve conflicts of interest.

At this point, we have laid the foundations for the chapters that follow. We have discussed what it means to create shareholder value and how a firm's strategy and organizational architecture interact in the value-creation process. We have shown how knowledge and incentives play key roles in the firm's organizational design, and we have developed some guiding principles for assigning decision authority and motivating employees to make value-enhancing decisions. We will now proceed to discuss each of the three legs of the organizational stool in greater detail. Although we address each leg individually, it is important to remember that they are fundamentally interdependent.

The First Leg: Decision Authority, the Level of Empowerment, and Centralization versus Decentralization

*T*he issue of centralization versus decentralization focuses on deciding where within the firm's hierarchy to assign decision authority. Recently the trend has been toward greater decentralization, motivated in part by increased global competition and changes in technology, as well as by the benefits of faster, more streamlined decision making. Nonetheless, it is worth reviewing the pros and cons of decentralized decision making. Determining where within a given hierarchical level to assign decision authority is primarily a function of the link between decision authority and knowl-

edge. A discussion of the decision process in general must distinguish between decision management and decision control in order to make the concept of empowerment more precise. Of course, employees have incentives to try to influence decision makers, and thus they can affect the optimal delegation of decision authority within the firm. Finally, there are trade-offs in assigning decision authority to one individual versus assigning it to a team. In keeping with our emphasis on balancing the three elements of organizational architecture, we note the importance of accompanying decentralization with an increased emphasis on performance measurement and incentive compensation in order to motivate the newly empowered decision makers to make value-enhancing decisions.

From Centralization to Decentralization and Back

Honda Motor Company was founded in 1948 by Soichiro Honda. Initially, decision making within the company was quite centralized. Mr. Honda made virtually all product and design decisions, while finance and marketing decisions were made by his partner, Takeo Fujisawa.

In 1973, Soichiro Honda retired. His successors adopted a more decentralized approach to decision making. Major decision-making authority was allocated among nearly thirty senior executives, who spent much of their time gathered at conference tables hammering out policies in informal sessions called *waigaya*—a Honda word meaning "noisy-loud." Engineers in research and development had responsibility for the design of new automobiles. Under this so-called Honda System, the company grew and prospered.

By the late 1980s, however, Honda's growth had stalled, and its profits had declined. Honda had lost market share in the Japanese auto market, falling from third to fourth, behind Mitsubishi, Nissan, and Toyota. Part of Honda's problem was that it hadn't responded to changing tastes in the Japanese auto market.

In April 1991, the new CEO, Nubuhiko Kawamoto, announced that he was radically changing the decision-making system at Honda by taking direct control of the company's automotive operations in Japan. He reasoned that the company had grown too large for group decision making:

> We'd get the people from research, sales, and production together and everyone would say "not this" or "not that." We'd talk but there would be no agreement. Product planning would be on a tight schedule but we would have another discussion, another study and more preparation. Finally, the decision would come months later.

The centralization of decision authority at Honda was seen as a cultural revolution. Even after Kawamoto obtained the retired Soichiro Honda's support for this radical change, Honda employees resisted. Despite their resistance, however, the system changed. By 1993, powerful "car czars" ran the development of new models, middle managers had clear job responsibilities, and, according to some insiders, Kawamoto's power exceeded even that once held by Soichiro Honda.

The first real test of the new management structure was the unveiling of the 1994 Honda Accord. The vehicle was priced competitively and was widely acclaimed a success—it was named one of the Top 10 Cars of 1994 by *Car and Driver* magazine and Import Car of the Year by *Motor Trend* magazine. In 1998, a new CEO, Hiroyuki Yoshino, took over at Honda. The Accord remained the top-selling car in the United States throughout the 1990s, and Honda reported record profits.

Honda is just one of many firms that changed the assignment of decision authority within its organization over the past decade. But in contrast to Honda, most firms have *decentralized* decision authority—

for example, by *empowering* employees. An example of this trend, again from the automobile industry, is Fiat. In 1992, Fiat announced that it was decentralizing certain decisions, assigning them to the operating levels and cutting management positions. Other firms that have decentralized decision authority include General Electric, Motorola, and United Technologies, to name but a few. In fact, the financial press is constantly reporting how companies have improved profits, quality, and customer satisfaction through employee empowerment and other changes in their decision-making systems.

These examples raise a number of important organizational questions:

- Can altering the assignment of decision authority really have an important impact on productivity and value?
- What factors affect the optimal delegation of decision authority within the firm?
- When is it optimal to delegate decision authority to a team of employees rather than to specific individuals?

Assigning Tasks and Decision Authority

Firms transform raw materials into products, which are sold to customers. This process typically involves many *tasks*. At Honda, for example, vehicles have to be designed, assembled, painted, sold, and delivered. An important element of organizational architecture is the way in which tasks are grouped and then assigned to specific individuals and/or teams within the organization (a topic we explore in more detail in the next chapter).

Through the process of designing the organization, specific *jobs* are created. For example, a secretarial job might be created by bundling together a set of clerical tasks and assigning them to an individual. Jobs have at least two important dimensions: the *variety of tasks* that the employee is asked to complete and the *decision authority* to determine when and how best to complete those tasks.

Jobs vary substantially in terms of the variety of tasks and the degree of decision authority. Some jobs consist of just a few tasks and very limited decision authority. An example is a typist in a typing pool who concentrates on a single task and has limited discretion as to what to do or how to do it. Other jobs consist of many tasks but still provide limited decision authority. For instance, clerical jobs may involve filing, typing, answering the phone, making travel arrangements, and scheduling meetings, but the people in these jobs have minimal decision authority. Still other jobs consist of a narrow set of tasks but provide broad decision authority. A sales representative may have decision authority over which customers to contact, what sales pitch to make, what prices to charge, and so on, yet he or she concentrates on one principal task—selling products to customers. Finally, there has been a trend toward creating jobs that are broader in scope and yet also retain broad decision authority.

As managers move up in the corporation, job design issues consume more of their time. For example, a department manager plays an important role in defining the tasks of each employee within the department. But the problem of allocating tasks to jobs is extremely complex. It involves the assignment of literally thousands of tasks and decisions. It also involves simultaneous consideration of other corporate policies such as performance evaluation and compensation policy—the other two legs of our organizational architecture stool.

To illustrate this problem, consider the issue of setting prices. We initially assume either that headquarters sets prices for the local units or that the local managers have the authority to set their own prices. If headquarters grants the local managers the right to set prices, it reduces its own decision authority and correspondingly increases the decision authority of the local managers. In reality, headquarters can grant the local managers some decision authority without giving them full pricing responsibility—for example, by allowing local managers to set prices within a given range (we call this *boundary setting*). A firm has centralized decision making if headquarters retains decision authority, and it has decentralized decision making if the decision authority is assigned to the local managers.

A second issue is *choosing where within a given hierarchical level a decision should be made.* The decision authority of local managers is greater if they are each given decision authority over pricing in their respective locations. Alternatively, headquarters might decide to increase the decision authority of only one of the local managers— for example, by letting one manager make all the pricing decisions for a region. The primary decision, then, involves centralization versus decentralization.

Centralization versus Decentralization

In deciding whether to centralize or decentralize decision making, managers must consider the pros and cons of each. The principal benefit of decentralization is that it strengthens the link between decision authority and local knowledge, as we have discussed in previous chapters, and encourages the conversion of employee expertise or wetware into techniques or software that can create value (see Chapter 3). A principal danger, of course, is that incentive conflicts increase as decision authority is pushed down into the organization to lower-level employees who may not see their primary goal as maximizing shareholder value. The benefits and costs of decentralized decision making are summarized in Table 4.1.

Benefits of Decentralization

Effective use of local knowledge. Decentralized firms are better able to take advantage of local knowledge within the organization. Line managers generally have more accurate information about the de-

Table 4.1 The Benefits and Costs of Decentralized Decision Making

Benefits	Costs
More effective use of local knowledge (conversion of wetware to software)	Incentive problems
Conservation of the time of senior management	Coordination costs and failures
Training and motivation for local managers	Less effective use of central information

mands and price sensitivities of particular customers in local markets than headquarters does. They are also more familiar with the quality and condition of their production and inventory. This information is potentially difficult to share. If headquarters makes all pricing decisions, for example, then either the firm must expend resources to make the relevant pricing information available to headquarters, or headquarters must make decisions without all the relevant knowledge. Decentralization links decision-making authority with local specific knowledge and can reduce the costs of information sharing and processing. More effective use of local knowledge is thus one of the major benefits of decentralized decision making.

With centralized pricing decisions, local managers must seek permission to change prices. Headquarters then has to deliberate and convey its decision back to the local managers for implementation. This process takes time, and as a result decision making is slower. Such delays can lead to lost profit opportunities. Granting decision authority to line managers generally promotes more rapid decision making and quicker responses to changing market conditions.

At Kodak in the late 1980s, for example, poor performance in the manufacture of black-and-white film motivated the company to abandon its centralized decision-making approach and assign primary responsibility for the entire flow of the process to self-directed work teams. The results of this reorganization were impressive. The "Zebra Team" cut production costs by some $40 million and inventory by about $50 million. In film finishing, what had formerly taken four to six weeks was routinely accomplished in two days. In film coating, what had taken forty-two days was done in fewer than twenty. New products were brought to market in half the time. Decentralization thus facilitated the conversion of employee wetware into software, thereby creating value.

In our earlier Honda example, in contrast, decentralized decision making was slower than centralized decision making. In Honda's case, however, decision authority was decentralized to a large team of top executives. The bottleneck was in the team dynamics, which we discuss later in the chapter.

Conservation of management time. If the CEO spends time making local pricing decisions, that time cannot be used for making other decisions. Another benefit of decentralizing operating decisions to local managers, then, is that it frees up senior managers to focus on strategic decisions such as which product lines to sell and how to promote them. As Alfred Sloan, former CEO of General Motors and an early proponent of decentralization, described:

> My office force is small. That means we do not do much routine work with details. They never get up to us. I work fairly hard, but it is on the exceptions . . . not on routine or petty details.

Training and motivation of line managers. It is important for firms to attract talented employees and to train them as eventual replacements for senior management. Decentralized decision authority promotes both objectives. Granting responsibility to local managers helps to attract and retain talented, ambitious people who are likely to value this aspect of the job. It also provides the experience in decision making that is important training for more senior positions.

Costs of Decentralization

Of course, there is a downside to decentralization, too. It can create incentive problems, coordination problems, and information-sharing problems.

Incentive problems. Decentralization links decision authority with local knowledge. However, line managers do not necessarily have strong incentives to maximize shareholder value. For example, consummating sales requires less effort if local managers can simply quote lower prices. In extreme cases, local managers might discount products to their friends or obtain kickbacks from customers in return for selling at low prices. Developing an effective control system to prevent such actions is rarely easy or inexpensive. Also, there is nearly always some loss in shareholder value because it generally is not cost-effective to perfectly align each employee's interests with those of the shareholders. Incentive problems usually become more severe the further down in the organization decision authority is granted.

Ideally, headquarters would like to measure the effect of the local managers' decisions on shareholder value and use compensation schemes to motivate value-maximizing behavior. But directly observing the effect on shareholder value of individual decisions within the firm is usually impossible. Compensation schemes can be based on performance measures such as internal accounting numbers, and local managers can be paid based on their units' total profits. However, developing effective compensation schemes and performance measures is not always straightforward. (These issues are discussed in the next several chapters.) The firm can use other mechanisms—such as direct monitoring—to reduce incentive problems, but none of these techniques is costless.

Coordination costs and failures. If local managers operate independently, they may overlook important interaction effects. For instance, lowering the price at one location might divert sales from other locations—especially if those locations are nearby and share local media. It might also be wasteful for local managers to conduct their own market analyses if their markets are similar; most of the information could be obtained by conducting only one survey, or more precise estimates might be derived by pooling the observations.

Less effective use of central information. Line managers do not necessarily have all the relevant information for making good operating decisions. For example, headquarters might have important knowledge and expertise concerning ways to solve pricing problems, having observed the effects of various policies implemented over time at multiple locations. Headquarters might also have important information about product costs, upcoming promotions, and successful new products. For instance, in 1997 Häagen-Dazs introduced a new ice cream flavor in Buenos Aires called *dulce de leche*, named after a popular local flavor. Within weeks it was the store's best seller. A year later, consumers from Paris to Los Angeles were enjoying the same flavor; in stores that carry *dulce de leche*, only vanilla sells better. Headquarters thus plays an important role in the process of converting employee wetware (in this case, the idea for the new flavor) into software (replicating the formula and marketing it throughout the entire chain of stores). To promote hot products across markets, firms are reassigning decision authority so that products that are hot in one market are spotted more readily and introduced into other regions. This often requires some centralization. In fact, Häagen-Dazs consolidated its international division in order to better swap ideas, Quaker Oats cut a layer of management and merged some foreign divisions in order to build better communications across regions, and McDonald's reorganized its U.S. structure to resemble its overseas organization in order to encourage cross-border ad campaigns and tie-ins.

In general, local managers have more limited experience and obtain direct information from only one location. There may also be economies of scale in having headquarters make operating decisions for all units within the firm (some decisions have to be made only once, rather than many times). And if industry conditions are such that rapid decision making involving central information is important, the benefits of centralization are even greater.

An important role of central management in a decentralized decision system is to promote information flows and coordinate decision making within the firm. These activities typically involve transferring information to local decision makers, which can be expensive. The value of central information and coordination will be lower, of course, when product demand and product costs for the local units are more independent (for example, when the locations are farther apart) and when more of the relevant knowledge for decisions is held by the local managers.

Illustrating the Trade-Offs

Over time, the costs and benefits of decentralization will vary. For example, the importance of local knowledge can change when competition increases or consumer demand shifts. Also, the costs of transferring information and controlling incentive problems can decline as a result of new technologies (such as fax machines and email). Thus, if the importance of local knowledge increases as competition becomes more global, the optimal level of decentralization also increases.

Our analysis of centralization versus decentralization can help to explain the changes in the assignment of decision authority at Honda Motor Company in 1991. Recall that after Soichiro Honda retired in 1973, the relevant knowledge for decision making was spread among many executives, making the benefits of decentralization high. During this period, Honda could be viewed as operating with an appropriately high level of decentralization. By 1991, however, Honda had grown tremendously, and consensus decision making was no longer effective.

Also, Nubuhiko Kawamoto, the new CEO, was a former Honda engineer with considerable experience in the process of designing automobiles. The benefits of decentralization were thus smaller than previously (when senior management had less of the relevant knowledge). In response to these changing conditions, Kawamoto decreased the level of decentralization. The reduction in the benefits of decentralization combined with an increase in the costs resulted in a lower optimal level of decentralization.

And sometimes there are external factors at work. Bombardier Inc., the Canadian railcar company, has twelve factories in Europe and is buying more. It could save millions of dollars by consolidating operations—but it chooses not to. "Local presence is very important," says one manager. And although formal local-content rules requiring foreign companies to use local workers are banned in Europe, the practice still exists informally. Public authorities fear political fallout from awarding contracts to companies with nonlocal workers. One venture capitalist remarks, "If you look at who wins orders, local content is still very important." These political pressures are causing companies like Bombardier to be more decentralized than they would be otherwise. However, Bombardier is trying to centralize certain functions in Europe, such as engineering and purchasing, to reduce costs.

How Decentralization Varies by Type of Firm

We have seen how the firm's business environment and strategy are major determinants of organizational architecture, focusing particular attention on three factors in the environment: technology, market conditions, and regulation (see Figure 1.1). The benefits of decentralization tend to be highest in rapidly changing environments.

Research suggests that larger firms with greater local specific knowledge, higher diversification, and less regulation are more likely to have a higher degree of decentralization. In unregulated industries where market conditions and production technologies change frequently, the timely use of local knowledge will be particularly important. In more stable environments, companies can use centralized decision making and concentrate on gaining economies of scale through large-scale standardized production.

The benefits of decentralization are also likely to increase as the firm enters more diverse markets. If a firm offers a broad array of products, senior managers are less likely to have the knowledge necessary for good operating decisions across the various businesses. Decentralization will frequently be more important for firms that are pursuing a strategy of developing differentiated products at premium prices. Such a strategy requires effective use of information about customer demand and competitor offerings, information that is often held by lower-level managers in the organization. With strategies that focus on low-cost production of standardized products, however, local knowledge is often less important.

Another element of business strategy is the degree of vertical integration—whether a manufacturing firm makes its own inputs or provides its own retail distribution and service network. As the firm becomes larger, either through vertical integration or through geographic expansion, the appropriate level of decentralization will generally increase because more decisions have to be made. Time and mental-processing constraints will prevent senior managers from making all major decisions.

Centralized decision making has particular advantages when coordination of activities within the firm is important. For instance, airlines using a hub-and-spoke arrangement schedule short-haul flights from the spokes to arrive at a central hub at roughly the same time so that passengers can easily connect to their next flights. Airlines using centralized scheduling are able to coordinate their flight schedules and arrange baggage connections at lower cost and affording greater convenience to customers than if schedules were determined by decentralized decision makers (for example, by the commuter airlines affiliated with the larger carriers). Similarly, it is important for large commercial banks to coordinate the development of automatic teller machines centrally, so that all branches use the same system. And many decentralized firms find ways of overlaying elements of centralization onto their organizations. McKinsey & Company, with over 8500 professionals working at over eighty offices spread across five continents, is one of the most prominent management consulting firms in the world. It is important for McKinsey to have relatively decentralized decision making because of the vast amount of local knowledge held by on-site professionals. Nonetheless, if McKinsey is to deliver consistent, state-of-the-art products, communication throughout the organization is important. In 1989, McKinsey formed its Rapid Response Team. The purpose of this team was to respond to requests about the best current thinking and practice by providing ready access both to documents and to experienced consultants. A computerized database catalogs printed material and the experience profiles of consultants throughout the organization. In 1991, the Rapid Response Team responded to over a thousand requests for information and assisted nearly a quarter of the firm's consultants and clients throughout the world. Again, some degree of centralization can facilitate the conversion of wetware into software.

Recent Trends

In the past two decades, global competition has increased tremendously in many industries. Consider, for example, the automobile, consumer electronics, and computer industries. Competition has placed pressures on firms to cut costs, produce higher-quality products, and meet the demands of customers in a more timely fashion. The information needed for improving quality, customer service, and efficiency is often found lower in the organization. Thus, competitive pressures have increased the benefits of decentralization for many firms.

Technology has prompted changes in the level of decentralization for two reasons. First, the rate of technological innovation has increased dramatically. Firms must respond quickly to the resulting changes in market conditions and production technologies or risk losing market share and profits. These developments can motivate firms to decentralize decision authority when important aspects of the knowledge about new technologies are more likely to be held by local managers. Second, new technologies such as cellular phones and email have significantly lowered the costs of sharing information. In some cases, these changes have worked to promote decentralization by reducing the costs and time required to transfer central information to local decision makers to coordinate and enhance decentralized decisions. Computers have also made it less expensive to track the sales and production costs of individual products, thus increasing the feasibility of developing more precise performance standards for local decision makers that can be used in incentive compensation plans.

In other cases, the effect has been in the opposite direction—it has become easier to transfer local information to headquarters, favoring centralized decision making. For example, computerized cash registers allow central tracking of inventory and can increase the benefits of centralized purchasing. Many of the restocking decisions within Wal-Mart are now handled by an automated system through which suppliers restock items at individual stores whenever the system indicates that inventories have fallen to a specified level. Managers at individual stores have little decision authority over inventory levels. Advanced networks are creating huge operational changes in financial services firms, such as online banking over the Internet. Call centers and loan processing used to be decentralized, but electronic networks are centralizing and consolidating these services as well.

Technological advances have also allowed many firms to flatten their management structures. T. J. Rodgers, CEO of Cypress Semiconductors, uses a computer system to track the daily objectives of every company employee. The company essentially has no middle management. To quote from an article in *Fortune:*

> The computer system allows the CEO to stay abreast of every employee and team in his fast-moving organization. Each employee maintains a list of 10 to 15 goals like "Meet with marketing for new product launch," or "Make sure to check with Customer X." Noted next to each goal is when it was agreed upon, when it's due to be finished and whether it's finished yet.
>
> This way, it doesn't take layers of expensive bureaucracy to check who's doing what, whether someone has got a light enough workload to be put on a new team, and who's having trouble. Rodgers says he can review the goals of all 1,500 employees in about four hours, which he does each week.

Traditionally, firms relied on middle managers to transmit information and instructions from senior management to lower-level employees. Middle managers have also played an important role in coordinating and monitoring the actions of these lower-level employees. But by facilitating communication between senior management and lower-level employees, newer computer technology has reduced the need for middle managers. Technology has also led to changes in the roles of middle managers. In many firms, middle management's role has shifted from being a conduit in the information flow to something that more closely resembles coaching a sports team—assembling the best group of players, helping the team to design winning strategies, providing motivation, and so on. And perhaps the most important aspect of this new role is to encourage employees to share their wetware and to be alert to opportunities to convert that wetware into software that increases shareholder value.

Lateral Decision Authority

While discussions of decision authority often focus on centralization versus decentralization, lateral issues can also be important. Questions relating to the assignment of decision authority within hierarchical levels arise frequently within organizations. For example, should personnel decisions be made within each individual division, or should this be the responsibility of a separate human resources department? Should a divisional manager be in charge of his or her own division's R&D, or should R&D be performed elsewhere in the organization? The firm can

- Grant local managers the decision authority for their own locations
- Grant decision authority to one local manager, who makes all operating decisions
- Ask the local managers to work as a team in deciding on operating policies

As in the centralization versus decentralization problem, the relevant factors in making this choice include the distribution of knowledge and the costs of coordination and control. For example, granting separate decision authority to local managers takes greater advantage of specific local knowledge. However, operating policies at the various locations will not necessarily be well coordinated. Alternatively, granting all decision authority to one manager promotes coordinated decision making and takes advantage of any economies of scale by having one person make all decisions; it might also be easier to oversee the decisions of only one person. But these advantages come at the potential expense of less effective utilization of the other managers' local knowledge. The value of the third option, granting decision authority to a team of managers, depends on a number of factors; we discuss this alternative next. Which of the three options is best depends on the specific circumstances facing the firm. For instance, having the local managers make independent decisions is likely to work better when the markets are more independent and the individual managers have more of the relevant local knowledge needed for making operating decisions.

Assigning Decision Authority to Teams

Sometimes a firm may want to assign decision authority to a team of employees rather than to one individual. We use the term *team* to refer broadly to the many different types of work groups that have decision-making authority (teams, committees, task forces, and so on). Firms grant decision authority to teams of employees for at least three basic purposes: to manage activities, to make products, and to recommend actions. Teams that manage activities are often composed of several individuals from different functional areas (for example, manufacturing, marketing, and finance). Teams that make products often operate at the plant level. For instance, some firms give teams of production employees the decision authority to set their own work schedules and assignments and to organize the basic production process. Because their purpose is to manage some particular business or subprocess, both of these types of teams tend to be relatively permanent. Teams that are formed to recommend actions, however, focus on specific projects and normally disband when the task is complete. An example is the Silver Bullet Team formed at Eastman Kodak to reduce the use of silver—the most expensive ingredient in making film (Kodak is the world's largest user of silver). But what are the pros and cons of group decision making relative to individual decision authority?

Benefits of Team Decision Making

Improved use of dispersed specific knowledge. The relevant knowledge for decision making is often dispersed among many people within an organization. For instance, the relevant knowledge for product design resides with a variety of employees, including scientists,

82

engineers, and sales personnel. Through the use of teams, the individuals with specific knowledge are involved directly in the decision-making process. By definition, specific knowledge is difficult to collect and transfer to a single decision maker. Also, it can be important for the individuals with the relevant knowledge to share information among themselves. When information is shared in a group setting, new ideas may be generated that would not occur in a series of bilateral dialogues between the central decision maker and the individual employees. Sharing information also makes employees better informed for future decisions and actions. Granting decision authority to a team encourages the members to communicate and to brainstorm. Final decisions are then made through consensus or some type of voting mechanism.

At Hallmark, for example, team decision making has proved more productive than centralized decision making. It used to take Hallmark about two years to bring a new card to market. A new card had to move through the various functional areas, such as art, design, production, and marketing. Some of these functions were located in separate buildings. This all took time. Now Hallmark uses teams organized around specific holidays. For example, one team might work on cards for Mother's Day and another on cards for Valentine's Day. Teams are given most of the decision authority for the design and marketing of cards for a particular holiday. Through this process, Hallmark has cut in half its time to bring new cards to market.

Employee "buy-in." Employees are sometimes suspicious of management-initiated decisions, believing that they benefit managers at the expense of lower-level employees. Granting decision authority to groups of employees can increase employee buy-in. Employees who take part in a decision process are more likely to support the final decision and to participate actively in its implementation, for at least three reasons. First, they will be better informed about the decision and thus more confident of its value. Second, employees may feel they have less to fear if they make the decision themselves or if the decision is made by other employees with similar interests. In such cases, there is less concern that the policy is prompted by some hidden agenda. Reduced concern about the effects of the decision increases employee buy-in, even when senior management might have reached the identical decision. Third, employees have stronger incentives to work at implementing decisions that they recommend because their reputations depend on the ultimate outcomes of the decisions.

Costs of Team Decision Making

Collective-action problems. Collective decision making is often slow. Recall how it took months for senior executives at Honda Motor Company to reach a consensus on policy decisions. Group decision making is also subject to manipulation and political influence. And group decisions are not always efficient or rational. (Consider the old saying that a camel is a horse designed by a committee.)

For this reason, not everyone likes empowerment. Consider the example of Eaton Corp., which adopted worker-empowered teams at a small forge plant in Indiana. Many workers liked the idea of being their own boss and not having time clocks or supervisors. Self-directed work teams were responsible for deciding who was hired and fired, disciplining their members, and organizing production. Managers became "vision supporters" and functioned like coaches. Everyone wore the same blue uniforms. New hires underwent a grueling interviewing process, often involving as many as thirteen interviews—some with team members. Employees were careful about endorsing people because if a person whom they endorsed failed, it would reflect badly on the endorser.

However, many employees had difficulty adapting to the subtle control mechanisms of self-directed teams. Instead of one boss, employees now had a hundred bosses—everyone else on their team. When one team mistakenly produced a batch of faulty parts, the entire team had to explain the mistake to the rest of the factory. Disciplining coworkers in open meetings turned out to be very uncomfortable for some people. In discussing such disciplinary team meetings, one employee remarked, "I'd rather a 'vision supporter' dealt with stuff like that." This plant now has one of the highest turnover rates among all of Eaton's factories, 10 percent annually.

"Free-rider" problems.   Each team member hopes that the other members will work diligently for the success of the team. Yet individual members have an incentive to slack off because they bear only their proportionate share of the effect of their diminished effort on the group's results. Free-rider problems are common in most group activities and become more severe as the size of the group increases. They can be reduced through appropriate performance evaluation and reward schemes, although these schemes can be costly to design and administer.

Management Implications

When will team decision making work best?   Some managers and consultants argue that team decision making is almost always better than individual decision making. Our discussion suggests that team decision making is more likely to be productive when the relevant knowledge for the decision is dispersed among individuals and when the costs of collective decision making and controlling free-rider problems are low.

Team decision making is a common component of total quality management (TQM) programs, and many firms have increased their use of team decision making in the last few years through the implementation of TQM programs. Yet experience indicates that the *indis-*

criminate use of teams in TQM programs can be counterproductive—in such cases, the costs exceed the benefits.

Optimal team size.   Increasing the size of the team clearly enhances the team's knowledge base. However, larger teams increase the incentives to free-ride and also reduce the ability to make decisions and work in a coordinated fashion (remember Honda's *waigaya* meetings). Investment banks tend to have small corporate finance teams, even though in the weeks preceding a deal the team members frequently work one-hundred-hour weeks, because a ten-person team working fifty-hour weeks will not be as productive as a five-person team working one-hundred-hour weeks. It can be very difficult to quantify these costs and benefits, but research indicates that effective teams will have no more than twenty-five members and are typically much smaller.

Monsanto Inc., for example, used two-person teams that merged R&D and commercial skills to gain a competitive edge over its biotech rivals by bringing new genetic technologies to market faster. How did this work? The team model consists of a scientist and a marketing or financial specialist who act as codirectors to oversee a Monsanto business, such as global cotton seed. The two work in adjoining cubicles and are called "box buddies." They jointly share all decision-making responsibilities and earn the same pay, benefits, and bonuses. In Monsanto's giant agricultural sector, thirty box buddies lead most of the crop teams. This is how Monsanto tries to tap into relevant knowledge for decision making. But constant communication and good relationships are necessary. Besides having adjacent offices, box buddies use advanced pagers, email, and videoconferencing. In most cases, the box buddies travel together. However, and perhaps ironically, when Monsanto and American Home Products tried to merge in 1998, the deal fell through because the two CEOs were to be co-CEOs—but they couldn't agree on how to become box buddies and share the top job.

Decision Management and Control

Thus far, our characterization of decision making has been rather simplified. In particular, we have been assuming that an employee either does or does not have decision authority. In reality, some aspects of a decision can be decentralized, while other aspects are made at a higher level. As we suggested earlier, for example, line managers might have the authority to set prices within some range but require approval from headquarters for larger price changes. Thus, the decision authority of an employee can be increased without granting the employee full responsibility for a particular decision.

A useful characterization divides the decision-making process into four steps:

- *Initiation:* Generating proposals for various decision options
- *Ratification:* Selecting one decision from among the options
- *Implementation:* Executing the selected decision
- *Monitoring:* Measuring the performance of decision makers and establishing rewards

Often, initiation and implementation authority are merged into what we refer to as the *decision management function*, and ratification and monitoring authority are similarly merged to form what we call the *decision control function*. Decision management authority and decision control authority are generally assigned separately.

Granting an employee both decision management and decision control authority will not typically lead to value-maximizing behavior. If line managers make decisions and there is no independent monitoring or control, the managers are more likely to use their decision management authority for their own benefit. When decision makers have no stake in the firm's cash flows, decision management and decision control should be separated. Only when the decision maker has the legal rights to the residual profits of the enterprise (the cash left over after all bills have been paid, including debt interest and taxes; see Chapter 2), are these incentives internalized, and only then does it make sense to combine decision management and decision control.

Separation of decision management and decision control. A prominent example of the separation of decision management and decision control is the presence of a board of directors at the top of the corporation. In large corporations, the residual profits belong to the shareholders. The management of the firm is primarily the responsibility of the CEO, who typically owns less than 1 percent of the firm's stock. To mitigate potential incentive problems, the shareholders grant ultimate decision control authority to the board of directors. The board ratifies major decisions initiated by the CEO. The board also has monitoring authority and the right to fire and compensate the CEO. However, since board members are rarely major shareholders, there is still a role for other parties that "monitor the monitor." This role is performed by holders of large blocks of stock (such as public pension funds) and by takeover specialists. If the board of directors does a poor job, the directors can be replaced through a proxy fight or a corporate takeover.

The board has a fiduciary responsibility to the company and to the shareholders to exercise its decision control authority. Failure to do so can be costly, as was seen in the Compuware sexual harassment case. In the spring of 1998, Sheila McKinnon charged her boss, Peter Karmanos, CEO of Compuware, with sexual harassment. Karmanos had founded Compuware and built it into a $1.1 billion software company, in which he held a 12 percent stake worth $656 million. At a May 29, 1998, meeting of the board of directors, Karmanos disclosed McKinnon's allegations. Compuware's general counsel, Thomas Costello, presented an eighteen-page report from an outside investigator who had been hired to look into the allegations, which concluded that "there is no independent support for McKinnon's claims." Within ninety minutes the board decided to terminate McKinnon, and two days later she was fired.

But the outside directors had failed to take control of the investigation. By permitting the general counsel, one of Karmanos's subordinates, to supervise the investigation, they allowed Karmanos to retain decision authority over an investigation into his own alleged behavior. Experts in employment law say, "Get out of the way. When such explosive charges reach all the way to the top, it's crucial that the board, not the CEO or other senior executives, take control of the matter immediately." To ensure a thorough investigation and to meet its fiduciary responsibility, the outside directors of Compuware should have conducted the investigation, including hiring outside counsel and investigators. And these investigators should have reported back to the board, not to the CEO. Four days after she was fired, McKinnon filed a lawsuit against Karmanos and Compuware alleging sexual harassment and retaliation. In March 1999 the suit was settled out of court for an undisclosed amount.

The principle of separation of decision management and decision control also helps to explain the use of hierarchies within organizations. In hierarchies, decision management is formally separated from decision control—that is, the decisions of individuals are monitored and ratified by other individuals who are above them in the hierarchy. The same employee may have both decision control and decision management authority—for example, divisional managers might have the authority to approve certain initiatives of lower-level employees, while at the same time requiring authorization for the division's capital expenditure plan—but the important thing is that one employee not have responsibility for both decision management and decision control with respect to the *same decision*. In smaller organizations, where there is only one person (or only a few people) with the relevant knowledge to make decisions, it is awkward to separate decision management from decision control, and the two functions are often combined. But in such cases, the decision maker also tends to be an owner, which forestalls any incentive problems.

Should the CEO and the Board Chair Be Separate?

Many commentators complain that boards of directors of U.S. companies fail to adequately discipline senior managers. Of particular concern is the common practice of combining the titles of CEO and chairman of the board. On the surface, this practice seems to violate the principle of separating decision management and decision control. Benjamin Rosen, chairman of Compaq Computer, has voiced this concern succinctly:

> When the CEO is also Chairman, management has *de facto* control. Yet the board is supposed to be in charge of management. Checks and balances have been thrown to the wind.

Large shareholder associations and pension funds have in recent years sponsored proposals at Sears Roebuck and other large firms calling for separation of the titles. Government officials have considered regulations to force this change.

Contrary to the allegations of reformers, however, combining the titles of CEO and chairman does not necessarily violate the principle of separation of decision management and decision control. The extreme case of no separation exists only when the board has the CEO as its only member. Indeed, the boards of several large U.S. companies, including American Express, Eastman Kodak, General Motors, IBM, and Westinghouse, fired their CEOs/chairmen in the 1990s.

It is estimated that the titles are combined in over 80 percent of U.S. firms. In the vast majority of the remaining cases, the chairman is the former CEO. In these firms, the current CEO is typically a relatively new appointment, who will assume the combined title after a short probationary period. Proponents of regulations to force firms to appoint an outsider as chairman are essentially arguing that almost all major firms in the United States are inefficiently organized. While this assumption might be correct, the reformers have presented no cogent argument for how such an important corporate-control practice can be value-decreasing and still survive in the competitive marketplace for so long across so many companies (economic Darwinism).

While management and control authority for a decision are often granted to individuals at different levels within the organization, they are sometimes granted to separate individuals at the same level of the corporate hierarchy. For example, the quality of the output of a manufacturing division can be monitored by a quality unit with equal status within the organization. Similarly, internal auditors often monitor units on the same hierarchical level.

The separation of decision management from decision control is not a new idea. The charters of the English trade guilds, which were formed during the twelfth century, contained provisions for the election of auditors from the general membership of a guild to audit the financial records of that guild. The Book of Ordinances of 1564 contains an "order for ye audytors" that provides for four auditors to be chosen every year to audit the accounts between Michaelmas (September 29) and Christmas. The guild officers thus had decision management authority, but decision control authority was vested in the team of member auditors.

Empowerment. The concepts of decision management and decision control are also useful in making the term *empowerment* more precise. When managers announce that they are empowering employees, they are sometimes unclear about what authority is being granted. This ambiguity can lead to disputes and conflicts between management and employees—such as when management reverses the decisions of employees who thought they had been empowered. The principle of separation of decision management and decision control suggests that empowerment should not mean that an employee has complete responsibility for a particular decision. An empowered employee may have the authority to initiate and implement decisions; however, managers still have an important role to play in ratifying and monitoring those decisions. Ratification does not necessarily require that an employee seek approval for every decision. In some cases, managers might want to preauthorize decisions within a particular range (*boundary setting*). In any case, headquarters would want to maintain monitoring authority over the decision. Often, conflicts over empowerment can be avoided by a careful initial discussion of what authority is actually being delegated to the employee.

Influence Costs

Up to this point, we have assumed that decision-making authority is granted either to an individual or to a team within the firm, and that once the authority is granted, the employee or team is actively involved in decision making (subject to ratification and monitoring by others). But firms sometimes use bureaucratic rules that purposely limit active decision making. For example, airlines allocate routes to flight attendants based only on seniority—there is no supervisor who decides which flight attendant gets which route. Similarly, some firms base promotions solely on years worked with the firm.

One benefit of this limited discretion in making decisions is that it discourages individuals from trying to influence decisions. Employees are often quite concerned about the effects on them personally of decisions made within the firm. For example, flight attendants certainly care about which routes they fly. Employees are clearly not indifferent to which colleagues are laid off in an economic downturn. These concerns motivate politicking and other potentially nonproductive *influence activities* within the organization, thereby wasting valuable time trying to influence decision makers. In vying for promotions, for example, employees might take actions that are intended to make other employees look bad.

From *Barbarians at the Gate* (by Burrough and Helyar):

The scramble to succeed Sticht as CEO of Reynolds Tobacco split the company into warring camps. People no longer pulled together for the company. Now they looked after the interests of the executive they hitched their star to: Wilson, Horrigan, or Abely. Preparing for a financial analysts' meeting, Wilson and Abely quarreled over who would speak first—a squabble Sticht finally had to settle. At a rehearsal for presentations to a company-wide conference, Abely had run over his allotted time when Horrigan stomped into the room. "What's that . . . doing up there?" he stormed. "It's my time." Abely ordered a feasibility study on spinning off Sea-Land. Wilson, to whom Sea-Land reported, got wind of it and confronted John Dowdle, the treasurer, who was doing the study. "I'm sorry, I can't tell you about that," Dowdle said. "Abely will fire me if I tell you." Horrigan hired a public relations firm to get him nominated for the right kinds of business and humanitarian awards to enhance his resume. Horrigan's big score: a Horatio Alger award.

Eliminating discretion in decision making reduces these types of influence activities because there is no one to lobby. But such a tactic can also be harmful to an organization. When individuals are competing for a promotion, they have an incentive to prove that they are the most qualified person for the job. The information that results from their efforts to demonstrate their qualifications can be useful in making better promotion decisions. However, this information comes at a cost—employees are spending time trying to sell themselves rather than designing, producing, or selling products. It makes sense to limit discretion in decision making when the firm's profits are largely unaffected by decisions that nonetheless have a large impact on the welfare of individual employees. For example, an airline's profits are basically unaffected by which flight attendant gets the Hawaii route versus the Sioux Falls route. In such settings, the firm can benefit from a bureaucratic approach to decision making.

In this chapter, we have observed that jobs have at least two important dimensions—the degree of decision authority and the variety of tasks—and we have discussed decision authority in greater detail. In the next chapter, we turn to the variety of tasks as it relates to the bundling of tasks into jobs, the assignment of jobs to business units, and the organization of business units—whether that organization is based on function, product, or geographic area. We also address matrix organizations.

CHAPTER 5

Decision Authority II: Bundling Tasks into Jobs and Jobs into Business Units

*H*ow the tasks within a firm are bundled into jobs and then into business units can dramatically affect the firm's profitability. We distinguish between two types of jobs: those with specialized task assignment and those with broad task assignment. The trend today is toward creating jobs with more decision authority and broader task assignment, and we provide some useful insights into the nature of this trade-off. Firms can then group jobs into business units on the basis of functional specialty, geography, or product, or some combination of the three. Functional units are likely to work best in smaller firms that have a limited number of products and operate in relatively well-defined environments. Larger, more diverse firms will generally find it desirable to form units based on product or geography, with operating decisions decentralized to the business-unit level. Some firms, however, maintain an overlapping structure of functional and product or geographic business units.

These matrix organizations are more common in product-oriented industries such as defense, construction, and consulting, as well as for the international operations of U.S. firms. In matrix organizations, individuals are more likely to focus on the overall business process rather than on their own narrow functional specialty, although the intersecting lines of authority can create problems.

Reconfiguring Jobs to Boost Productivity

IBM Credit Corporation is a wholly owned subsidiary of IBM. Its major business is financing installment-payment agreements for IBM products. With assets valued at over $15 billion, IBM Credit would rank in the *Fortune* 100 finance companies on a stand-alone basis. In 1993, IBM Credit was touted in the financial press for having lowered the time required to process a credit application from six days to four hours. This decrease in cycle time was achieved through a major rebundling of the tasks performed by individual employees. Prior to this reengineering, individuals performed narrowly assigned tasks. For example, one employee would check the applicant's credit, and another would price the loan. Employees were grouped by functional specialties to form the basic business units of the firm, such as the credit and pricing departments. After the reengineering, applications were handled by "caseworkers" who processed applications from start to finish. The basic business structure of the company was correspondingly altered. The results at IBM Credit suggest that the way in which tasks are bundled into jobs and jobs into business units can dramatically affect a firm's productivity.

The issues involved in bundling tasks into jobs are obviously quite complex. Nonetheless, the problem is economic in nature—managers face a set of *economic trade-offs* when they bundle tasks. As in the case of decision authority, we can provide useful insights into the nature of these trade-offs by offering some simple examples.

Specialized versus Broad Task Assignment

FinWare, Inc. (a fictitious company), is a distributor of financial software. Its customers include individual consumers and small businesses. Within FinWare, there are two primary activities or *functions*: software sales and after-sales service (helping customers install the software in their systems and managing interfaces with other programs). Thus, FinWare must perform four basic tasks—sales and service for each of its two customer groups. Of course, these four basic tasks could be subdivided into a much larger number of individual tasks. To keep our discussion manageable, however, we will ignore this finer partitioning, although our analysis can be readily extended to cover such a subdivision.

FinWare operates in multiple locations throughout the country. At its newly opened East Coast office, each of the four tasks is expected to require four hours per day. Thus, the firm must hire two full-time employees for this office. The obvious alternatives for structuring the two jobs are (1) to have each employee specialize in one function (either sales or service) and perform that function for both customer groups, or (2) to have one employee provide both sales and service for individual consumers and the other employee perform both functions for business customers. We refer to the first alternative as *specialized task assignment* and the second as *broad task assignment*. The pros and cons of the two approaches are summarized in Table 5.1.

Advantages of Specialized Task Assignment

Using specialized rather than broad task assignment has at least two important benefits:

- *Exploiting comparative advantage.* Specialized task assignment allows the firm to match people with jobs based on skills and training, and correspondingly permits employees to concentrate

Table 5.1 Costs and Benefits of Specialized Task Assignment*

Benefits	Costs
Comparative advantage/economies of scale	Forgone cross-benefits
Lower training costs	Coordination costs
	Functional myopia
	Reduced flexibility

*Incentive issues can favor either specialized or broad task assignment, depending on the nature of the production technology and information flows.

on their particular areas of expertise. For example, FinWare can hire salespeople to sell and technicians to provide service. The principle of comparative advantage suggests that this specialization will often produce higher output than having individuals perform a broad set of tasks, because there are potential economies of scale in concentrating on a smaller number of tasks.

- *Lower training costs.* With specialized task assignment, each employee is trained to complete one basic function. With broad task assignment, employees are trained to complete more than one function, and this training can be more expensive. For instance, suppose the service function at FinWare requires a skilled technician with an advanced college degree, whereas the sales function requires an individual with only a high school diploma. Specialized task assignment will allow FinWare to hire one person with an advanced degree and one high school graduate. With broad task assignment, the required level of education is usually the highest level required for any of the assigned tasks. Thus, broad task assignment will require FinWare to hire two people with advanced degrees and to train each of them to perform both functions. Since it costs more to hire a person with an advanced degree than to hire a person with only a high school diploma, broad task assignment will be more expensive than specialized task assignment.

Adam Smith on the Economics of Specialization

With specialized task assignment, employees concentrate on performing a narrow set of tasks. Adam Smith, an important eighteenth-century economist and philosopher, was among the first to recognize the potential gains from this type of specialization. In his classic book *The Wealth of Nations,* he explained how a number of specialized employees, each performing a single step in the manufacturing of pins, could produce far more output than the same number of generalists making whole pins. Smith presents the following description of a pin factory using specialized employees:

> One man draws the wire, another straightens it, a third cuts it, a fourth points it, a fifth grinds it at the top for receiving the head; to make the head requires two or three distinct operations; to put it on is a peculiar business, to whiten the pins is another; it is even a trade by itself to put them into the paper.

Smith argued that a small factory with ten specialized employees could produce about 48,000 pins a day, whereas ten employees working independently could not have produced twenty pins per day.

Disadvantages of Specialized Task Assignment

While specialized task assignment has some advantages relative to broad task assignment, it also has drawbacks:

- *Forgone cross-benefits.* Sometimes, performing one task can lower the cost of performing another task if the same person does both tasks. For example, important information about a customer's service requirements might be acquired through the sales effort. This information is less likely to come to light if sales and service are handled by separate people. Or consider the case of two employees on an automobile assembly line. The first attaches the door to the car frame, and the second attaches the latching mechanism and makes sure that the door latches to the frame. If the first employee does not align the door correctly, the second will have more difficulty getting the door to latch properly. Combining the two tasks into one job increases the care the employee will take in checking for proper alignment before attaching the latch.

- *Coordination costs.* The activities of specialized employees must be coordinated. For instance, FinWare would have to establish procedures for transferring sales orders to service technicians. Also, it might have to appoint a manager to handle exceptions to these procedures (for instance, before committing to the purchase of the software, a customer might demand authorization for specialized installation).

- *Functional myopia.* With specialized task assignment, employees tend to concentrate on their own individual functions rather than on the overall process of providing sales and service to customers. For example, a salesperson who is compensated primarily through commissions will have incentives to sell software to a customer even if that sale will generate large service costs, as when the software is not well matched with the customer's existing computer system.

- *Reduced flexibility.* When task assignment is specialized and only one person is trained to perform a particular function, what happens when that person is sick or on vacation? Also, having only one person trained to do a job can place the firm at a disadvantage when bargaining with that employee over salary and other benefits. These problems will be more severe in small companies, since large companies are more likely to have several people who are trained to perform any given task.

Incentive issues. Our discussion of the costs and benefits of specialized versus broad task assignment has focused on informational and technological considerations, but incentive issues can also be important. From an incentive standpoint, it is sometimes better to have employees concentrate on a narrow set of tasks, while in other circumstances a broad set of tasks is preferable.

With broad task assignments, the firm is concerned not only with how hard employees work but also with how they allocate their effort among their assigned tasks. For instance, senior managers at FinWare would be concerned with how employees balance their sales and service efforts. Designing an evaluation and compensation scheme that motivates an appropriate balance of effort is complicated by the fact that often the effort exerted on some tasks is more easily measured than the effort exerted on other tasks. At FinWare, the sales effort can be easily measured by sales volume, but the quality of after-sales service might be quite difficult to measure—there are no good direct indicators of service quality, and poor quality might reveal itself only over time (primarily as customers fail to make repeat purchases). If FinWare pays a sales commission, employees with broad task assignments will concentrate on sales at the expense of providing good after-sales service to customers; selling has an immediate impact on their income, while providing better service affects their income only through its eventual effect on repeat purchases. FinWare can reduce this incentive to misallocate effort by not paying a sales commission, but then employees will have relatively low incentives to work at either task. Another potential response to this problem is to use specialized task assignments. The salesperson could be provided with high-powered incentives to concentrate on sales, and the service person could be evaluated and rewarded on the basis of more subjective measures, such as customer satisfaction surveys.

Some situations require the coordinated execution of several separate tasks that individually are difficult to assess. In such cases, it can make sense to assign all the tasks to one individual and make that person accountable for the final product, as IBM Credit did. For instance, in the example of attaching doors and latches to automobiles, assigning both tasks to one employee makes it easy to identify who is to blame if the door does not latch properly. At FinWare, a customer's failure to make a repeat purchase might be due to either poor sales effort or poor service. Having one employee responsible for both sales and service facilitates identification of the employee responsible for the customer's unhappiness.

Productive Bundling of Tasks

The decision concerning specialized or broad task assignment depends on the technological, informational, and incentive issues that have just been discussed. The degree to which tasks are related *within* versus *among* functional areas is likely to be of particular importance in making this decision. At FinWare, the success of specialized task assignment depends largely on the degree of similarity between the selling efforts for the two customer groups. If there are only minor differences between selling to individuals and selling to businesses, training employees in consumer sales will adequately prepare them to do business sales. In contrast, if the selling tasks are quite different, little is gained by training one employee to perform the two selling tasks as opposed to training separate employees. In this situation, any economies of scope that result from specializing in sales are likely to be small. Similarly, the costs of specialized task assignment at FinWare depend on how closely tasks are related across functional areas. When they are basically unrelated (for instance, when little valuable information about service is gained through the sales effort and vice versa), little is lost by having employees concentrate on a single function. In such cases, it is also relatively easy to develop routine procedures to coordinate the work of the individual specialists. Ultimately, the degree of relatedness among tasks depends on the way specialized knowledge is created and the costs of transferring that knowledge. It also depends on the technology used in the production process.

Our FinWare example is quite simplified. In most settings, more complicated task divisions are clearly possible. For instance, the selling function might have two phases, the initial contact and closing the deal. The initial contact requires less specialized product and service knowledge than closing the deal but is potentially more time-consuming. Here, it might be better for a salesperson to handle the initial contact and to schedule a joint call by both the salesperson and the service person to close the deal. Or, at some locations, more complete specialization might be feasible. For instance, an employee at an office with a larger sales volume could concentrate solely on selling to individuals. While our basic FinWare example does not deal with these more complicated considerations, it nevertheless isolates some of the key issues in deciding how to configure tasks into jobs.

Forming Business Units: Function versus Product or Geography

Our discussion of specialized versus broad task assignment highlights the trade-offs involved in bundling tasks into jobs. Managers are confronted with a similar set of trade-offs when they bundle jobs into business units such as departments, divisions, and subsidiaries. There are two standard methods of grouping jobs into business units: by function and by product and/or geography.

Grouping people together within a business unit lowers the costs of communication and coordination among the people *within the unit.* For instance, the people within a unit often report to the same manager, who facilitates information flows and coordination. (These information flows are critical to the process of converting employee wetware into value-creating software.) Employees are also likely to form closer working relationships if they share the same workspace— especially if they are evaluated and compensated on the basis of business unit performance. However, managers must then devise methods of coordinating activities *among interdependent business units.* For instance, rules and procedures must be developed for interunit activities, managers must be appointed and given the authority to rule on exceptions to these procedures, and liaison staff and coordinating committees must often be appointed to address interunit issues. In summary, there is a trade-off between the benefits that come from grouping people together and the costs of coordinating the activities of this group of people with the activities of other units. In addition, it is also important to consider incentive issues—some groupings make it easier to devise productive performance evaluation and reward systems than other groupings do. Some of the coordination problems that can arise within a functional organization are highlighted by the process that Cadillac formerly used for developing new products. Under this process, engineers were grouped by narrow functional specialty and charged with completing a related set of tasks:

> The designer of the car's body would leave a hole for the engine, then the power-train designer would try to fit the engine into the cavity, then the manufacturing engineer would try to figure out how to build the design, and finally the service engineer would struggle to invent ways of repairing the car. The results were predictable. On one model, the exhaust manifold blocked access to the air-conditioning compressor, so seasonal maintenance meant removing the exhaust system. On another model, the connection between the spark plugs and the spark plug wires was so tight that mechanics tended to break the wires when they pulled them off to check the spark plugs.

Automobile companies have been able to reduce problems of this type by moving to a system of "concurrent engineering" in which everyone affected by a design participates in the design process as early as possible. Often, companies use development teams that are charged with the entire process—these development teams group jobs by product rather than by function.

Grouping Jobs by Function

Grouping jobs by functional specialty, such as engineering, design, sales, finance, and so on, is sometimes referred to as the *unitary* or *U form* of organization because it places each primary function in one major business unit (rather than in multiple business units). Individual jobs are characterized by specialized task assignment. At FinWare, for example, all the sales jobs in the organization could be grouped together to form a sales department, and all the service jobs could be grouped together to form a service department. These departments would then be charged with managing their particular functions across the firm's entire product line. Figure 5.1 shows what the organization chart for FinWare would look like if the company were organized by function. Senior management plays an important role in defining the organizational architecture, coordinating activities among departments, making key operating decisions, and setting corporate strategy. For example, detailed procedures for transferring sales orders to the service department must be established. Exceptions and special cases are handled by senior management and/or by coordinating commit-

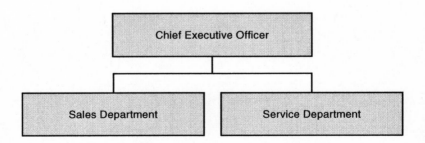

Figure 5.1 FinWare as a functional organization.

tees (which often include senior division managers and corporate staff).

Grouping Jobs by Product or Geography

In a *multidivisional* or *M form* of organization, jobs are grouped into a collection of business units according to product or geographic area. Operating decisions on product offerings and pricing are decentralized to the business-unit level. Senior management is responsible for major strategic decisions, including the organizational architecture and the allocation of capital among the business units. Figure 5.2 shows how the organization chart for FinWare would look if the company were organized by product or geography. With a product organization, the company is divided into a business products division and a consumer products division. Each of these divisions then has its own sales and service departments that focus on the particular products handled by that division (jobs within the business units are often grouped by functional area). In the geographic organization, the company is divided into a West Coast division and an East Coast division. In this

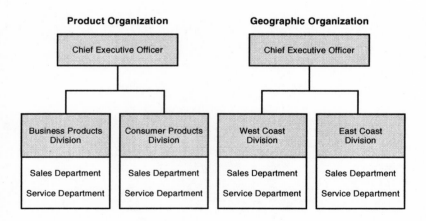

Figure 5.2 FinWare as a product and geographic organization

case, the sales and service departments within each business unit serve both individual and business customers within the unit's geographic area.

Trade-Offs between Functional and Product or Geographic Business Units

Benefits of functional business units. There are at least three major benefits to grouping jobs by function. First, such a grouping helps to promote effective coordination within the functional areas. For instance, a supervisor in the service department can assign employees to specific projects based on their current workload and expertise. It is also easier for functional specialists to share information if they are in the same department. For example, if a service technician develops a new solution to a problem (wetware), that employee's supervisor can help promote its use by training other technicians within the department (conversion to software). Second, a functional grouping helps to promote functional expertise. Employees focus on developing specific functional skills and are directly supervised by knowledgeable individuals who can assist and support this development. Third, there is a well-defined promotion path for employees. Employees tend to work their way up within a functional department—for example, from salesperson to local sales manager to district sales manager. Having a well-defined promotion path can reduce employee uncertainty about career paths and thus make it easier to attract and retain qualified employees.

Problems with functional business units. Although a functional grouping has advantages, it also has disadvantages. First, there is the issue of using senior management's valuable time to coordinate functions and make operating decisions—time that might be used more productively for activities such as strategic planning. Second, there can be significant, time-consuming coordination problems among de-partments. Let's suppose that FinWare is organized by function. When the sales department makes a sale, the order must be communicated to the service department, which in turn must schedule the required customer service. This process can cause lengthy delays in serving the customer. Moreover, important information can be lost in these communications between departments. Third, employees sometimes concentrate on their own functional specialties to the detriment of the overall goal of satisfying customers. For instance, the sales depart-ment might focus on achieving the department's goals, even if that focus imposes costs on other departments in the firm. A salesperson might promise a customer rapid installation even though the workload of the service department is already high. Finally, in some businesses, a familiarity with a variety of functions can be important for career advancement, so that well-defined functional career paths are less val-uable. Table 5.2 summarizes the benefits and costs of a functional organization.

Benefits of product or geographic business units. An advantage of the M form of organization for large corporations—especially those

Table 5.2 Benefits and Costs of Functional Organization Relative to Product or Geographic Organization

Benefits	Costs
Improved coordination among functional specialists	Less effective use of local product or geographic information
Development of functional expertise	Inappropriate use of senior management time
Well-defined promotion path	Coordination problems among business units
	Functional focus—it is more difficult to design compensation plans that promote a focus on profits and customers

in dynamic environments—is that decision authority for operations is assigned to individuals lower in the organization, where the relevant knowledge is typically found. Managers of business units are compensated on the basis of the performance of their units; this provides them with incentives to use their knowledge more productively. Decentralizing decision authority to business-unit managers also frees senior management to concentrate on other, more strategic issues. The separation of the corporate office from operations allows senior executives to focus their attention on the overall performance of the corporation rather than on specific aspects of the functional components. A product or geographic focus also promotes coordination among the functions that are involved in producing and marketing a particular product or serving a given geographic area.

Problems with product or geographic business units. Business-unit managers tend to focus on the performance of their own units. This focus is consistent with maximizing shareholder value so long as the unit manager's actions do not adversely affect the performance of other business units. Shareholder value is then simply the sum of the values of the individual units. But to maximize shareholder value, managers must take into account any important interdependencies among units, such as overlap in customers, interunit transfers of intermediate products, and common resources. If managers focus on their own units and do not consider these interdependencies, overall shareholder value suffers. If FinWare were organized geographically, for example, the West and East Coast divisions might compete against each other for a national customer and reduce the overall profits of the firm by selling products at a lower price than if they coordinated their marketing. This problem can be mitigated by forming *groups* of interrelated business units and basing a component of unit managers' compensation on overall group performance. However, as we discuss in later chapters, developing a compensation scheme that appropriately motivates unit managers is not easy. Splitting functional personnel among business units also forgoes potential economies that might result from combining similar specialists within one business unit.

Where functional business units work best. Functional grouping works best in small firms with a limited number of products. In these firms, it is relatively easy for senior managers to coordinate operating decisions among departments in a timely and informed fashion. In large firms with more diverse product offerings, however, senior executives are less likely to have the relevant knowledge for making operational decisions for the company. In addition, with a functional organization, senior management will have to spend more time on operating and coordination issues rather than on major strategic issues facing the firm. In such firms, grouping by product or geography will often be the preferred alternative.

Another factor in the desirability of functional business units is the rate of technological change in the industry. Technological change broadly includes new products, new production techniques, and organizational innovations. Functional business units are more effective in environments with more stable technology, since in such environments frequent communication among functional departments and specialists is less important and interactions can be handled through routine rules and procedures. In addition, senior management is likely to possess more of the relevant knowledge for coordinating functional areas because the relevant knowledge base remains relatively constant.

In less stable environments, direct communication among functional areas is more important, and new situations that will challenge established coordination procedures are more likely to arise. In addition, senior managers are less likely to have all the relevant knowledge needed to address these challenges. The frequent introduction of new products increases the benefits of communication between salespeople and design engineers concerning customer demands and preferences. Similarly, it is important for development and manufacturing personnel to share information when production techniques and technologies are changing more frequently.

Finally, in a rapidly changing environment, there will tend to be more uncertainty about the appropriate organizational architecture. When divisions are organized around products or geography, different divisions can experiment with different architectures. For example, when Citibank began making a market in swaps, it opened trading desks in New York, Toronto, London, and Tokyo. The different operations competed for business not only with other financial institutions but also with each other. By encouraging experimentation with the architecture of these businesses, Citibank exploited the benefits of economic Darwinism within the firm. As the divisions' experience grew, the best procedures were made standard across the bank and became part of Citibank's corporate software. Thus, in a more dynamic environment, a product or geographic organization probably works better.

Operating Environment, Strategy, and Architecture

In previous chapters we have discussed how organizational architecture is influenced by the firm's business environment and strategy. Both elements also affect the workability of functional versus product or geographic organizations.

The experience of large U.S. firms at the beginning of the twentieth century illustrates the influence of the environment and strategy on business-unit design. The first large firms in the United States were the railroad companies, which emerged around 1850. These firms initially organized around basic functions, such as finance, pricing, traffic, and maintenance. The late 1800s saw an increase in the number of large firms in industries such as steel, tobacco, oil, and meatpacking. Most of these firms followed the lead of the railroads and organized around basic functions. As companies like DuPont, General Motors, and General Electric continued to expand—both geographically and in the number of product lines they offered—they began to struggle in markets in which they faced smaller competitors. Their organizational structures did not fit their changing environments or strategies. In response, these companies began experimenting with different organizational forms. Many large companies adopted the multidivisional or M form of organization. Economic historian Alfred Chandler notes that

> The inherent weakness in the centralized, functionally departmentalized operating company . . . became critical only when the administrative load of the senior executives increased to such an extent that they were unable to handle their entrepreneurial responsibilities efficiently. This situation arose when the operations of the enterprise became too complex and the problems of coordination, appraisal, and policy formulation too intricate for a small number of top officers to handle both long-run, entrepreneurial, and short-run, operational administrative activities.

Similarly, in the 1950s, most of the *Fortune* 500 oil companies were organized into functional departments. But when these companies began having trouble competing with smaller corporations, they started to experiment with their organizational architectures, and the design that appeared to work best was the multidivisional form of organization. Some of the firms organized around geographic areas, while others organized around product lines. Companies that switched to the M form early outperformed other companies that switched later. By the middle 1970s, most large oil companies had switched to the multidivisional form of organization. Those that did not switch tended to be smaller companies that performed well using the old structure.

Matrix Organizations

Some firms attempt to capture the benefits of both the functional and the product or geographic organizations by using overlapping business-unit structures. These *matrix organizations* have functional departments such as finance, manufacturing, and development. But employees from these functional departments are also assigned to business units organized by product or geography, or for special projects. Matrix organizations are characterized by intersecting lines of authority in which two or more lines of responsibility can run through the same individual. Individuals typically report to both a functional manager and a product manager. The functional departments usually serve as the primary mechanism for personnel functions and professional development. The functional managers typically have primary responsibility for performance reviews (since they have better technical knowledge for evaluating an employee's performance). Product managers provide input into these reviews.

Intel Corporation's organizational structure in 1992 provides an example of a matrix organization. The company was organized around five major product groups: entry-level products, Intel products, microprocessor products, multimedia and supercomputing components, and semiconductor products. Intel staffed these groups with people from the basic functional groups: corporate business development, finance and administration, marketing, sales, software technology, and technology and manufacturing. Thus, individual workers were members of both product and functional groups.

Matrix organization is prevalent in industries such as defense, construction, and management consulting. These industries are characterized by a sequence of new products or projects (for example, building a new airplane or a new shopping mall). Individuals are assigned to work in teams on particular projects, and when a project is completed, the individuals assigned to it are reassigned to new project teams. Given the nature of the projects in these industries, it is important for individuals from different functional areas to communicate and to work together closely. For example, a successful airplane design must meet the demands of the customer; thus, there are benefits from the use of product-oriented teams. However, it is critical that the plane be aerodynamically sound. Thus, these projects also benefit from a high level of functional expertise, which is promoted by maintaining functional areas.

Figure 5.3 shows how FinWare might look if it adopted a matrix organization. The firm maintains functional divisions for sales and service. Employees from these divisions are simultaneously assigned to either the business products unit or the consumer products unit ("teams"). Functional managers focus on managing their particular function across both products, while product managers focus on managing particular products across both functions.

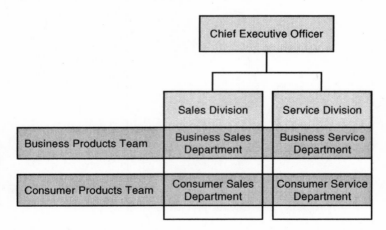

Figure 5.3 FinWare as a matrix organization

A potential advantage of a matrix organization relative to a functional organization is that employees are more likely to focus on the overall business process rather than on their own narrow functional specialties. And in contrast to a pure product or geographic organization, functional supervision is maintained; there is a mechanism for helping to ensure functional excellence and for providing clearer opportunities for advancement and development.

But while matrix organizations tend to look good on paper, they can be difficult to implement effectively in practice. Potential problems with the matrix form of organization arise from the intersecting lines of authority. Employees who are assigned to a product team do not automatically have strong incentives to cooperate with other members of the team or to be concerned about the team's success. Rather, they may be more concerned with how their functional supervisors view their work, since their functional supervisors are responsible for their primary performance reviews. Moreover, employees often see themselves as representatives of their functional areas. They may be excessively concerned about how the decisions made by a product team will affect their particular area. These problems can be reduced by appropriate design of the performance evaluation and reward systems. Individuals will be more concerned about the output of a product team if their compensation depends on team output. A related problem with matrix organizations is the potential for disputes between functional and product managers and the difficulties in resolving such disputes. Enron may have encountered such difficulties, with functional personnel (legal and risk management) coopted by earnings-driven executives. Finally, having both a functional and a product manager can increase influence costs (see Chapter 4)—employees have two supervisors to influence, not just one. For instance, nurses might lobby their nursing supervisors as well as physicians for good performance reviews.

Mixed Designs

Often, firms organize their business units in more than one way. For example, J. P. Morgan Chase uses three types of business units for its different banking activities. Some activities are organized by product, some by geography, and some by customer. Chase Delaware handles the bank's credit card business. Individuals and middle market firms are served geographically. And large corporate customers are served by specific teams, which generally operate out of New York City; these teams are frequently set up by industry. Large multinational corporations often use a matrix organization for their international divisions (with overlapping country and product managers), while their domestic business units are organized by function, product, or geography.

Network Organizations

Some firms (or even groups of firms) have experimented with other methods of organizing business units, one of which is the so-called *network organization*. Network organizations are divided into work groups based on function, geography, or some other dimension. The relationships among these work groups are determined by the demands of specific projects and work activities rather than by formal lines of authority. These relationships are fluid and frequently change with changes in the business environment. The Japanese *keiretsu,* which is an affiliation of quasi-independent firms with ongoing relationships that ebb and flow, is an example of a network organization. Networks can facilitate information flows and cooperative undertakings among work groups. However, their heavy reliance on implicit understandings and informal relationships can lead to misunderstandings or opportunism.

Recent Trends in Assignment of Decision Authority

Traditionally, firms have created jobs characterized by limited decision authority and narrow task assignments. In turn, these jobs have tended to be grouped by functional specialty—either at the overall firm level or at the business-unit level. During the past decade, however, there has been a significant shift toward empowering employees by granting them greater decision authority and broader task assignments. Many companies have also shifted from functional business units toward more product-oriented organizations. These changes have been motivated by increased global competition and the rate of technological change. In addition, the workforce of today is better educated than it was in the past, and modern production techniques rely more heavily on technical expertise than on brawn.

Over the past few decades, the increased level of competition in many industries has been driven by such things as loss of patent protection, reduced transportation costs, deregulation, and improved technology. It has called for dramatic responses. During the 1980s, Xerox CEO David Kearns faced a strong increase in foreign competition; this prompted him to shift Xerox's focus toward improving customer service and product quality. To achieve these objectives, Xerox substantially reassigned decision authority by empowering workers and moving away from a functional organization. In Kearns's words:

> About the only consoling factor was that I knew we weren't the only ones in the soup. Global competition had set upon this country, and everyone was vulnerable. American business was threatened not only by Japan and Korea. Europe was mobilizing into a potent force that demanded serious consideration. And yet, as I looked around me, I saw that so many great and admired companies were doing nothing but sitting on their hands. Like us, they

were kissing away their businesses and laying the groundwork for their own destruction.

After my string of trips to Japan and after deep introspection about Xerox's strengths and flaws, the solution began to point in one direction. Our only hope for survival was to urgently commit ourselves to vastly improving the quality of our products and service. This was something a lot of corporations talked about, but it was extraordinarily difficult to do. It meant changing the very culture of Xerox from the ground up. Everyone from the cleaning people to the chairman would have to think differently.

To further illustrate some of the factors that have motivated organizational changes, let us examine IBM Credit Corporation in more detail. For our purposes, we will consider the four basic functions that IBM Credit must perform: checking the applicant's credit, pricing the loan, writing the contracts, and sending the final document package to the applicant. Of course, this characterization is simplified, but we can use it to illustrate the main points of our analysis.

Prior to its reengineering, IBM Credit was organized around these four basic functions: It was divided into functional departments— credit, pricing, contracts, and documents—with each department reporting to the general manager. Employees were typically assigned a specialized set of tasks within their functional area and were given limited decision authority on how to complete those tasks. For example, a clerk in the credit department might have the simple task of logging applications using prescribed methods. Coordination across functional departments was handled by senior management, often through formal rules and procedures. For example, there were procedures for transferring credit applications among the various functional departments. Department heads served together on committees to assist in this coordination process. With this architecture, customers received relatively poor service, and it was difficult to provide a customer with timely information about the status of an application. However, each application was subjected to a careful credit check, and each stage of the process was conducted by functional experts.

When IBM was the only major producer of mainframe computers, the loss of customers because of delays in processing financing applications was not of great concern. The emergence of Japanese competitors such as Hitachi, however, and the prospect of a substantial decrease in sales increased the pressure on IBM to change its business strategy to focus more on customer service and to shorten the time required to process a credit application.

New information and computer technologies enabled IBM Credit to develop internal systems that would support an organizational change. For instance, before the reengineering, some of the information necessary for processing a credit application was stored in a manual filing system. Thus, it made sense to assign certain tasks to individuals who were familiar with the system and were located in close proximity to it. Computerizing the system allowed employees throughout the firm to access the database directly—a change that permitted the firm to reassign tasks more easily. Similarly, IBM Credit was able to develop computer programs to assist less skilled personnel in pricing loans. Such systems made functional expertise less important, thereby diminishing one of the advantages of the old organizational architecture.

In the face of competitive pressures and new technologies, IBM Credit completely changed its assignment of decision authority. Under the new structure, individual caseworkers have the primary decision authority and responsibility for completing all the steps in the credit process. Each financing request is assigned to one caseworker, who checks the applicant's credit, prices the deal, draws up the contracts, and compiles the documentation. Employees have substantial decision authority in completing these tasks, and the functional business units of the firm have largely been abandoned, although some functional specialists remain in the organization to help the caseworkers with difficult or unusual cases. Performance evaluation and reward systems were correspondingly changed to focus more specifically on processing times and customer service. With this new organizational architecture, IBM Credit can process a credit application in about four hours, and customer satisfaction has increased as a result.

Another example of a firm that reorganized along these lines is GTE, the telephone company. GTE's functional organization—with separate departments for repairs, billing, and marketing—often frustrated customers, who found it difficult to locate the right person in the company to address a particular problem. Because of increased competitive pressures, GTE decided that it would have to offer its telephone customers dramatically better customer service. Rather than making incremental improvements in each of its functional departments, GTE decided to reorganize around the basic process of providing customer service. Customers wanted one-stop shopping—they wanted to have one number to call to fix an erratic dial tone, question a bill, sign up for call waiting, and so on, at any time of the day. GTE began meeting this demand when it set up its first pilot "customer care center" in Garland, Texas. Preliminary data from this and other pilot projects indicated a 20 to 30 percent increase in productivity. Customers also reported better service.

IBM Credit and GTE are but two examples of the many firms that have undertaken similar restructurings. This reengineering process seeks to create value by drawing on the experience and abilities (or wetware) of the employees to improve the firm's software by carefully examining and reconfiguring the tasks involved in the firm's operations. The success stories from these restructurings have led some management consultants to advocate widespread change for all firms throughout the world. Nonetheless, a firm should not be restructured unless management has carefully considered whether a reassignment of decision authority is warranted given the firm's particular business environment and strategy. Although changes in technology and competition have altered the appropriate assignment of decision authority in many firms, these shifts have not occurred in all industries. Narrow task assignment and functional specialization are probably still effective for many firms in relatively stable industries. Consider, for example, a coal-mining operation—it probably makes sense to have some employees concentrate on mining the coal, while other employees sell it and still other employees deliver it.

Ultimately, of course, the key to any successful restructuring is communication. The 1993 movie *Six Degrees of Separation* popularized the famous Harvard University experiment in which randomly selected people in Kansas were handed a letter addressed to people they did not know in Massachusetts. They were asked to forward the letter to an acquaintance who might bring it closer to the "target." On average, it took five intermediaries before the letter reached the recipient. Yet if communication in a large global corporation required moving through five people (even with email) before finding the right person to respond to a query, the delay and distortion of the message could be significant and valuable business opportunities could be lost. Interestingly, two researchers at Cornell University have developed a mathematical model that shows how a few well-placed individuals in the organization who cut across traditional boundaries can greatly increase both the speed and the accuracy of communication. In undertaking a restructuring, senior managers should think about the strategic placement of key individuals who will help maintain the flow of information that is so important to the success of the firm.

In discussing decision authority, we have attempted to identify the relevant issues rather than provide pat answers. Managers at individual firms should consider these issues in light of their own circumstances when deciding whether to centralize or decentralize, whether to use individual or team decision making, or whether to organize by function or by product line. Once those decisions have been made, the next problem is how to measure the performance of the various individuals and business units within the firm. We now turn to this second element of organizational architecture.

CHAPTER 6

The Second Leg: Performance Evaluation

*T*his chapter and the next describe the performance evaluation system—the second leg of the three-legged stool that constitutes the firm's organizational architecture. Performance evaluation and compensation systems together motivate value-adding decision making and effort. Performance evaluation involves assessing individual employees as well as business units; this chapter focuses on individual performance evaluation. Ideally, managers would like to be able to measure every employee's contribution to shareholder value, both for feedback purposes and as a basis for compensation. Instead, they must rely on proxies such as output (for example, pieces produced) relative to some "normal" level of output. But many employees have multidimensional jobs, some aspects of which are more easily quantifiable than others. Evaluating an employee on the basis of only the quantifiable aspects of a job will lead the employee to deemphasize the other aspects. Subjective performance appraisals can be used either alone or to supplement any quantifiable measures of output, although subjective reviews are vulnerable to inaccuracy, bias, and favoritism. And with much of the work today being done in team settings, we discuss how to evaluate individual performance within such a setting. The most important point with respect to per-*

formance evaluation is that the greater the reliance on incentive pay, the more precisely the employee's output must be measured in order to reduce the effect of factors beyond the employee's control. Since most employees are risk-averse, reducing random fluctuations in compensation can increase shareholder value.

Performance Evaluation That Works

Lincoln Electric Company, headquartered in Cleveland, Ohio, manufactures welding and cutting supplies and industrial electric motors in numerous plants around the world. The company has set sales records in every quarter since mid-1993 and is often cited as a model of productivity gains and cost savings.

At the heart of Lincoln Electric's success is a strategy of building quality products at a cost lower than its competitors' and passing these savings on to customers. In part, Lincoln has implemented this strategy with an employee incentive system that uses a pay-for-performance compensation plan to foster labor productivity increases. The wages that production employees receive are based entirely on piecework. In addition, employees receive year-end bonuses that average approximately 100 percent of regular compensation.

A key element of Lincoln's organizational architecture, and the topic of this chapter, is performance evaluation. There are two components of Lincoln's performance evaluation: the number of pieces produced and a merit rating. The first component is an objective, readily quantifiable performance measure for each production employee—the employee's wage is equal to a piece rate times the number of good units produced. (Employees are not paid for defective units.) The piece rates, set by the time-study department, allow employees producing at a standard rate to earn a wage comparable to the wages for similar jobs in the local labor market. However, by working hard—in some cases even through meals and breaks—

employees can double and sometimes as much as triple their pay. Moreover, Lincoln's policies prohibit piece-rate changes simply because an employee is making "too much" money. Finally, any employee who has been at Lincoln for at least two years is guaranteed employment for at least thirty hours per week.

The second component of Lincoln's evaluation system is the employee's merit rating. These ratings are used to determine the employee's share of the bonus pool. Although there is substantial annual variation, the size of the bonus pool is approximately equal to total wages and is about twice Lincoln's net income after taxes. An employee's merit evaluation is based on his or her dependability, quality of work, output, ideas, and cooperation, assessed primarily by the employee's immediate supervisor.

Several important observations emerge. First, Lincoln's performance measurement system is an integral part of the company's strategic focus on efficient production. Lincoln reinforces that focus through its compensation system, which relies on information from the performance evaluation system—the two systems are linked. Finally, the firm uses performance measures that are objective and explicit (units produced) as well as other measures that are fairly subjective (dependability and cooperation).

The Contribution to Value

In general, there are at least two reasons to evaluate employee performance. First, a performance evaluation provides employees with feedback on ways in which they might increase their productivity. For example, additional training in particular areas might be indicated. This information is also useful to managers, who want to assign employees to jobs that will make the best use of their skills. Second, a performance evaluation provides an indication of an individual employee's contribution to shareholder value, which in turn is used in

determining rewards and penalties—wages, raises, bonuses, promotions, reassignments, demotions, and dismissals. These two purposes
create different incentives. If evaluations were used exclusively to
provide feedback, employees would be less likely to try to distort
their evaluations to make themselves look better. But when employees
are rewarded on the basis of the measured performance, they have
more incentive to find ways to inflate their evaluations. Management's
task is to work around these incentives to find reasonably accurate
performance measures that will tie in to the strategic objectives of the
firm and help to motivate value-adding effort and decision making.

In Chapter 2, we established that shareholder value is measured
by the present value of all cash flows accruing to the shareholders.
The firm's stock price is the obvious barometer of intrinsic shareholder value. Ideally, then, we would like to measure the employee's
performance by his or her individual contribution to the change in
stock price after a day's work. But of course this is utterly infeasible.
Shareholder value is determined by the collective actions of employees throughout the firm—the impact of one employee's efforts simply
cannot be detected that precisely. And shareholder value is also affected by random factors from outside the firm, such as conditions in
the general economy—changes in the tax code, regulations, the Federal Reserve rate, unemployment figures, oil prices, and so on—that
are well beyond the individual employee's control. Even when it
seems that an employee's contribution might be clearly reflected in
the stock price, as when a scientist in the research lab discovers a
new wonder drug and the stock price goes up $20, that employee has
also contributed to shareholder value in other ways that are not so
readily measured, such as by guiding the work of other researchers.
And the $20 price increase also reflects the efforts of those who as-
sisted in the scientist's discovery. We therefore must look for other
measures that can serve as proxies for an employee's actual contribution to value. In using these measures, the firm typically strives to

capture the employee's productivity or output, as determined by the employee's skill level and training and by the amount of effort he or she exerts. Different measures will correspond to the employee's actual productivity to varying degrees. If output and quality are easily measured, piecework may correspond quite closely to performance, provided that output is not affected by factors for which the employee cannot be held responsible, such as random machine failures or the quality and timely availability of parts and supplies. Other measures such as the number of hours worked will correspond somewhat less closely to performance—the employee may be at his or her desk, but whether productive energy is being expended is another matter. No performance measure is perfect, but they all provide a basis for assessing an employee's contribution to shareholder value.

In choosing among the various measures of performance, managers must keep several things in mind. First, the cost involved in evaluating an employee's performance must not exceed the gains from doing so. The gains generally stem from the incentive effect of tying compensation to performance, but there are attendant costs, too, including those arising from employees' efforts to beat the system. Second, because an employee's productivity is subject to random factors beyond the employee's control (weather, delivery schedules, raw material quality, and so on), a greater reliance on output-based incentive pay will cause greater variability in the employee's compensation. Average pay will then have to be higher to compensate employees for the greater variability, since most employees require additional compensation for risk. But higher average compensation means lower shareholder value. In these cases, it will make sense to design a (perhaps costlier) measurement system that will gauge employee performance more precisely in order to reduce the impact of random factors on compensation. Thus, the degree of incentive pay and the care with which performance is measured are jointly determined. Because the two legs of the stool are complements, *greater reliance on incentive compensation should be accompanied by an increase in the precision with which employee performance is measured.*

Setting Performance Benchmarks

Suppose an employee's output is easily measured—units assembled, items sold, tires changed, and so on. Management's first task is to determine a "normal" level of output in order to be able to judge whether a particular employee's performance is "good" or "bad." Pay scales can then be set so that the earnings of an employee who produces a normal level of output will be competitive with market rates of pay, perhaps adjusted for other factors such as training and experience. There are at least two ways to establish these performance benchmarks: time-and-motion studies and historical production data analysis.

Time-and-Motion Studies

In time-and-motion studies, industrial engineers determine the most effective work method by estimating how much time a particular task requires or, equivalently, how much output can be produced in a certain period of time. Time studies employ a wide variety of techniques for determining how much time a particular activity requires under certain standard conditions. Motion studies involve the systematic analysis of work methods, taking into account the raw materials, the design of the product, the process, the tools, and the activity at each step. In the course of determining the amount of time a particular activity should take, industrial engineers often discover ways of redesigning the product or process to reduce the time required and thereby improve the firm's software. Time-and-motion studies can be expensive in terms of the engineering time used in the studies, and they should be redone whenever product designs change or new equipment is introduced. They also suffer from potential bias because of employees' incentives to establish lower quotas by deliberately un-derperforming during the study period.

Past Performance and the Ratchet Effect

Performance benchmarks can also be established using historical data on past performance. Unfortunately, this method often leads to what is called the *ratchet effect*, which refers to the practice of basing next year's standard of performance on this year's actual performance. Per-formance targets are usually adjusted in only one direction: upward. A bad year causes subsequent years' targets to be reduced very little, if at all. This "ratcheting up" of standards discourages employees from exceeding their quotas, so as not to raise the standard for future periods by too much. There are many illustrations of the ratchet effect:

- Companies often base a salesperson's bonus on the salesper-son's success in meeting target sales, with target sales being based on the previous year's sales. If salespeople expect an un-usually good year, they may try to defer some sales to the next fiscal year. For instance, they might take a customer's order but delay processing it until the following fiscal year.
- In the former Soviet Union, central planners would set a plant's production quota based on past output. Plant managers who met their targets received various rewards, while those who missed their targets were punished. This created incentives for man-agers to exceed the quota but just barely, so as not to have future quotas set "too high."
- An automobile engine assembly plant mandated a labor pro-ductivity goal each year. Each department's target was based in part on the previous year's productivity plus an increase. This created incentives for managers to defer making major produc-tivity improvements in any one year, preferring instead to spread them over several years.

Lincoln Electric avoids the problems of the ratchet effect through its policy that the piecework rate cannot be changed even if an employee is making "too much" money. Once a piecework rate is set by the time-study department, it remains in effect until production methods or processes are changed, or until an employee challenges the rate and a new time study is conducted.

Job rotation can also reduce problems caused by the ratcheting up of each year's performance targets. If an employee knows that next year someone else will have to beat this year's sales figures, he or she will sell more now. Of course, this benefit must be weighed against the costs of frequent job rotation, such as the damage to customer relationships.

Measurement Costs

When it is difficult to quantify the employee's output, performance evaluation becomes much more complicated—and interesting. For example, your server at a restaurant might appear to have performed well. But you begin to suspect that you were served caffeinated instead of decaffeinated coffee at 2 A.M. when you still cannot sleep. The quality of a patent attorney's work is not known until a challenge to the patent is filed. Students' performance on standardized tests captures only part of a teacher's output. A research scientist's output can be difficult to quantify. While almost everything—even effort—is observable at some cost, the cost is not always justifiable. For example, in jobs that require physical effort, an employee's level of effort might be measured by attaching a heart-rate monitor to the employee or by videotaping the employee at work. But there are a host of problems that could arise with these methods, not the least of which would be the annoyance of the employees.

Often, elaborate accounting systems that keep track of sales, parts, output, quality, or divisional profits must be developed and maintained. Computer systems and software that are capable of producing detailed reports can be expensive and complicated. And additional management and clerical time is often required to ensure the accuracy of the reports, particularly if the measures are used to determine compensation. High measurement costs can thus lower the net benefits of tying pay to performance. When the firm relies heavily on incentive-based pay, however, higher measurement costs are generally justified in order to allow the firm to quantify the impact of factors beyond the employee's control for which the employee should not be penalized. Clearly, then, reducing measurement costs can have a significant impact on shareholder value. In fact, new technologies and software have greatly increased the ease and accuracy of tracking performance. As a result, managers are incorporating performance measures in their evaluations of both individuals and business units to a greater extent.

Lower-cost performance measurement also affects organizational architecture, which can in turn drive strategy. For example, most people view coin-operated laundries as dingy, hot, and generally unattractive operations, typically run by sole proprietors. But new national chains are now beginning to emerge. Duds 'n Suds offers cocktails along with clothes cleaning. SpinCycle and Laundromax are national chains with full-time attendants, industrial-strength machines, televisions, air conditioning, and other amenities. At the heart of this change is the use of debit cards, which has eliminated the use of coins altogether, thereby facilitating performance measurement, reducing employee theft, and bringing about the transformation of mom-and-pop Laundromats into corporate chains.

In some cases, of course, it makes sense to rely on more readily available proxies for employee performance. For example, managers are often evaluated on the basis of the accounting profits of their divisions, even though what the firm is ultimately interested in is the shareholder value created by its managers. Shareholder value includes not only short-term divisional cash flows but future expected cash flows, and not only for the manager's own division but for other divisions whose performance may be indirectly affected by the manager's efforts. Accounting profits are merely a proxy for shareholder value. Similarly, schoolteachers are often evaluated on the basis of their students' performance on standardized tests, even though the school is ultimately interested in broader, harder-to-measure indicators of learning. Whether a particular measure is "good" for purposes of performance evaluation depends on whether that particular measure captures the effects of the employee's efforts on the broader target, which is shareholder value. For example, if paying a manager based on divisional profits motivates more diligent effort on the part of the manager, which in turn has the effect of increasing shareholder value, then divisional profits are a good performance measure. On the other hand, to the extent that incentive pay based on divisional profits motivates actions that do not enhance value (such as forgoing profitable long-term opportunities because of a negative impact on near-term profits), divisional profits are a poor performance measure.

Horizon Problem

Objective measures of output frequently focus on the near term because of the difficulty of measuring the future consequences of today's decisions. But short-term performance measures can cause employees—especially those who are about to change jobs or leave the firm—to concentrate their efforts on producing short-term results. For example, a sixty-four-year-old salesperson who works on commission and who expects to retire at age sixty-five has little incentive to develop or even maintain long-term customer relationships.

Gaming

If the measure of output is not directly related to shareholder value, then employees' attempts to increase their reported output (to improve their performance evaluations) might actually be value-reducing. Recall from Chapter 3 the costs that Sears incurred when its mechanics charged customers for unneeded or undone car repairs. And there are other examples. A salesperson might offer customer discounts in order to shift sales from one evaluation period to another. An employee who is paid on the basis of his or her output might reduce quality in order to increase output. A refuse hauler who is compensated on the weight of trash delivered to the landfill might use a fire hose to top off the load with water before weighing in at the truck scales.

Seemingly objective measures of performance, such as sales or output, can create incentives for employees to take value-reducing actions (such as lowering product quality) in order to increase their measured performance. The designers of the performance evaluation system must try to anticipate these perverse incentives. For example, an old, marginal mine remained open for years because it had one very rich pocket of ore that the managers of the mine held in reserve instead of mining all at once. Whenever the yield of ore from the mine fell below an acceptable level, the managers would mix in a little of the high-grade ore to raise the yield and keep the mine open. Similarly, insurance agents at Prudential engaged in "churning" to boost sales and increase their commissions: They would persuade customers to use the cash values on their existing policies to purchase bigger policies, telling them that it wouldn't cost anything. The new policies were in force long enough for the agents to collect large commissions. But once the premiums on the new policies exhausted the cash values on the old policies, many policyholders, some of them elderly, were hit with big, unexpected premium bills. Customers who couldn't pay lost their insurance coverage. In 1997, Prudential agreed to a $410 million settlement on a class-action lawsuit related to deceptive sales practices.

Relative Performance Evaluation

To reduce the effect of random factors that are beyond the employee's control, management can look at the average output of all employees. Using the output of other employees to adjust an individual employee's output in the compensation contract is called *relative performance evaluation.* For instance, studies have shown that turnover among the managers of subsidiary banks in multibank holding companies is greater when their bank's performance is poor relative to the median bank's performance within the holding company; this suggests that multibank holding companies are comparing the performance of their subsidiary banks in an attempt to filter out external factors in making compensation and retention decisions. Even CEO compensation (salary plus bonus) depends on relative performance evaluation: A study of the CEOs of large, publicly traded U.S. corporations found that their compensation is higher when their firm's stock price is higher and when the market or industry index is down.

Using the output of other employees as a reference measure tends to work best when all members of the reference group are subject to similar random events—they all sell or manufacture the same products and face the same competitive and economywide factors. However, forming a reference group from employees inside the firm can have drawbacks. In most cases, employees' jobs are not identical. For instance, some salespeople have large, established territories, whereas others have small, developing ones—and customer types can vary dramatically among sales territories.

If the average performance of an internal reference group is used to determine normal performance, the group has incentives to punish extremely productive employees who raise the average, or "rate busters." In the classic research study known as the Hawthorne experiments (see Chapter 3), employees were observed actually hitting colleagues who exceeded the commonly accepted output rate. Thus, employees may collude to hold down the benchmark. Or instead of working diligently and increasing their own performance, coworkers might sabotage their peers within the reference group. Alternatively, employees might try to have themselves assigned to a weak reference group so that their performance will appear to be above average. Clearly, a relative performance measurement system creates strong incentives for employees to improve their own relative standing. And some employees will go to outrageous lengths when their advancement is based on relative peformance evaluation, as the following story illustrates:

> I was recently talking to a friend of mine who works at a big bank. When I asked him about his new promotion, he told me how he got it. He managed to crack the network messaging system so that he could monitor all the memos. He also sabotaged the work group software and set back careers of a few naive souls who didn't realize that someone was manipulating their appointment calendars. They would miss important meetings and be sent on wild-goose chases, only to look like complete buffoons when they showed up for appointments that were never made. By the time any of these bumpkins knew what hit them, they had a new vice president.

Some firms employ external benchmarking to overcome the lack of an internal reference group or to avoid the pernicious effects of employee sabotage and collusion. Firms can exchange information directly or through a trade association that aggregates information across several firms to mask individual firm data. Thus, the average performance of other firms is used as the reference measure. But even if firms are willing to share data, such cooperation is potentially illegal under antitrust laws. Moreover, employees in outside firms may not be subject to the same random events as the benchmarking firm's employees.

Subjective Performance Evaluation

Most jobs have multiple dimensions. For example, baseball players have to field balls, get hits (ranging from bunts to home runs), run bases, and generally support the team. It is difficult to specify and measure all aspects of the job. If output is measured using only explicit performance measures and explicit measures are available for only certain aspects of a job, employees will emphasize those aspects to the detriment of the others. For instance, if a veteran ballplayer were evaluated solely on his hitting, he would have less incentive to spend time mentoring young ballplayers. Often, therefore, a firm will augment objective, explicit measures of output with subjective yet more comprehensive measures of performance.

Subjective performance reviews are conducted primarily because it is impossible to accurately measure all the dimensions of the employee's output that are of value to the firm. In fact, few employees are evaluated by objective measures alone. For example, most employees receive annual performance reviews from their supervisors. These reviews are often the basis for setting salaries and promotions. Even when compensation is based entirely on objective measures such as number of pieces produced, the firm reserves the right to fire employees for low-quality production, tardiness, inability to get along with coworkers, or other unsatisfactory behavior. For example, Lincoln Electric bases factory employees' wages entirely on piecework—an objective measure. But in addition to this objective measure, Lincoln also uses a subjective merit evaluation to set the employee bonus.

Multiple Tasks and Unbalanced Effort

The most important reason to use subjective performance measures is that employees have numerous tasks, not all of which are quantifiable. As discussed in Chapter 4, multiple tasks are assigned to one employee because it is efficient to bundle the tasks. For example, a salesperson might be expected to sell products to existing customers, contact potential new customers, and fill out sales reports; these tasks are all part of selling the product.

Suppose an employee assembles welders and also trains new employees to assemble welders. The first activity is easily measured, perhaps by counting the number of welders assembled; the second is more difficult to assess. If the employee's evaluation is based primarily on the easily measured task (assembling welders), he or she has an incentive to concentrate on that activity and will not necessarily allocate adequate time to training. Remember: *You get what you pay for—and frequently, that is all you get.*

Recall from Chapter 4 that this multitask problem can affect job design. For example, the firm might want to have certain employees concentrate only on assembling. These employees could be evaluated on their output of assembled welders. Other employees could then concentrate on training new assemblers and correspondingly could be evaluated on the basis of the performance of the trainees after they leave training. If the tasks are separated, the employees can be given more focused incentives to perform their one task. Alternatively, an employee's performance evaluation can incorporate subjective reviews of those aspects of the job that are less readily measured. Welder assemblers can be evaluated on the basis of both units assembled and the supervisor's assessment of their performance in terms of the quality of instruction, the degree of patience, and how the trainees subsequently perform as assemblers.

Subjective Evaluation Methods

There are two widely used subjective performance appraisal systems: standard rating scales and goal-based systems. Standard rating scales tend to be less explicit and more subjective.

Standard rating scale systems. Standard rating scales require the evaluator to rank the employee on a number of different performance factors, using, say, a five-point scale: substantially exceeds requirements, exceeds requirements, meets all requirements, partially meets requirements, or does not meet requirements. The different performance factors vary among positions within the firm, but they often include variations of the following:

- Achieves forecasts, budgets, and objectives.
- Organizes effective performance through oral and written communications.
- Sets and attains high performance goals for self and group.
- Updates knowledge of job-related skills.
- Emphasizes teamwork among subordinates.
- Identifies and resolves problems.
- Evaluates subordinates objectively.
- Ensures equal opportunities for all subordinates.

After ranking the employee on each of these narrow criteria, the evaluator then assigns a rating for the employee's overall performance on the job: excellent, better than satisfactory, satisfactory, needs further improvement, and unsatisfactory. Most subjective performance appraisals also contain a section in which the supervisor provides detailed comments on the employee's strengths and weaknesses and offers specific recommendations for improvement and further development.

Review systems of this kind are not new, and much of what is new is merely the jargon invented by consultants to make these systems appear to be a valuable innovation. For example, 360-degree performance evaluations are a means of formally capturing input from the bottom up rather than just from the top down, and they offer the potential for a broader scope of information about an employee's performance. And yet privately held W. L. Gore & Associates, manufacturer of Gore-Tex waterproof fabric, has been using 360-degree evaluations as part of its performance feedback since 1958. Under this system, annual evaluations of all employees are gathered from peers, subordinates, and superiors. The evaluations are anonymous and rate employees on their contribution to the success of the business during the past year. All ratings on each employee receive equal weight. Compensation committees composed of sponsors with specialized knowledge of the department use the rankings to award pay increases or performance warnings. This is essentially just a classic ratings-based system.

Goal-based systems. In a goal-based system, each employee is given a set of goals for the year. For example, a goal might be to "hold training sessions for all employees in the department by November 1" or "hire four additional qualified members of minority groups." These goals tend to be more objective and easier to measure than the vague performance factors used in the standard rating scales, such as "emphasizes teamwork." Nonetheless, the goals are still more subjective than standard piecework measures. At the end of the year, the supervisor writes an overall evaluation of the employee based on the extent to which the goals have been achieved. Evaluators then review the assessments with their supervisors to help ensure the accuracy of the review and promote consistency of criteria across employees.

In general, an employee's immediate supervisor does the employee's performance evaluation. However, some firms have experimented with peer evaluation, especially in situations where teams are important. The benefit of peer evaluation is that an employee's peers have more information about typical performance in group assignments and the employee's actual contribution to the team. But peer evaluation can create tensions within the team. For example, some team members might systematically lower everyone else's ratings in order to make themselves look better. Or well-liked team members may be rated highly in order to increase their chances of being promoted to supervise their former peers. Finally, teammates might decide to collude to give everyone high performance ratings.

Problems with Subjective Performance Evaluation

There are several potential problems with subjective performance evaluation. For one thing, disciplining employees and informing them of their shortcomings are unpleasant tasks, even when doing so is clearly appropriate from a shareholder value viewpoint. To avoid conflicts with subordinates, supervisors are normally reluctant to give adverse performance ratings. What frequently happens is that supervisors compress ratings around a norm rather than distinguishing between good and bad performers. Worse, a supervisor might rank employees based on his or her own personal likes and dislikes rather than on the employees' job performance. The resulting inaccuracy and bias in the performance evaluation system lower morale and with it the employees' incentives to work diligently, thereby lowering overall firm performance.

Research confirms the tendency of managers to assign relatively uniform performance ratings to employees. A study of 7000 performance ratings by managers and professionals in two firms showed that 95 percent of all appraisals were in just two categories: good and superior (outstanding). A survey of employee attitudes at Merck & Co., a large U.S. pharmaceutical firm, reported the following:

- "Managers are afraid to give experienced people a 1, 2, or 3 rating. It's easier to give everyone a 4 and give new people a 3.
- "Charlie's been in that job for 20 years. He hasn't done anything creative for the last 15 years. Do you think my manager would give him a 3 rating? No way! Then he'd have to spend 12 months listening to Charlie complain.
- "What's the use of killing yourself? You still get the same rating as everyone else, and you still get the same 5 percent increase. It's demoralizing and demotivating."

This evidence suggests that low-rated, disgruntled employees can make life miserable for their supervisors. In response, supervisors bias their evaluations. Hence, performance ratings are inaccurate appraisals of an employee's true performance. Biased, inaccurate appraisals reduce employees' incentives to work harder and can lead to the promotion of less-qualified people. The problem here lies not in the evaluation system per se, but rather in the incentives for the evaluators. Of course, this gets back to our earlier observation that the precision with which performance is evaluated is critical. The bottom line is that a subjective rating system is, by definition, imprecise, and thereby gives rise to bias and inaccuracy.

At Lincoln Electric, however, supervisors are evaluated and compensated on the basis of how well they evaluate lower-level employees—which is determined by how well those employees subsequently perform. Also, employees can discuss their ratings with senior management. Problems of bias are likely to be lower if the supervisor is held accountable for the future performance of individuals who are promoted based on the supervisor's recommendation.

To overcome the tendency to rate all employees "above average," some firms require that a fixed fraction of employees be assigned to each category (that is, the supervisor must rank a certain percentage of the employees as poor performers). Jack Welch reportedly insisted on this sort of distribution at GE. However, these forced distributions may not accurately reflect the true distribution of performance in each work group, especially in smaller groups. For example, having to rank one of four employees as poor might compel the supervisor to underrate a solid performer, thus leading to greater inaccuracies than would result from a merely biased supervisor. Nor do forced distributions necessarily reduce the "retribution effect" imposed on the supervisor. Under a forced distribution, supervisors might still assign ratings based on the potential disagreeability of the employee rather than on the employee's true performance.

141

Subjective appraisal systems certainly have their detractors. A survey by the Society for Human Resource Management concluded that more than 90 percent of subjective appraisal systems are unsuccessful. One management consultant describes annual job performance reviews as a "deadly disease." He asserts that virtually every survey finds that most employees who get these reviews and most supervisors who do them rate the process a resounding failure. Consulting firms find that advising companies on how to improve their appraisal process is a lucrative and fast-growing business. Many managers find performance appraisals an annual irritation—they pull out last year's review and hastily update it.

Consultants disagree about the cause of these problems. Some claim that the process does not work because of forms that are outdated or that were designed by personnel specialists with limited input from the managers who would actually be using them. Others argue that supervisors are poorly trained to conduct appraisals and give feedback, or that supervisors dislike giving negative feedback and employees have a hard time accepting criticism. One consultant recommends that companies teach "everyone how to give and receive good feedback" (which invariably elicits groans of "No—not more HR training sessions!"). Other consultants suggest at least twice-a-year reviews and more frequent informal feedback. Formal written appraisals are often used by employers to combat wrongful-discharge lawsuits. However, such systems can backfire when employees who have received acceptable reviews are let go. An interesting aspect of a subjective rating system is that an employee is less likely to be successful in a lawsuit involving subjective performance measurement than when the employee can document that a firm reneged on promises of advancement involving objective performance measures. While subjective performance systems are universally criticized, they are pervasive—suggesting that despite their drawbacks, they have few substitutes.

Combining Objective and Subjective Performance Measures

Most performance evaluation systems have both objective and subjective elements. Objective measures consist of items like output and sales that can be easily quantified and explicitly measured. Subjective measures consist of judgments about employee performance (the year-end evaluation from a supervisor). Like Lincoln Electric, many organizations that use objective measures also use subjective measures to evaluate the same employee. For example, investment banks pay bonuses on the basis of fees generated by the employee, but also use subjective measures such as the "quality of the deal." As the accuracy of either measure decreases, more weight will be placed on the other in determining performance.

Because the costs and benefits of objective and subjective measures vary among jobs, some firms will use only objective performance measures, others will use only subjective measures, and still others will use mixtures of both. However, employees performing similar tasks in similar industries tend to have similar performance evaluation systems because the advantages and disadvantages of alternative evaluation methods will also be similar. If objective performance measures are not readily available or are very costly to develop, the firm will tend to place a greater reliance on subjective evaluations. Indeed, given today's complex job assignments, basing employee pay on only quantifiable performance measures can be a serious mistake. Often, the key is to design a subjective performance evaluation system that addresses the concerns raised in this chapter. And sometimes the best the firm can do, given the costs inherent in developing a performance measurement system, is to simply pay all employees a straight salary or an hourly wage with cost-of-living increases. Such a system will generate fairly low-powered incentives, but it may still be preferable to a poorly designed or overly costly performance-based incentive plan.

Objective and Subjective Performance Evaluation at Fiat

The Italian firm Fiat, with over 250,000 employees in sixteen operating sectors, combines both objective and subjective performance reviews into a single, integrated system. In the 1980s, Fiat introduced a formal management by objectives (MBO) evaluation program for its five hundred highest-level managers. Under the MBO program, annual bonuses of up to about 30 percent of base salary are awarded for meeting objectives.

Managers have a set of objectives tailored to their specific situations. Managers in charge of profit centers have profit and debt objectives. Profit targets are defined in terms of net profit before taxes. Because Fiat had a dangerously high level of debt in the 1980s, profit center managers' objectives also included reductions in borrowings. Besides these specific financial objectives, managers have other performance indicators, such as increasing sales in particular markets, completing an acquisition, improving product quality or customer service, and introducing new products or processes.

Even if managers meet their particular objectives, no bonus will be paid unless the larger group achieves its goals. For example, the Fiat Group has sixteen sectors, each headed by a manager. If the entire Fiat Group fails to meet its objectives, none of the sixteen sector managers receives a bonus, even if some of them achieved their goals. Each manager has a set of weightings attached to each objective: 20 to 40 percent for profits, 10 to 20 percent for reducing debt, and 10 to 15 percent for each of three or four other performance targets. Each objective is scored on a five-point scale, with 3 being the minimum acceptable score. Superiors set the targets for each objective. Performance ratings vary from 1 to 5, depending on the difficulty of the particular objective.

A manager who gets a performance rating below 3 receives no bonus. A performance rating of 3 carries a bonus of 12 percent of salary. A manager with a rating of 4 receives an 18 percent bonus, and one with a 5 receives a 30 percent bonus. The median manager's rating is between 4.1 and 4.4. In any given year, about 10 percent of the managers are rated below 3.0, and about 15 percent are rated 4.9 or better.

The performance evaluation system at Fiat is similar to those used by large U.S. corporations.

Team Performance

One complaint of the employees at Lincoln Electric is that their pay suffers when the employees that precede them on an assembly line are unable to keep them supplied with work. These team production effects can make evaluating the performance of individual team members quite complicated. Of course, if a manager is on the assembly floor, he or she will be able to observe the employees' effort, efficiency, and attitude and can readily assess the degree to which a particular employee's production was affected by factors beyond his or her control. But sometimes there is no measure of individual output; only team output can be observed. In these cases, team members must be evaluated, at least in part, on team output. Using team output focuses team members on a common objective and helps to promote cooperation. However, paying team members on the basis of group output creates incentives for individual employees to free-ride—to slack off, knowing that the effect of one member's lesser effort is spread across the whole team. These incentives are lower in smaller teams. But as team size grows, free-rider problems can become enormous.

Free-rider problems can be reduced by evaluating team members not only on team output but on other measures as well, such as the number of hours worked, a supervisor's subjective evaluation of how hard they are working, and peer evaluations. Peer reviews are often important in evaluating the individual performance of team members because teammates have the most accurate knowledge of how a team member has performed.

Consider a team of employees formed to work on a project. Such projects build leadership skills and give employees experience in working together as teams. They also enhance productivity by allowing employees to share their expertise and by enabling all team members to benefit from other employees' experience to a much greater extent than if they all worked individually. (In other words, the employees' wetware is more effectively employed in developing corporate software.) Perhaps most important, teams build employees' management experience, because one of the key tasks for a new team is to develop the internal architecture for the group. Our three-legged stool again comes into play. Decision authority over various aspects of the project must be assigned among the team members, and the team members must decide how to evaluate the work efforts of each member in order to ensure a high-quality project. The team must also have some system of rewards and penalties in order to motivate a consistent level of effort. Within a team, as in a family, this system is frequently social (excluding a slacker from team meetings, designating the hardest-working team member to speak for the group, etc.).

The manager overseeing the project typically will evaluate all team members on the basis of the quality of the final project. Some managers will go further and rely on formal peer reviews to evaluate the contribution of individual members to the project. For example, each team member can rate all other team members on a five-point scale according to qualities such as the following:

- Expresses opinions freely.
- Comes to meetings prepared.
- Takes the initiative.
- Accepts criticism.
- Listens to others.
- Delegates authority.
- Shares information freely.
- Bases decisions on sound data.
- Values all customers.
- Recognizes others' contributions.

These reviews can reduce individual members' incentives to slack off and thus can increase productivity. But they can also lead to backstabbing and employees' spending more time lobbying peers for good reviews. Such problems will tend to be greater if the team is formed for a single project; projects with overlapping members will tend to have greater incentives to resolve these conflicts.

In a much-touted move designed to empower workers, cut down on monotony, reduce stress, and thereby increase productivity, well-known jeans manufacturer Levi Strauss installed multitask teams in its U.S. plants in the early 1990s, replacing its old piecework system. Instead of individual employees specializing in zipper sewing or belt-loop attaching, teams of twenty to thirty employees were responsible for completing individual orders by assembling full pairs of pants. In essence, jobs were redesigned from being functional to being more multitask and process-oriented (recall Chapter 4). Employees were evaluated and rewarded on the basis of team output. But this created free-rider problems, which in turn led to absenteeism and slacking off, causing tempers to flare. Supervisors on the plant floor spent more time intervening to prevent "big fights." One plant manager reported, "Peer pressure can be vicious and brutal." Before the multitask teams were initiated, each employee received two weeks of training in group dynamics and an additional one-day seminar devoted to "let's-get-along sessions" with private consultants. These training sessions appeared to neither prevent nor resolve the conflicts. Moreover, productivity fell and costs rose. The quantity of pants produced per hour fell to 77 percent of preteam levels. At one plant, the cost of stitching a pair of Dockers went from $5 before teams to $7.50 with teams.

By 1997, Levi's share of the domestic men's denim jeans market had fallen to 26 percent, from 48 percent in 1990. In 1997, Levi closed eleven U.S. plants and laid off 6400 employees. Despite the company's vows to preserve the team strategy at its remaining U.S. plants, many of the plants are unofficially going back to individual piecework. Robert Haas, Levi's CEO, admits, "Teams created pressures and tensions and a lot of unhappiness, and some people would rather go back. Ours is a culture of experimentation and novelty, and we're not always successful."

Despite experiences like the one at Levi Strauss, teamwork has become almost a sacred cow to American businesses. Yet one survey by Mercer Management found that only 13 percent of 179 teams received high ratings. "Somehow, we have to get past this idea that all we have to do is join hands and sing *Kum Ba Yah* and say, 'We've moved to teamwork.'" Many companies are narrowing the focus and time horizon of teams. A team manager at Texas Instruments counsels that not everyone has to be on a team and that only 5 percent of its workforce are on self-directed teams.

Teams fail for several reasons:

- *The mental opt-out.* Busy managers feel compelled to sit through endless team meetings and frequently "surrender by withholding any real effort." Fully half the decisions reached by teams are never implemented.
- *Dueling advice.* "Teams start out with everyone very polite. Then they start to storm." Several months can pass before things settle down.
- *Old-fashioned pay schemes.* When companies move to teams, they often keep their old individual performance measures and pay systems instead of moving to team-based pay systems to reward the entire team for meeting goals. But if the legs of the stool are not coordinated, the stool will not be functional. The performance measurement system must be adjusted to incorporate a reasonable basis on which to evaluate the performance of individual employees as well as teams. And a manager who has been assigned the decision authority for performance evaluations must have access to information on actual performance.

148

Sometimes that information can best be obtained from the team members themselves.

Government Regulation

Since the 1960s, federal laws in the United States dealing with affirmative action and equal employment opportunity (EEO) have had a profound effect on both performance evaluation systems and reward systems. Federal and state legislation and court actions have forced companies to document their compensation and promotion decisions to demonstrate that their actions are related to performance and are not influenced by the employee's race, religion, sex, age, or national origin. As a result, labor laws and court decisions have had a significant impact on performance appraisal systems. In deciding cases involving alleged discriminatory employment practices, courts look more favorably upon companies with the following characteristics:

- The firm's job descriptions are clearly written and well defined.
- The appraisal system has clear criteria for evaluating performance, such as written objective scales and dimensions.
- There are specific written instructions on how to complete the performance appraisal.
- Employees are provided feedback about their performance appraisal.
- Higher-level supervisors' evaluations are incorporated into the appraisal system.
- Individuals who receive similar evaluations in the firm are treated equally and consistently.

While these characteristics appear to be sensible and even laudable, government regulation has also had negative side effects. The law does not permit companies or employees to opt out of these regulations. The potential for legal scrutiny of the firm's performance evaluation systems pushes these systems to become more formal and more extensive. Every action and every appraisal must be documented, and the volume of paper alone is daunting, to say nothing of the amount of employee time spent on this documentation. A firm's human resources department typically assumes the role of ensuring that the firm is complying with labor laws, and there has consequently been enormous growth in the size of human resources departments.

But a performance appraisal system that meets these regulatory criteria is not necessarily the one that would maximize shareholder value. For example, many Japanese managers try "to make everybody feel that he is slated for the top position in the firm" by delaying performance appraisals and differentiation among cohorts for twelve to fifteen years after an employee joins the firm. This lack of annual feedback to employees would probably run afoul of affirmative action laws in the United States and thus would be strenuously opposed by both the legal and human resources departments at most large corporations. Hence, U.S. firms find it more difficult to use less formal, more subjective performance evaluation systems than do their foreign competitors, even though such systems might be value-enhancing for some firms in a less regulated setting. Government regulations thus cause U.S. firms to spend more money than they otherwise would on appraisal systems that document to a court's satisfaction the firm's compliance with affirmative action regulations. But the extent to which regulations cause firms to deviate from their optimal performance appraisal systems can lead to even greater value erosion. This is an example of how regulation affects the firm's optimal choice of organizational architecture and hence shareholder value.

Evaluating individual performance is rarely easy, but we have tried to highlight some of the major considerations. We now turn to measures of division performance.

CHAPTER 7

Divisional Performance Measurement

*L*arge companies, particularly those with multiple lines of business, are typically organized into business units or divisions. This type of structure provides senior managers with information about the profitability or efficiency of the different lines of business within the firm and creates accountability and incentives for the operating managers charged with running those businesses. The business units within the firm can be set up as cost centers, expense centers, revenue centers, profit centers, or investment centers. Each type of center will have a different level of decision authority and will accordingly be evaluated on the basis of different performance measures, such as costs, revenues, profits, or value added. Because the business units within a firm often provide products and services to one another, the reported performance of each business unit will depend on how those products and services are valued, which involves setting appropriate transfer prices. Transfer pricing is one of the thorniest issues that managers face: It not only changes how the firm's profits are allocated among business units but also affects the firm's total profits by altering the operating decisions of individual business units. Transfer pricing and performance measurement in general rely on internally generated accounting numbers, but the accounting sys-

*tems of most firms are designed for decision control (decision ratifi-
cation and monitoring) rather than for decision management
(decision initiation and implementation). We discuss the trade-off between these two applications and the general impression among managers that most accounting systems are simply not up to the task when
it comes to providing information for decision management.*

Performance Measures Matter

CSX is a Fortune 500 transportation company that provides freight
shipping and related services via its rail, truck, and cargo ship fleets.
Some years ago, CSX reorganized and changed the way it evaluated
its internal divisions: it adopted Economic Value Added (EVA), which
is measured by the after-tax operating profit of a division minus a
charge for the capital invested in the division. The capital charge is
calculated by taking the division's after-tax cost of capital and mul-
tiplying it by the amount of capital employed in the division. The
EVA of one of CSX's major divisions was negative, meaning that the
capital employed in the division was not earning an adequate return
and shareholder value was being destroyed. The CEO of CSX informed the division managers that if they were unable to raise EVA
to break even, the division would be sold.

After several years on EVA, freight volume had increased by 25
percent, the number of freight trailers was down to 14,000 from
18,000, and the locomotive fleet had shrunk from 150 to 100. Under
the old performance measurement system, managers were not charged
for the cost of the capital employed by their business units, and so
they treated the existing stock of containers and trailers as essentially
free. Under the new system, rather than permitting trailers and containers to sit idle, managers were motivated to either use them or get
rid of them. Containers and trailers were loaded and back on the
tracks in five days rather than sitting idle for two weeks, and the

division's EVA was in the black. CSX's stock price rose from $28 when EVA was first adopted to $75 five years later; the S&P 500 was up approximately 80 percent over the same time period. (CSX's stock has since underperformed the S&P 500, in part because of its $10 billion purchase of Conrail.)

Measuring Divisional Performance

Like individual performance measurement, divisional performance evaluation serves two basic purposes: feedback on how the firm is doing—which units are creating value and which are destroying value—and input to the reward system. Ultimately, what matters is a business unit's contribution to shareholder value as determined by the present value of net cash flows. But different measures can serve as proxies for value. Moreover, decision authority is assigned to different business units in different ways, and performance must be evaluated and rewarded accordingly.

The business units of the organization are, in effect, production teams. For example, the maintenance department maintains the facilities; the marketing division structures and implements marketing plans; research and development explores potential new products; and operating units provide products and services to customers. Depending on its degree of decision authority and the way in which its performance is evaluated, each business unit will generally fall into one of five categories: cost centers, expense centers, revenue centers, profit centers, and investment centers. For instance, CSX changed from evaluating some of its divisions as profit centers to evaluating them as investment centers. We describe these different types of centers next.

Cost Centers

Cost centers are responsible for producing a stipulated level of output, and a cost center's efficiency is measured and rewarded according to how fully it achieves this objective. Cost-center managers typically have decision authority over the mix of inputs—labor, materials, and outside services—used in production, and they are evaluated on the cost efficiency with which they use these inputs. Since they are not responsible for selling products, they are not judged on revenues or profits.

Evaluating the performance of a cost center requires that its output be measurable. Moreover, central management specifies the cost center's output or budget and must therefore possess the necessary expertise to do so. Manufacturing departments like the welder assembly department at Lincoln Electric are normally cost centers. The output of the welder assembly department is measured by counting the number of welders completed. Cost centers are also common in service organizations such as CSX's railcar maintenance department (where output is measured by the number of railcars serviced), bank check processing departments (where output is measured by the number of checks processed), and hospital food services departments (where output is measured by the number of meals served). In addition to the quantity of output, central management must monitor output quality, because unit managers may try to meet their cost targets by substituting inferior inputs and reducing quality. Thus, Lincoln Electric must have mechanisms to ensure that the assembled welders meet quality standards, which requires that the firm be able to assess quality at reasonable expense.

There are various objectives for evaluating cost center performance. Two of the more widely used are

- Minimize costs for a given output
- Maximize output for a given budget

To maximize shareholder value, managers must produce the appropriate level of output at minimum cost (without sacrificing quality).

Cost-center managers focus primarily on the second aspect—cost control. Their basic task is to choose the most efficient input mix, and thus the first evaluation criterion focuses directly on cost minimization. For example, if the manager of the railcar maintenance department is told to service one hundred railcars per day, that manager is evaluated on his or her ability both to meet this production schedule and to control the cost of servicing the one hundred railcars. The quantity decision has already been made by central management. Minimizing costs given a prespecified quantity (and quality) is consistent with maximizing shareholder value, provided the target level of output is the optimal level.

The second evaluation criterion, which is to maximize output given a specified budget, is essentially equivalent to the first criterion as long as the specified budget is the minimum budget necessary for producing the target level of output. For example, the manager of the railcar maintenance department might be given a fixed budget and evaluated on the basis of the number of railcars serviced according to quality specifications. With either criterion, the manager has incentives to select the cost-minimizing input mix to produce the target level of output.

In both cases, the manager is constrained—in the first case by the target output level and in the second case by the budget. Central management must choose either the optimal output level or the correct budget for efficient production of this output level. In either case, however, the cost-center manager has incentives to reduce costs (or increase output) by lowering quality, so the quality of production in cost centers must be monitored.

Cost-center managers are sometimes evaluated on the basis of minimizing average cost. But it is important to understand that shareholder value may not be maximized at the point where average costs are minimized. In Table 7.1, for example, profits are maximized by selling six units, yet average unit cost is minimized by producing nine

Table 7.1 Minimizing Average Cost Does Not Yield the Profit-Maximizing Level of Sales

Quantity	Price	Revenue	Total cost	Total profits	Average cost
1	$35	$ 35	$ 78	$−43	$78.0
2	33	66	83	−17	41.5
3	31	93	90	3	30.0
4	29	116	99	17	24.8
5	27	135	110	25	22.0
6	25	150	123	27	20.5
7	23	161	138	23	19.7
8	21	168	155	13	19.4
9	19	171	174	−3	19.3
10	17	170	195	−25	19.5

units. Maximum profits occur when incremental costs and incremental revenues are equal—but this need not be where average unit costs are lowest.

Because average unit costs tend to decline as production increases (if incremental unit cost is constant), a cost-center manager who is evaluated on the basis of minimizing average unit costs has an incentive to increase production, even when inventories are mounting. Focusing on average costs can create incentives for cost-center managers to either overproduce or underproduce, depending on how the value-maximizing output level compares to the level at which average costs are lowest. Cost centers work most effectively when the cost-center manager has expertise in determining the optimal input mix and central managers have a good understanding of the business unit's cost functions and are able to determine the value-maximizing output level, monitor quantity as well as quality, and establish appropriate rewards.

Expense Centers

Areas such as personnel, accounting, patenting, public relations, and research and development are often organized as expense centers.

Like cost-center managers, expense-center managers typically have fixed budgets and are asked to maximize service or output. A major difference between expense centers and standard cost centers, however, is that expense centers' output is measured more subjectively. Thus, an expense center is basically a cost center that does not produce an easily measurable output.

The difficulty in quantifying the output of an expense center has several implications. The manager of an expense center—for example, the director of human resources—is given a total budget and told to provide as much service as possible. Because the cost per unit of output is difficult to measure, the users of this expense center generally are not charged directly for the center's services, but rather are allocated a portion of the cost as overhead, either as a fixed amount or through a cost allocation system based on some factor such as head count. Hence, they tend to overconsume the expense center's services, with the result that the center's manager—the human resources director—regularly requests larger budgets. Central management has difficulty determining the budget that maximizes shareholder value, again because output is not easily measured. Expense-center managers may derive additional benefits from managing larger staffs (empire building), which further reinforces the tendency of these centers to grow faster than the firm as a whole. And if the central budget office tries to cut the human resources department's budget, the HR director might threaten to reduce the services that are most highly valued by users within the firm, thereby enlisting their support in lobbying against the proposed budget cuts.

There are a number of ways to evaluate expense centers. One is to benchmark their budgets against those of similar expense centers in similar-sized firms, if this information is available. Another is to reorganize the firm and place the expense center under the control of its largest user, who then has not only more knowledge about the expense center's value but also the decision authority to set the expense center's budget. The danger here, of course, is that under this reorganized structure, the business unit controlling the expense center will supply too little of the center's service to other business units within the firm.

Revenue Centers

The idea behind a revenue center is to hold the manager of the center accountable for selling certain products; revenue centers organize the marketing activities of selling, distributing, and sometimes servicing finished products received from manufacturing. For example, a regional sales office might be evaluated as a revenue center. The regional sales manager is given a budget for personnel and expenses and has decision authority over how to deploy this budget to maximize revenue. In general, though, the regional sales manager has limited discretion in setting the selling price.

Like cost centers, revenue centers can have various performance objectives. One objective is to maximize revenue given the selling price (or quantity) and the budget for personnel and expenses. That is, the revenue center is told the price of each product it sells and is given a fixed operating budget. This objective is consistent with maximizing shareholder value provided central management chooses the correct price/quantity combination for each product sold by the revenue center. Giving a revenue-center manager decision authority over product pricing can undermine value creation if units are sold below the profit-maximizing price in order to boost revenues.

Revenue centers work best if sales managers are knowledgeable about the demands of the customers within their sales districts and understand how to sell products effectively, and if central managers can determine the correct price/quantity combination and the optimal product mix. Otherwise, salespeople may shift their efforts toward selling products that generate more revenue rather than selling products that generate greater shareholder value.

Profit Centers

A profit center is often composed of several cost centers, and possibly expense and revenue centers as well. Profit-center managers are given a fixed capital budget and have decision authority over the input mix, the product mix, and selling prices (or output quantities). Profit centers work well when the knowledge required to make decisions about the product mix, quantity, pricing, and quality is specific to the division, as when the profit-center manager rises through the ranks within the division, and when this information is not readily transferred—typically because it is complex and highly detailed.

Profit centers are usually evaluated on their actual accounting profits, which is consistent with shareholder value objectives to the extent that accounting profits are related to the underlying cash flows. Measuring profits seems straightforward, but there are two complications: how to price transfers of goods and services between business units (transfer pricing) and which corporate overhead costs to allocate to specific business units. In every large firm, managers constantly debate these two issues. (We examine transfer pricing later in this chapter.)

In general, when there are significant interdependencies among business units, motivating managers of individual profit centers to maximize the profits of their own units will not maximize overall shareholder value. In focusing on their own profits, unit managers may ignore the effects of their actions on the sales or costs of other units. Suppose Chevrolet, in trying to increase its profits, decides to improve its car quality. This can affect consumers' perception of the average quality of all General Motors cars—including Buick's perceived quality. An enhanced reputation for Chevrolets thus helps Buick. But if Chevrolet receives no credit for the improvement in Buick's profits, it will tend to underinvest in quality enhancements. To help managers internalize both the positive and the negative effects of their actions on other profit centers, firms often base incentive compensation not just on the profits of the manager's own business unit, but also on the profits of a group of related profit centers and/or on the firm's total profits. Unless the group and/or the entire firm reach a certain profit target, no individual profit-center manager receives a bonus.

Investment Centers

Investment centers are similar to profit centers except that they typically have additional decision authority for capital expenditures and are evaluated on measures such as return on investment. Investment centers are most appropriate when the manager of the unit is in a position to anticipate and evaluate investment opportunities and is knowledgeable about the unit's operating decisions.

An investment center often comprises several profit centers. For example, suppose the consumer electronics group of an electronics firm comprises three profit centers: television, DVD, and stereo. The group manager has decision authority over the amount of capital invested in consumer electronics and is evaluated on the return on invested capital. There are two commonly used measures of performance for investment centers: return on assets and residual income (or Economic Value Added).

Accounting ROA. The most commonly used measure of investment-center performance is return on assets, or ROA. ROA is the accounting net income of the investment center divided by the total assets employed in the investment center. It has intuitive appeal because it can be compared to external market-based returns to provide a benchmark for a division's performance. (For firms with debt financing, it is important to add back interest expense to accounting income before comparing ROA with the firm's external market-based yields.) However, using ROA can create problems. It does not accurately measure the division's economic rate of return because accounting income (the numerator) is not always an accurate measure of economic profit, which represents the change in value over the period, and accounting assets (the denominator) do not necessarily reflect the current value of the division's investment base. Accounting rules tend to be conservative; they dictate that accounting net income exclude some value increases and include some value declines. For example, accounting net income excludes any appreciation in land value until the land is sold, but it recognizes declines in the market value of an asset even if the asset has not been sold. Also, accounting depreciation does not necessarily reflect the change in the economic value of the depreciable assets and therefore distorts both income and assets.

Perhaps more significant, the investment-center manager will be inclined to reject otherwise-profitable projects whose ROAs would nonetheless lower the center's overall ROA. For example, suppose the center has an ROA of 19 percent, 4 percentage points above its 15 percent cost of capital (the rate of return the firm must pay in order to raise capital). A new investment project with a 16 percent ROA is available. Taking on this project would increase shareholder value because the ROA is above the cost of capital of 15 percent. However, accepting the project lowers the investment center's ROA. If the center is evaluated on the basis of maintaining or increasing its ROA, the investment-center manager will reject the project, even though its rate of return exceeds the firm's cost of capital and would thus increase shareholder value. There are other problems with ROA as well. For example, riskier projects should be evaluated using a higher cost of capital. If managers are rewarded solely for increasing their ROA without being charged for any additional risk imposed on the firm, they have an incentive to plunge the firm into risky projects (although the manager's risk aversion will tend to check this tendency). Finally, a manager who is evaluated on the basis of ROA and who is near retirement might accept projects that will boost ROA immediately, even if they are uneconomic in the long run—this is just another example of the horizon problem (see Chapter 6).

Accounting residual income. To overcome some of the incentive problems of ROA, such as the incentive to forgo projects with ROAs that are above the cost of capital but below the division's average ROA, some firms use *residual income* to evaluate performance. When the residual-income approach is used, business-unit performance is measured by subtracting the dollar cost of capital employed in the business unit from the operating profits of the business unit. For example, suppose a division has operating profits of $20 million, total assets of $100 million, and a cost of capital of 15 percent. Its ROA is 20 percent, which is above its cost of capital. The dollar cost of capital employed is $15 million (15 percent of $100 million), so residual income is $5 million ($20 million less $15 million). Under the residual-income approach, accepting a new project with an ROA of less than 20 percent but more than 15 percent increases residual income and therefore also increases shareholder value, even though it lowers average ROA.

Nonetheless, residual income (and its variant, Economic Value Added) has its own problems. Like ROA, it relies on accounting measures of profits and assets, although adjustments can be made to bring these numbers more into line with economic reality. And since residual income is a straight dollar figure, larger divisions tend to have larger residual incomes than do smaller divisions, which makes comparisons among investment centers of different sizes difficult. Implementing the residual-income approach also requires that central management estimate the cost of capital for each division. In principle, each division will have a different required cost of capital to control for risk differences. However, these risk adjustments can prompt divisional managers to lobby central management to reevaluate their risk and lower their required capital costs. And, again like ROA, residual income measures performance over a single year. It does not measure the impact of today's decisions on future cash flows. For example, current-period residual income (and ROA) can be increased by cutting maintenance, but at the expense of future cash flows and hence shareholder value.

The different types of business units are appropriate in different circumstances. Table 7.2 summarizes our discussion of the various types of business units. Note the balance between the performance measure and the level of decision authority. Also note the linkage between the decision authority assigned to each center and the location of the relevant knowledge. For example, if a center does not have expertise in customer demand, it does not have decision authority for pricing and hence is evaluated as a cost center.

To ensure that the three-legged stool remains balanced, performance rewards must be tied to performance evaluations. For example, in addition to introducing EVA, CSX also changed its management compensation plan and introduced a stock incentive program. Therefore, CSX changed both its performance measurement system and its performance reward system to reinforce its new corporate focus on shareholder value creation. We address reward systems in more detail in the next two chapters.

Transfer Pricing

Whenever business units within a company transfer goods or services among themselves, a *transfer price* must be established for the goods and services exchanged in order to measure the business units' performance. For example, suppose a large chemical company is organized into profit centers. Besides selling to outside customers, these profit centers sell intermediate products to other profit centers within the company. In order to measure the performance of the various profit centers, each of these internal transactions requires a transfer price. The "buyer" pays the transfer price; the "seller" receives the transfer price.

Table 7.2 Summary of Cost, Expense, Revenue, Profit, and Investment Centers

Unit type	Performance measures	Decision authority	Typically used when
Cost center	Minimize total cost for a fixed output Maximize output for a fixed budget	Input mix (labor, material, supplies)	Central manager can measure output, knows the cost functions, and can set the optimal quantity and appropriate rewards. Central manager can observe the quality of the cost center's output. Cost center manager has knowledge of the optimal input mix.
Expense center	Minimize total cost for a fixed level of service Maximize service for a fixed budget	Input mix (labor, material, supplies)	Output is difficult to observe and measure.
Revenue center	Maximize revenues for a given price (or quantity) and operating budget	Input mix (labor, material, supplies)	Central manager has the knowledge to select the optimal product mix. Central manager has the knowledge to select the correct price or quantity. Revenue center managers have knowledge of the demand of the customers in their sales districts.

Table 7.2 Summary of Cost, Expense, Revenue, Profit, and Investment
Centers (*continued*)

Unit type	Performance measures	Decision authority	Typically used when
Profit center	Actual profits Actual profits compared to budgeted profits	Input mix Product mix Selling prices (or output quantities)	Profit center manager has the knowledge to select the correct price/quantity. Profit center manager has the knowledge to select the optimal product mix.
Investment center	Return on investment Residual income EVA	Input mix Product mix Selling prices (or output quantities) Capital invested in center	Investment center manager has the knowledge to select the correct price/quantity. Investment center manager has the knowledge to select the optimal product mix. Investment center manager has knowledge about investment opportunities.

Some managers view the transfer pricing problem as unimportant from the overall firm's perspective. They think that changing transfer pricing methods merely shifts income among divisions, and that, other than relative performance evaluation, little is affected. But this is a mistake: *The choice of transfer pricing method does not merely reallocate total company profits among business units—it can affect the firm's total profits.* Think of the firm's total profits as a pie. The transfer pricing method not only changes how the pie is divided among the business units, but it also changes the size of the pie. Managers make investment, purchasing, and production decisions on the basis of the transfer prices they face. If these transfer prices do not accurately reflect resource values, managers will make inappropriate decisions and shareholder value will be reduced.

For example, suppose the cost to the firm of producing an intermediate chemical is $20 per kilogram, but the transfer price is $30. The division using the chemical will consume too little of it because that division's manager will have an incentive to shift to other inputs that in reality are more expensive, thereby reducing shareholder value. Also, because transfer prices affect managers' performance evaluations, incorrect transfer prices can result in inappropriate promotion and retention decisions.

Taxes can also be an important factor in determining an optimal transfer price. If the buyer and seller divisions are in different countries with different tax rates, then headquarters should set the transfer price in such a way as to allocate as much profit as possible to the division in the country with the lower tax rate. Of course, international tax treaties and local regulations limit the degree to which firms can exploit transfer pricing methods for tax purposes, and in the late 1980s the United States began imposing stiff penalties on tax underpayments caused by transfer pricing issues. In fact, 30 percent of all U.S. corporate tax adjustments each year involve transfer prices. To streamline the resolution process, the IRS instituted an Advanced Pricing Agreement Program, wherein a taxpayer team and an IRS team work together to develop an acceptable transfer pricing method. As long as the taxpayer complies with the agreement, the IRS will not challenge subsequent years' transfer prices. The IRS had negotiated about 350 such agreements by the end of 1999. Nonetheless, in November 2001 Senator Byron Dorgan of North Dakota released a report claiming that multinational corporations had avoided paying $45 billion in U.S. taxes through the judicious use of transfer pricing.

Some consultants advocate using two separate transfer pricing systems, one for tax purposes and the other for internal decision making, even though maintaining two systems can be costly. Jay Tredwell, director of CEO solutions for Answer*Think* Consulting Group, says, "Having a separate system can give senior managers a better view of . . . real profitability [as opposed to] their 'tax profitability.'" However, Michael Patton, a partner at Ernst and Young, counters,

> An essential problem with separated reporting is that transfer prices already reflect the profitability of a division or project. If you are trying to make decisions about new activities or facilities, and trying to judge their returns on invested capital, you need good benchmarks to judge these by, and good transfer prices provide part of that. Basically, then, the question is whether your current transfer prices reflect economic reality or not. If they do, there's little need for a new system. If not, the tax authorities may have a question or two for you on audit in a few years' time.

Transfer prices are more prevalent than many managers realize. For example, firms often have extensive charge-back systems for internal service departments. Consider the charges that the advertising department receives for janitorial services, telephones, security services, data processing, legal services, and human resources. Most firms charge inside users for these internally provided services. These charge-back systems are simply internal transfer prices. Because the use of transfer prices (including charge-back systems) is widespread and because transfer pricing affects performance measurement and hence the rewards that managers receive, disputes over transfer prices between divisions are virtually inevitable. Transfer pricing is a continuing source of tension within firms, and many managers in multidivisional firms are involved in a succession of transfer pricing battles over the course of their careers.

Economics of Transfer Pricing

The optimal transfer price for a product or service is its opportunity cost—the value forgone by not using the product in its best alternative use. Unfortunately, as we will see, this rule, while simple to state, is often difficult to implement in practice.

Opportunity costs.   To illustrate the concept of opportunity cost, we focus on two of a firm's business divisions—manufacturing and distribution. Manufacturing furnishes a product to distribution for external sale. The incremental or marginal cost of production is $3 per unit, and manufacturing has excess capacity. Distribution can sell the product for $5 per unit, net of its selling costs.

If a unit of product is manufactured and transferred, the firm incurs $3 in production costs. Transfers to the distribution center do not preclude production for alternative uses. Each transferred unit simply increases total production costs by $3. Therefore, the opportunity cost of a transfer is $3. Moreover, a transfer price of $3 creates optimal incentives for both divisions. Distribution is willing to pay the transfer price of $3 because it can sell the product at a profit. Manufacturing is willing to supply product at $3 because it can cover its costs.

As this example is meant to suggest, the marginal cost of producing the unit is generally its opportunity cost. However, this is not always the case. Suppose manufacturing can produce a unit for $3 and can then either transfer that unit to distribution or sell it directly to an outside customer for $6—but because of limited capacity, it cannot do both. In this case, by transferring the unit to distribution, the firm forgoes a $6 direct sale. Thus, even though the incremental production cost is still $3, the opportunity cost of an internal transfer is now $6, because that is the value forgone by not selling it directly (the best alternative use). The distribution center will not buy the product at a $6 transfer price because its net selling price is only $5. However, this decision is optimal from the firm's standpoint because profits are maximized by producing the unit and then selling it directly to the outside customer for $6.

Transfer pricing with limited information.   If central management knew the opportunity cost of internal transfers, it could simply mandate the correct transfer prices. Determining the opportunity cost, however, requires information on costs, revenue, capacity, and alternative uses. If all this knowledge were readily available at central headquarters, there would be no reason to decentralize decision making within the organization, and transfer pricing would not be an issue. Central management would have the relevant knowledge and could retain the authority to make the production decisions; if decision authority were delegated for other reasons, central management could easily monitor the process. In reality, of course, much of this information is not readily available to central management, especially in large, multidivisional firms.

Suppose that the manager of manufacturing is the only person with detailed knowledge of that division's marginal costs and that he or she wants to maximize the manufacturing division's profits. If manufacturing can set the transfer price, it will attempt to set the price above its incremental cost in order to increase its *measured* profits—even if distribution is allowed to purchase the product on the outside. When this happens, the firm manufactures and sells too few units of the product. Manufacturing's higher profits lead to lower-than-optimal production levels and reduced shareholder value.

The basic problem is that distribution overestimates the *opportunity* cost to the firm of producing extra units of the good because of the artificially high price set by manufacturing. Hence, from the firm's standpoint, distribution buys less than the optimal quantity to be sold in the external market. The transfer price that maximizes shareholder value in this example is the incremental production cost of the unit. But that transfer price would force the manufacturing division to report a lower profit.

This discussion illustrates the basic incentive problems associated with internal transfers. Opportunity cost is the transfer price that maximizes shareholder value. But because division managers tend to have better knowledge of opportunity costs than senior management does and because transfer prices are frequently used in performance evaluation and in setting managerial rewards, division managers have incentives to influence the transfer price to their own advantage.

To complicate matters further, the information necessary to calculate opportunity costs is especially difficult for senior management to obtain because opportunity costs depend on the firm's alternative uses of the product or service. Central management is likely to know less about these alternative uses, and the resources used to make the product, than does the manager of the division that produces the product. Moreover, the alternative uses will change as the firm's business opportunities change. For example, sometimes the division has excess capacity, and manufacturing can sell the product both internally and externally. At other times, manufacturing has only enough current capacity to produce for either the inside or the outside buyer. This specialized knowledge of the alternatives resides primarily with the division managers.

Further problems arise when either distribution or manufacturing has the decision authority to set the price of the goods or services transferred and the other division cannot purchase or sell outside. If manufacturing has the decision authority, it will tend to set a price above its opportunity cost in order to increase its profits, and distribution will then purchase fewer units than it would purchase at the correct (lower) transfer price. But if distribution has the decision authority, it will set a transfer price below the opportunity cost in order to increase its measured profits, and manufacturing will then supply too few units at this lower cost. If central management knew the opportunity cost, it could dictate both the transfer price and the quantity to be transferred.

Common Transfer Pricing Methods

The correct transfer price, then, is opportunity cost. But, as we have also noted, determining opportunity costs is difficult, in part because the information needed to calculate these costs lies with operating managers, who have incentives to conceal it. To address this problem, companies sometimes hire outside experts to conduct special studies of the firm's cost structure. However, not only are such studies expensive and time-consuming, but their findings will become outdated as soon as the firm's business opportunities or productive capacities change. On the other hand, if senior management simply assigns the decision authority over the transfer price to either manufacturing or distribution, prices are likely to be set incorrectly, resulting in too few units transferred and lower shareholder value.

Because determining opportunity costs is a difficult undertaking, managers resort to various approximations. We discuss the four most prevalent methods for setting transfer prices: market price, marginal production cost, full cost, and negotiated pricing. Each of these four methods works in some situations but not in others. For example, if the divisions operate in different countries with different tax rates, then the choice of method will be driven in part by tax considerations. Our aim is to describe these basic alternatives and set forth their advantages and disadvantages so that managers can select the best transfer pricing method for their particular circumstances.

Market-based transfer prices. The standard transfer pricing rule offered by most books is this: *If there is a competitive external market for the product, the product should be transferred at the external market price.* If manufacturing cannot cover its costs (including capital costs) at the external price, then the company is better off not producing internally and should instead purchase the product in the external market. If distribution cannot make a long-run profit at the external price, then the company is better off not transferring the intermediate product and should instead sell it directly in the external market.

In short, the use of market-based transfer prices is assumed to produce the correct make-versus-buy decisions. At the same time, however—and this is what makes the issue of transfer pricing so difficult—in circumstances where the firm is most likely to produce a product internally, the external market price is *least* likely to provide an accurate measure of the opportunity cost of internal production. An intermediate product may not be available from other firms, or the product that is produced externally may not be identical to the product that is produced internally. In the former case, there is no market price; in the latter, the market price will be an unreliable guide to opportunity cost. And even when there are virtually identical cheaper external products, producing internally can still make sense if it improves quality control, ensures timeliness of supply, or protects proprietary information. When these factors are included in the analysis, the external market may no longer be cheaper. For example, Kodak, like many companies, has outsourced a variety of activities, but it has kept its Eastman Gelatine facility in Peabody, Massachusetts, to maintain the quality of a critical input. The gelatine from the plant is shipped to various Kodak plants and mixed with other chemicals to create a photosensitive emulsion on strips of film. Poor-quality gel will overexpose the film, as George Eastman discovered in 1930 when a bad batch of gelatine nearly ruined him. He founded Eastman Gelatine shortly thereafter.

Marginal-cost transfer prices.   If there is no external market for the intermediate product, or if synergies or quality concerns cause the market price to be an inaccurate measure of opportunity cost, then the incremental or marginal production cost may be the best transfer price. Marginal cost represents the value of the resources employed to produce the last unit. As with other transfer pricing methods, however, there are problems with using marginal production cost as a measure of opportunity cost. If all of manufacturing's output is transferred internally and marginal cost is below the average total cost, manufacturing's fixed costs will not be recovered. Thus, manufacturing will appear to be losing money. Of course, if central management knows the magnitude of the fixed costs, it can budget for this loss. But, once again, if central management knows the magnitude of the fixed costs, then it probably knows the marginal cost, and thus there is little reason to have a separate business unit and transfer pricing system in the first place.

One variation of marginal-cost transfer pricing is the use of a two-part price—all transfers are priced at marginal cost, but distribution is also charged a fixed fee. Distribution pays the marginal cost for the additional units and buys the number of units that maximize firm profits. Unlike straight marginal-cost pricing, this variant allows manufacturing to cover its full cost and earn a profit. The fixed fee represents distribution's right to acquire the product at marginal cost, and it is set to cover manufacturing's fixed cost plus a return on invested capital.

Another problem with marginal-cost transfer pricing arises when the marginal cost per unit is not constant as volume changes. Suppose the marginal cost per unit increases as volume expands (say, a night shift is added at higher hourly wages). If marginal cost is greater than average cost and all users are charged the higher marginal cost, the total paid by all the users will be greater than the total cost of manufacturing. Users who do not expand their volume will still see their costs increase. In such cases, conflicts will arise within the firm over the appropriate measure of marginal cost and whether marginal cost should be charged to *all* users or just to those users whose demand for additional volume required the increased level of output, thereby prompting the addition of the night shift.

A similar problem arises when manufacturing approaches capacity. Let's assume that manufacturing is considering a $2.5 million outlay to add more capacity. The $2.5 million is a variable cost in the long run, but it increases short-run fixed costs (depreciation, utilities, and maintenance). Thus, there will be disputes about whether the costs of the additional capacity should be included in the transfer price. What makes such conflicts so difficult to resolve is that there is no objective method for calculating marginal costs. They are certainly not reported in *The Wall Street Journal.* Instead, they have to be estimated, normally as "variable costs," from accounting records. While most of the components of marginal cost are easily observed, such as the cost of direct labor and direct material, some components are quite difficult to estimate. For example, how much of the electricity bill is fixed, and how much is variable? Since these classifications are to some extent arbitrary, time and other resources are wasted as managers in manufacturing and distribution debate various cost terms and their applications—and as senior managers are forced to spend time arbitrating such disputes.

Moreover, under marginal-cost transfer pricing, manufacturing has an incentive to convert a dollar of fixed costs into more than a dollar of marginal costs—such as by using high-priced outsourcing of parts instead of cheaper internal manufacturing—even though this clearly reduces shareholder value. For manufacturing, the use of outsourcing can remove the burden of any fixed costs, while distribution, as well as the firm as a whole, bears the extra cost of such decisions.

Full-cost transfer prices.   A simple, objective, hard-to-change transfer pricing rule can sometimes lead to higher shareholder value even if it is technically less accurate. In some firms, transfer prices are based on full accounting costs simply to avoid wasteful disputes over measuring marginal costs. Since full cost is the sum of fixed and variable costs, full cost cannot be changed simply by reclassifying a fixed cost as a variable cost.

The problem, however, is that full-cost transfer pricing frequently causes distribution to purchase too few units. Full-cost accounting generally overstates the opportunity cost to the firm of producing and transferring one more unit internally. As a result, distribution will buy too few units internally. Full-cost pricing also allows manufacturing to transfer any production inefficiencies to distribution. Thus, manufacturing has less incentive to be efficient under a full-cost transfer pricing rule. To be sure, marginal-cost transfer prices also allow manufacturing to export some of its inefficiencies to distribution, but the problem is not as pronounced as under full-cost pricing. And allowing distribution to purchase externally as well as from manufacturing forces manufacturing to remain competitive.

Despite these problems, however, full-cost transfer pricing is quite common. In various surveys of corporate practice, full-cost transfer prices are used 40 to 50 percent of the time. In most cases, moreover, the definition of *full cost* includes direct materials and labor and also a charge for overhead. One reason for the popularity of full-cost transfer pricing is the ability of this method to deal with changes in capacity. As a plant begins to reach capacity, opportunity cost is likely to rise because of congestion and the cost of alternative uses of now-scarce capacity. Hence, opportunity cost is likely to be higher than direct materials and labor costs. When a plant approaches capacity, then full cost does not overstate opportunity cost and in fact might be a closer approximation to it than just the cost of materials and labor.

Perhaps the most important benefit of full-cost transfer pricing, however, is its simplicity, and hence its ease of implementation. It is more difficult for operating managers to manipulate full-cost than marginal-cost calculations, so senior management has to field fewer calls to arbitrate disputes over calculating the transfer price. Nonetheless, managers should consider whether full-cost pricing is optimal for their particular situation. If the opportunity cost differs materially from full cost, the firm's forgone profits can be substantial and shareholder value will not be maximized.

Negotiated transfer prices.   Transfer prices can also be set by ne-gotiation between the divisions involved. This method can result in transfer prices that approximate opportunity cost because manufac-turing will not agree to a price that is below its opportunity cost and distribution will not pay a price that is above the external market price. With negotiated transfer prices, the two divisions have an incentive to set the number of units at a level that maximizes the combined profits of the two divisions. Once the value-maximizing number of units is agreed on, the transfer price determines how the total profits are divided between the two divisions.

While negotiation is a fairly common method of setting transfer prices, it, too, has its drawbacks. It is time-consuming, and it can lead to conflicts among divisions. Divisional performance measurement becomes dependent on the relative negotiating skills of the division managers. Moreover, if the divisions negotiate a transfer price without at the same time agreeing on the quantity to be transferred at that price, there is no guarantee that they will arrive at the transfer price that maximizes shareholder value.

Jon Flexman, former CFO at Hewlett-Packard, oversaw a mish-mash of interdivisional transfer pricing mechanisms based on both financial and tax accounting regulations: "We . . . reward managers based on their product margins, as they are created by our transfer-pricing system." Managers "often get caught up in negotiations with each other" to produce profits for their division and for themselves personally. This produces a set of final output prices that restricts what sales representatives can charge end users. A manager at Answer*Think* Consulting Group complains, "The biggest problems are when the measured profitability of a business unit has more to do with the skill of its manager in negotiating transfer prices within the company than [it does with] its economic profits and the factors that drive share-holder-value creation."

Reorganization: The Solution if All Else Fails

In some cases, transfer pricing conflicts among profit centers can become quite contentious, especially when the volume of transactions among divisions is large. In such cases, a small change in the transfer price can have a large impact on a division's reported profits. Hence, the potential for (and destructive effects of) opportunistic transfer pricing actions by operating managers is substantial.

If transfer pricing becomes sufficiently divisive, the best solution may be to reorganize the firm. For example, senior management could combine two profit centers with a large volume of transfers into a single division. Alternatively, it might convert manufacturing into a cost center rather than a profit center and compensate the operating head on the basis of efficiency of production. Or the divisions could be organized as cost centers, with pricing and quantity decisions made at the central office.

Internal Accounting and Performance Measurement

The internal accounting system performs an important role in creating incentives for employees to maximize shareholder value. Accounting measures of costs, revenues, profits, return on investment, and residual income are used in performance evaluation, and accounting costs are frequently used as transfer prices. This section elaborates on the role of accounting within the firm.

Uses of the Accounting System

Many people think of the accounting system in terms of the firm's external financial reports to shareholders, tax authorities, regulators, and lenders. But these external financial reports (both quarterly and annual) aggregate an enormous amount of internal accounting data.

Internally, managers rely on detailed operating reports of expenses, product costs, inventories, and customer account balances from the accounting system, all of which are generally computer-accessible.

Management uses internal accounting reports for two general purposes: decision management and decision control. As discussed in Chapter 4, the decision-making process is divided into decision management (initiation and implementation) and decision control (ratification and monitoring). Managers frequently have authority over both decision management and decision control—but not normally for the same decisions. Senior managers in the firm tend to be responsible for decision control, while responsibility for decision management tends to be delegated to managers at lower levels in the firm. But to exercise either decision management or decision control, managers require information, much of which is generated by the accounting system.

Decision management typically requires estimates of future costs and benefits. Before deciding to build a new plant, the manager must evaluate alternative uses of this plant; evaluating a new marketing initiative requires judgments about likely future sales and competitors' responses. Managers frequently use accounting-based data as inputs for these types of decisions because accounting numbers provide a starting point in forecasting the future financial consequences of proposed actions. Similarly, most firms have accounting-based budget systems. Managers forecast costs and revenues for the next year in preparing their budgets. This process encourages managers to be forward-looking, to coordinate their operations with other managers who are directly affected by their decisions, and to share specialized knowledge of their markets and production technologies. Accounting-based budgets provide the framework for such coordination and knowledge sharing.

Accounting budgets also serve to hard-wire the process of converting wetware into software (see Chapter 3). For example, suppose a production employee discovers a faster way to set up the machines. This wetware is converted into a plant production policy—a new setup algorithm—and becomes part of the firm's formula for value creation. Next year's budget will be adjusted to incorporate fewer labor hours for machine setups. If the setup efficiencies do not materialize as planned, the accounting system will report this in the form of unfavorable variances from budget.

While accounting systems are helpful for decision management, they are generally more useful for decision control (ratification and monitoring). In fact, accounting systems evolved primarily for this purpose. Internal accounting systems protect against fraud, embezzlement, and theft of company assets. They also provide a scorecard for how a business unit has performed historically by measuring its costs, profits, or residual income. Of course, decision monitoring can be based on aggregate data to average out random fluctuations. Instead of monitoring every machine setup, it is usually more effective to aggregate all setups occurring over a week or a month and make sure that the average setup cost is within acceptable levels.

Monitoring is by definition a historical function and is well served by the accounting system. But because accounting systems are primarily used for decision control—to prevent malfeasance and to measure past performance—they are often found wanting when it comes to providing managers with the information they need for decision management. Accounting systems are based on historical costs and historical revenues and in this sense are backward-looking.

Trade-Offs between Decision Management and Control

To the extent that accounting systems are used primarily for monitoring purposes, accounting measures are not designed for use by the people being monitored—the operating managers. As a result, these managers tend to be dissatisfied with financial measures as a basis for making operating decisions. The data rarely provide sufficient detail for decision making. In response, operating managers develop their own, often nonfinancial information systems to provide more of the data that they need for decision management. But at the same time, they rely on the output of the accounting system to monitor the managers who report to them. One survey confirmed that managers rely on nonfinancial data (labor counts, units of output, units in inventory, units scrapped) to run their day-to-day operations. Still, when they are asked about their "most valuable report in general," they say that it is the monthly income or expense statement because this is one of the measures that is used to judge their performance.

In choosing among alternative accounting systems, managers must make trade-offs between decision management and decision control. All accounting (and nonaccounting) performance measures are prone to manipulation. Managers can choose accounting methods that reduce expenses and increase reported earnings, thus artificially raising ROA. Investment-center managers can also increase ROA by rejecting (or terminating) profitable projects with ROAs below the average ROA for their division. Most accounting measures are short-term measures of performance. They all suffer from the horizon problem, wherein retiring managers emphasize short-term performance at the expense of future cash flows. Therefore, any accounting-based performance measurement system requires careful monitoring by senior managers to control behavior by lower-level managers that is not consistent with maximizing shareholder value.

Of course, using the same numbers for many purposes helps to control any incentives to distort the numbers for any one purpose. And although managers have considerable discretion, accounting methods are regulated—managers must choose accounting methods from among those permitted by generally accepted accounting principles (GAAP), and external, third-party auditors ensure the accuracy and consistency of the accounting reports. Most firms employ a single accounting system for multiple purposes (making adjustments as necessary): shareholder reports, taxes, internal decision management and control, and regulation. Debt agreements, management compensation plans, and financial reports all use these accounting-based numbers.

But no performance measurement and reward system works perfectly; no system eliminates all opportunities for managers to increase their well-being at the expense of the shareholders. The key question is: Does the system outperform the next best alternative after all the costs and benefits are factored in? It is important to avoid the "Nirvana fallacy," which suggests that a system should be discarded if it allows any managerial opportunism, no matter how minor. The Nirvana fallacy arises when a real system is compared to an assumed but unachievable "perfect" system. Economic Darwinism would suggest that by virtue of the fact that they have survived, most accounting systems are useful.

We turn next to compensation and reward systems, which rely on the performance evaluation system.

CHAPTER 8

The Third Leg: Compensation

*T*here are two important objectives in compensation policy: (1) to attract and retain qualified employees and (2) to motivate employees to be more productive. This chapter focuses on the first objective, attraction and retention, although we discuss some incentive-related issues as well. (The next chapter examines incentive compensation in more detail.) There are various factors involved in setting the appropriate level of pay, including the nature of the job itself. It is important to strike a balance between low wage rates—which on the surface would appear to save the firm money, but which can lead to excessive turnover and a less-qualified applicant pool—and high wage rates—which will limit turnover, but over time will affect the firm's ability to compete in its product markets. Some degree of turnover is useful, of course, to bring fresh ideas and talent into the organization. There are pros and cons to long-term employment relationships, and these relationships can be improved through different compensation schemes, including wage premiums, seniority-based pay, and promotions. Fringe benefits are another important component of compensation, and we discuss the mix between salary and fringe benefits as well as the choice among fringe benefits.

Compensation Structure Matters

In the late 1980s, RKO Warner Video owned and operated twenty-four video stores; it was then one of the larger video chains in the New York City area. It had an enormous inventory and offered high-quality service and attractive decor. Although the company was reasonably successful, senior management was concerned about two human resource problems. First, employee turnover was "unacceptably high." Second, "the quality and consistency of performance by store managers varied considerably across the chain." Store managers were responsible for organizing the racks, keeping the store clean, opening on time, returning tapes to racks promptly, ordering product from the warehouse, and keeping checkout times short. However, RKO's reward system did not motivate an adequate level of effort on these tasks—its organizational architecture was poorly designed.

To address these concerns, RKO adopted a new bonus plan for store managers. The aims of the plan were twofold. First, the company wanted to raise the level of compensation in order to "attract and keep qualified store managers." Second, RKO wanted to structure the compensation package in a way that would motivate managers to "be more conscientious and take pride in their work."

The new plan had a substantial impact on the level of pay and made RKO more competitive in the local labor market. Before the plan went into effect, RKO store managers received annual salaries ranging from $21,000 to $28,000. The new bonus plan was targeted at increasing compensation by about 15 percent, depending on performance. In fact, during the first quarter under the new bonus plan, two store managers received substantially more in bonus pay than in base salary. RKO was thus able to adjust its pay scheme to attract and retain employees. Although less successful from an incentive standpoint, the plan also motivated some operational improvements.

By structuring compensation appropriately, managers can make employees better off and also increase shareholder value. Individuals will reject a potential employment relationship unless they expect to earn at least as much as they could earn elsewhere for performing similar tasks. If they are not as well off as they would be in their next best alternative, they will quit and go to work for another firm (or withdraw from the labor force). The level of compensation is a key factor in attracting and retaining qualified employees. But shareholders must also receive an adequate return on their investment, or they will invest elsewhere. Paying employees more than the competitive rate results in a cost disadvantage that in the long run can drive the company out of business. Managers thus have incentives to design compensation packages that allow the firm to attract, retain, and motivate skilled employees, but at a reasonable cost.

Human Capital and the Level of Pay

The hiring decisions of all firms in the market determine the demand for labor. The supply of labor is determined by the decisions of individuals as to whether to accept the given wage rate or stay out of the labor force. The market wage rate then equates supply and demand. If a firm pays too little (below the prevailing wage), it will be unable to attract qualified employees or will have high turnover. This principle motivated RKO to raise its level of pay. Overpaying will result in low turnover and long queues for job openings (witness the large number of applications for a teaching position in many suburban public schools). However, a firm that overpays will capture less value than firms that do not overpay.

And compensation goes hand in hand with decision authority and how tasks are bundled into jobs (see Chapter 5). In 1993, aircraft engine manufacturer Pratt & Whitney was on the verge of closing its North Berwick plant (Maine's largest factory) because of high operating costs and inefficiencies. But a new plant manager overhauled operations. Before he joined the firm, there were 129 job classifications, 90 of which contained only one or two people. He broadened job descriptions and found that eighteen inspectors could do 15 percent more work than twenty-eight had done five years earlier. He eliminated automatic pay raises and tied pay to the level of training rather than to seniority. As workers received training for each job level and as they shouldered more responsibility, their pay increased. Shop-floor wages varied between $9 and $19 per hour, with the higher wages going to people who were running special cost studies or quality projects—tasks that had previously been done by managers. The plant's overall operating costs per hour fell 20 percent in two years, without employees taking a pay cut.

Human Capital

Employees vary in their abilities, skills, and training. *Human capital* is a term that characterizes an individual's set of skills (part of the individual's wetware). The value of these skills is determined by supply and demand in the marketplace. Individuals invest in their human capital through education and training. The return on this investment consists of the higher wage rates that come from having more valuable human capital—hence college graduates typically earn more than high school graduates.

It is useful to distinguish between *general* and *specific* human capital. General human capital consists of training and education that is equally useful to a broad variety of employers. Investments in general human capital include obtaining an MBA degree, mastering the general principles of engineering, or learning popular word processing programs. Specific human capital, on the other hand, consists of knowledge and training that are more valuable to one particular employer than to other employers. Investments in specific capital include such things as learning the details of a particular firm's accounting system or product lines.

Typically, employees pay for their own general training. The gains from general training go principally to the employees, rather than to the firms employing them—if a firm does not pay the employee the market price for these new skills, the individual can move to another firm that is willing to pay. Correspondingly, employees are reluctant to invest in specific training, since it does not increase their market value. Thus, firms generally must pay for specific training. (We discuss exceptions to these generalizations later in the chapter.)

Compensating Wage Differentials

Jobs vary along many dimensions, including the quality of the work environment, geographic location, length of commute, exposure to danger, characteristics of coworkers, and degree of monotony. Given comparable salary offers, individuals choose the job with the most desirable characteristics (such as attractive location and low risk of injury). To attract employees to less desirable jobs, firms must increase the level of pay.

The *extra* wage that is paid to attract an individual to a less desirable job is called a *compensating wage differential*. For instance, RKO probably had to pay more to attract a manager to work at night in a more dangerous location than to attract a manager to work during the day at a safer location; it had to offer "combat pay." In fact, firms in general have to pay compensating differentials in order to attract employees to staff their night shifts. Variation in job requirements for education, skills, and training also account for differences in pay. For example, an office job in a pleasant work environment might pay more than the relatively less pleasant job of sanitation worker simply because the skills required for the office job are higher. However, sanitation workers will be paid more than similar unskilled labor engaged in more pleasant tasks because it is more difficult to attract and retain sanitation workers.

Compensating wage differentials have two important effects. First, all societies have relatively unpleasant tasks that must be performed, such as those of morticians and sanitation workers. Compensating differentials attract people to these jobs and reward them for their efforts. And the individuals who accept unpleasant tasks tend to be the ones for whom the unpleasant aspects of the job are least bothersome. For example, if a wage premium is offered for working in a noisy factory, the people who are most likely to apply are those who are the least bothered by noise. Individuals who are significantly noise-averse would choose to work in a quiet environment at a lower wage. But compensating wage differentials cause employers with unpleasant work environments to have higher labor costs. Employers can thus reduce their labor costs by enhancing their work environments, provided they can do so at reasonable cost (the incremental cost of providing a more pleasant environment must not exceed the incremental savings in labor costs).

In essence, there is a job-matching process in labor markets whereby firms offer and individuals accept jobs in a manner that makes the most of their relative strengths and preferences. Firms have incentives to reduce the risk of injury in order to reduce wage premiums. In turn, the people who take risky jobs are likely to be those who are the most tolerant of risk—individuals *self-select* on the basis of their preferences. For example, fisheries often find it too expensive to reduce the risk of injury beyond some level, and thus they must offer wage premiums to crews of fishing boats. Individuals applying to work on these boats are likely to be among those who are most willing to place their lives at risk on the job. Because of this self-selection, the compensating differential is less than it would be if the firm attempted to hire a randomly selected person from the population. A firm that can provide a safe environment at a low cost will offer low-risk jobs and lower wages; these positions will then be filled by more risk-averse employees.

Because employees who accept dangerous jobs at a higher wage generally consider themselves better off than if they were working in safer environments at lower wages, regulations that force firms to provide safer work environments can make employees worse off by eliminating the compensating wage differential. In the summer of 1994, Labor Secretary Robert Reich charged a Bridgestone Tire subsidiary with 107 safety violations and levied a fine of $7.5 million. The labor secretary ostensibly took this action on behalf of the employees at the tire plant. To quote the secretary, "American workers are not going to be sacrificed at the altar of profits." Reich was "amazed" when the employees and the local community failed to support his action. Indeed, one employee went so far as to indicate that the secretary "didn't know what the hell he was doing." This lack of employee support might reflect two considerations. First, employees might worry that the cost of complying with the regulations would lead to layoffs or wage cuts. Second, pay will generally be lower in a safer environment. Thus, employees who self-select a relatively less safe work environment are potentially made worse off by this type of regulatory action.

The overall costs and benefits of regulatory intervention are hard to estimate. On the one hand, employees might mistakenly believe that a plant is safer than it really is (although it is not clear why the government would be better informed about the level of safety at a plant than the employees who work there). Moreover, employees who are hurt on the job can impose costs on society through subsidized medical care and disability payments. Still, it is clear that employees do not always believe that they benefit from government actions "on their behalf."

Costly Information about Market Wage Rates

It is not always obvious what the going wage rate should be. For one thing, compensation levels in many labor markets are not readily observable; firms generally do not share complete information about compensation. Moreover, individuals vary in their characteristics and rarely are perfect substitutes for one another. Thus, the wage paid to one individual is not necessarily indicative of what it would cost the firm to hire someone else. It is therefore not always obvious whether a firm is underpaying or overpaying its employees. But if a firm is inundated with qualified applicants when it advertises a job opening and its turnover rate is low, it is likely that the firm is paying *above* the market wage rate. In contrast, if the number of applicants is low and turnover is high, the firm is probably paying *below* the market rate.

For example, when Nucor's mill in Darlington, South Carolina, advertised to fill eight openings, over 1300 applicants showed up, creating such a traffic jam that the state police had to be called out. Unfortunately, the police force was a bit thin—three officers were already at Nucor applying for jobs. Even if the number of applications at Nucor included many unqualified candidates, the sheer size of the applicant pool certainly suggests that Nucor was paying above the market wage rate for these particular jobs.

In choosing the rate of pay, it is important to consider the trade-offs between incremental compensation and turnover costs. Turnover costs include the costs of recruiting and training employees as well as the cost of the reduced productivity that results from employing inexperienced personnel. In addition, if employees expect that they will be working for the firm for only a short time, they are less likely to be concerned about how their actions affect the long-run cash flows of the firm. For instance, a salesperson might push to make a sale in order to collect a commission, even if he or she knows that the customer will be unhappy with the product and will avoid future purchases. Turnover costs can also arise when employees who leave a firm take customers and trade secrets to competing firms. Nonetheless, turnover can have beneficial effects on the firm—for example, it brings "new blood" and fresh ideas and talents to the organization.

With intense competition for skilled employees, especially for managers, companies are resorting to a variety of tactics other than raising the level of pay. Key employees may receive retention bonuses of 15 to 50 percent of one year's pay, spread over three years, if they remain with the firm. After NYNEX and Bell Atlantic merged, top managers were promised retention bonuses above $1 million if they stayed at least three years. No one left.

Often under the guise of "increasing corporate loyalty," firms seek ways to attract and retain managers. To reduce turnover rates, employers are revamping rigid pay systems to make it easier for employees to move laterally and enhance their skills while still increasing their earnings. New career-development programs help employees plan their next moves up the corporate ladder. Citibank's program for 10,000 managers reviews each manager twice a year to assess future career moves. International Paper requires managers to discuss career desires with employees annually, in addition to the employees' annual performance reviews. Booz Allen has a rotation program for its consultants that permits more flexible workdays, thus making it easier for employees to balance work and family life. One Booz Allen consultant whose parents developed health problems was assigned a stint as a college recruiter. This flexibility gave him more time to help his parents. Now, when headhunters call him, he says, "I made a commitment to the firm, and they made a commitment to me." Many of these programs are nonpecuniary forms of compensation that certain employees value enormously.

The number of outside job offers made to existing employees can also give an indication of market wage rates. While such offers provide important information about the market value of existing employees, managers must be careful in deciding whether to match these outside offers. Failure to do so can result in the loss of valued employees. But a policy of matching all outside offers encourages employees to solicit such offers, which not only takes time away from work but also increases the likelihood that employees will receive offers that entice them to leave the firm. Of course, there are some compensation differentials, principally related to lifestyle, that most firms cannot match.

Internal Labor Markets

Although we said earlier that it is usually the employee who pays for general training and the firm that pays for specific training, many firms invest in general training—for example, paying tuition for an employee to obtain an MBA—and many employees invest their own time and effort in developing firm-specific skills. Such firms are usefully characterized as having *internal labor markets,* with outside hiring focused primarily on filling entry-level jobs, while most other jobs are filled from within the firm. Firms with internal labor markets establish *long-term relationships* with employees. One study found that the typical employee between ages forty-five and fifty-four had been with his or her current employer for at least ten years.

Established career paths and the prospect of promotions play important roles in firms with internal labor markets. Rather than simply reflecting outside market conditions, the rates of pay (discussed in more detail iater in the chapter) and job assignments in internal labor markets are often determined by administrative rules and implicit understandings. Firms can also have more than one internal labor market. For example, the internal market for white-collar employees may be very different from the internal market for blue-collar employees.

Japanese firms were once known for their extensive use of internal labor markets. Many Japanese executives spent their entire careers with the same firm. Senior executives virtually never moved from one major firm to another, and firms rarely went outside to hire for any position other than an entry-level job. Turnover was extremely low. Pay was tied largely to seniority, and the differences in pay among employees were small relative to the differences in American companies. These small pay differentials would be difficult to maintain if there were an active outside labor market in Japan because market pressures would tend to bid up the salaries of the stronger performers.

But poor performance over the last decade has placed pressures on Japanese firms to reconsider their policies of lifetime employment guarantees. Mitsubishi employees, for example, used to be lords of the universe. Hired from the top universities and treated like the elite, they had good jobs, security, and lifetime employment. But then the bubble burst. Now, recent hires quit and look for new jobs. There is no longer the same sense of security as before. As more firms abandon their policy of lifetime employment, the outside labor market is becoming more active.

Reasons for Long-Term Employment Relationships

There are several advantages to the long-term employment relationships found in internal labor markets. Long-term relationships provide employers and employees with incentives to invest in firm-specific training. Moreover, the prospect of a long-term relationship with a firm provides powerful incentives for employees to work productively because they have more to lose if they are dismissed. Another major advantage lies in the reduction in search, relocation, retraining, and other costs incurred by both the employer and the employee in the course of a change in employment. Finally, a long-term relationship gives managers more time to learn about the skills, work habits, interests, and abilities of individual employees, making it easier to match jobs and employees within the firm. Firms with well-developed internal labor markets have few surprises when they fill higher-level positions.

Costs of Internal Labor Markets

However, not all firms have active internal labor markets. Some firms rely heavily on outside markets to fill positions at all levels, which suggests that in some cases the costs of internal markets can be greater than their benefits. One potentially important problem with internal labor markets is the restricted competition for higher-level jobs within the organization. If a firm considers only internal candidates for higher-level jobs, it will not always hire the most qualified person—who may be someone from outside the firm. The likelihood of finding a desirable candidate in the outside labor market is highest when the job does not require specific training. Thus, firms are more likely to use internal labor markets where specific training is important. Indeed, firms in the steel, petroleum, and chemical industries, where complicated production technologies can take a long time to learn, tend to rely more heavily on internal labor markets, while firms in the shoe and garment industries do not.

Eastman Kodak had a long history of filling senior positions exclusively with long-time employees. An advantage of this policy is that senior executives have extensive experience with the firm and detailed knowledge of the company. The prospect of promotion and long-term employment also provides important motivational effects. A disadvantage, however, is that sometimes the best people for senior jobs are outsiders. During the late 1980s and early 1990s, shareholders placed intense pressure on Kodak's board to appoint outsiders to senior positions. Many shareholders felt that hiring outsiders was necessary to bring new skills and vision into the firm. In late October 1993, Kodak announced that it had hired George Fisher, CEO of Motorola, as its new CEO. The stock market greeted this announcement with an 8 percent increase in Kodak's stock price (from the close of the market on October 26 to the close on October 28), representing a $1.6 billion increase in the overall value of the company.

Career Paths and Lifetime Pay

Employees who take jobs at firms with internal labor markets often expect to spend much of their careers at the same firm. Thus, in considering an entry-level job, prospective employees will generally focus on their entire stream of earnings over their anticipated career path. For example, an individual might accept a job at Firm A that pays less than another job offered at Firm B if he or she anticipates faster or more reliable growth in compensation at Firm A.

The fact that individuals tend to base their employment decisions on career earnings gives firms with internal labor markets more flexibility in setting the level and time profile of pay. These firms will not need to pay the market wage rate at each point in time. Rather, compensation can vary over a career path, as long as the overall value of the earnings stream is competitive at each point in time—i.e., it is worth as much as earnings streams offered by competing firms in the labor market.

There are at least three ways in which firms can use their flexibility in setting the level and time profile of pay to enhance employee motivation. These methods are wage premiums, seniority-related pay, and tying major pay increases to promotions.

Wage Premiums

In many jobs, it is difficult to monitor employees' actions. As we discuss in Chapter 6, it is difficult to measure an employee's contribution to value, which can make it difficult to devise incentive compensation schemes that effectively motivate desired behavior. For example, manufacturing companies want production employees to work hard, but it is difficult to measure employee effort with great precision. In addition, piece rates or other output-based compensation can discourage employees from paying appropriate attention to product quality.

One way to motivate employees in these cases is to pay compensation that is *above* the market rate. Paying such a premium obviously increases labor costs. However, it can have the desirable effect of motivating employees to work harder because individuals who are paid a wage premium realize that if they are fired, they will have difficulty finding another job that offers a similar wage premium. This effect will be stronger for employees who have longer time horizons with the firm, since they have more to lose. Wage premiums also provide incentives for employees to stay with the firm, which can be particularly important when the employee has firm-specific human capital; such employees are less easily replaced.

Job seniority and pay. Compensation typically increases with seniority within the firm, in part because of the increases in productivity that come with experience. As an employee ages, however, the increases in productivity typically do not keep pace with the increases in compensation. Mandatory retirement ages served to put a cap on this disparity until amendments to the Age Discrimination Employment Act in 1978 and 1986 precluded mandatory retirement for most workers in the United States. Firms now frequently offer attractive packages to encourage older employees to retire.

One explanation for this typical pattern of productivity and compensation is that it gives employees stronger incentives to add value. When the employee is first hired, he or she is underpaid relative to his or her potential productivity, often with the understanding that the initial period of employment will serve as a training period. Over time, of course, the employee's productivity will increase as he or she becomes more experienced—but the employee's compensation will increase at a faster rate, eventually overtaking and then surpassing his or her productivity. The employee is underpaid in the early years but is willing to continue working for the firm because of the expectation of being overpaid in subsequent years. Under this compensation scheme, younger employees have incentives to make investments in firm-specific human capital and to work hard in order to avoid being fired and losing future wage premiums. Older employees continue to work hard because they are being paid more than they can earn at other firms relative to their productivity, despite any decline in their productivity in later years.

Firms with this type of compensation policy have short-run incentives to fire older employees, as these employees are being paid more than they are worth. Unjustified firings of older employees, however, are not usually in the long-run interests of such firms because they undermine the credibility of the compensation plan—younger employees will no longer believe that hard work will lead to wage premiums when they get older. Of course, firms cannot pay premiums to all older employees for an indefinite period and stay in business. To survive in a competitive marketplace, these firms will adopt policies such as attractive retirement packages to help ensure that older employees retire when they reach a certain age. Increased labor market mobility, along with the higher likelihood of layoffs in general (perhaps stemming from lower growth rates), also tends to undermine such a system.

Promotions. Firms typically have hierarchical levels, with positions at a given level paying more than positions at lower levels. Employees move up in the hierarchy through promotions based on their skills and ability. The competition for promotions can be viewed as contests or tournaments among employees. Employee productivity is then higher as they try to win these contests. Sometimes, firms actually run "horse races" among internal candidates. Under this procedure, the candidates are notified that they are competing for a job that has higher pay and prestige. General Electric ran such a horse race to fill the CEO position when Reginald Jones retired in 1981. The winner was Jack Welch. Welch's successor, Jeffrey Immelt, won in a similar horse race in late 2000. The two other GE executives in the running landed on their feet, however: W. James McNerney, Jr., was immediately picked by 3M Corporation to be its new chairman and CEO, and Robert Nardelli was tapped to become president and CEO of Home Depot.

In addition to matching people with jobs on the basis of skills and ability, promotions obviously play an important role in providing incentives within many organizations. One benefit of using a promotion-based incentive scheme is that it commits the firm to serious performance reviews of its employees. Promoting the wrong person to a job can be a costly mistake, so employers have incentives to conduct in-depth performance reviews to reduce the likelihood of making such errors. Typically, the employee with the best *relative performance* is chosen for promotion, which means that employees are less likely to be rewarded or penalized for factors beyond their control—common "shocks" that affect all the contestants in the promotion contest are filtered out of the decision (see Chapter 6).

Promotion-based schemes have several significant drawbacks, however. First, judging people on relative performance can undermine employee cooperation, and some employees might even sabotage the work of others. Second, promotions can be a rather crude tool for providing incentives because the chance for promotion occurs only at occasional intervals, and the employee is either promoted or not. Monetary incentives, such as bonus payments, are more flexible. Third, the so-called Peter Principle holds that employees are promoted until they reach jobs that they cannot handle. Fourth, employees do not always value promotions. For example, research scientists and software developers often do not want higher-level administrative positions. Finally, because promotions can be based on subjective judgments rather than just on objective productivity measures, promotion contests can prompt employees to expend their time and energy in lobbying for promotions, at the expense of their work-related responsibilities.

Despite these drawbacks, promotions are used throughout the world for motivating employees, although lately the prospects for promotion in many firms have dimmed as a result of flatter management structures (the reduction in middle-management positions) and a slowing in growth rates. This development has lowered incentives for many employees, who worry that their chances for promotion are slim even if they do a good job. In response, firms have tried to restore employee incentives by adopting more explicit pay-for-performance plans. The American Productivity and Quality Center reports that 75 percent of employers in the United States have an incentive plan (such as a profit or gain-sharing plan) for rank-and-file employees and that roughly 80 percent of these plans have been adopted since 1983.

Influence Costs

Coworkers frequently compare compensation levels. Employees use information about the pay of other employees to challenge compensation decisions or to lobby for pay increases. Some managers try to minimize pay differentials to cut down on this type of influence activity, but doing so comes at a cost: Poorly performing employees are likely to be paid too much relative to more productive employees, who are likely to be undercompensated and will tend to look for better opportunities outside the firm. Of course, managers try to keep their compensation decisions confidential, but it is difficult to prevent coworkers from sharing information on their compensation, particularly in small departments or in public institutions (where public disclosure of pay levels is often mandatory).

Sometimes firms run into such problems in tight labor markets, where it is not uncommon for new hires to be paid more than the people who were recruited a few years earlier. At Price Waterhouse (now PricewaterhouseCoopers) in 1998, Scott Sanster, a strategy consultant, said, "This year, MBAs are being offered salaries and sign-on bonuses nearly 30 percent higher than what I got. It can be a real morale buster." A company spokesperson contended, "We are keeping pay increases at a level roughly equal to the increase in starting salary." Employees often feel frustrated when new hires earn more than experienced workers. Some managers downplay this problem and take the attitude that an employee who has been at the firm for only a short time is unlikely to move to a new company for a 5 to 10 percent pay increase. But other companies, in order to keep their best and brightest, are bumping up the pay of those employees semiannually or even quarterly.

To address these problems, managers often develop methods of evaluating and comparing jobs within the organization. One popular method is the Hay System. Under this system, each job within the organization is evaluated on such factors as required know-how, problem-solving skills, the number of people supervised, and accountability. Based on this evaluation, each job is assigned a total number of points and given a position within the firm's hierarchy. Jobs at a particular level in the hierarchy have similar compensation ranges. For example, jobs at one level might pay from $50,000 to $55,000, depending on the employee's experience and qualifications. While salaries reflect external market rates to some extent, emphasis is placed on internal consistency among jobs (equal pay for equal work). Internal consistency appears to reduce employee complaints about compensation policies and helps to protect the firm against liability in discrimination suits. However, relating pay to factors such as the number of employees supervised can lead to empire building by managers.

The Mix of Salary and Fringe Benefits

Most employees receive a significant amount of their compensation in the form of *fringe benefits*—compensation that is either in kind or deferred. Examples of in-kind payments are health insurance and membership in a company fitness center, where the employee receives a service instead of cash compensation. Payments to pension plans are examples of deferred compensation. For the typical American employee, about 75 percent of the total compensation package is pay for time worked, and about 25 percent is fringe benefits. Based on the cost to the employer, the most important fringe benefits are pensions, medical and life insurance, and pay for leave time (vacations and sick or other leave). Many employees also receive benefits such as company-paid education, dental care, discounted meals, and subsidized recreation programs. In a 1998 survey of more than 2000 college graduates, job benefits ranked in importance as follows: medical insurance, pension benefits, annual salary raises, and dental and life insurance.

There are many different types of fringe benefits. To attract scarce engineers and programmers, the connectivity software firm WRQ in Seattle, with 800 employees, must make its recruiting appeal heard over the "giant sucking sound" of crosstown rival Microsoft (with some 50,000 employees). Microsoft offers a stock plan that has transformed many of its employees into millionaires. WRQ offers a work environment with employee-friendly policies: team management, reasonable and flexible hours, time off for volunteer work, natural light from a ten-story atrium, massages, napping and breast-feeding rooms, and balconies overlooking the lake. Such policies have allowed WRQ to recruit more experienced people—especially more women—and to experience only half the turnover of other software companies. A former Microsoft employee now at WRQ, a man of thirty-one with a wife and a new baby, used to enjoy his work at Microsoft, but does not miss the thirteen-hour days and being on call around the clock.

By taking advantage of employee preferences for a less stressful job environment, WRQ is able to compete for talent effectively.

Employee Preferences

Salary and fringe benefits are typically not perfect substitutes from an employee's point of view. One reason is taxes—certain fringe benefits (such as health insurance) are not subject to income taxes when they are received by the employee. For example, an employee who wants to purchase an insurance policy costing $3000 would prefer that the firm provide the policy; otherwise, the employee must buy the policy with after-tax dollars (an employee in a 40 percent tax bracket would have to receive $5000 in salary to purchase the policy). Moreover, a firm may be able to provide group insurance at a lower cost per employee than individual employees would have to pay if they purchased their own insurance. The potential cost advantage of employee group health and life insurance has two main components: a broader risk pool (countering the tendency for less-healthy individuals to sign up for the most extensive coverage) and lower administrative and selling expenses. On the other hand, some employees will prefer $3000 in cash to $3000 in fringe benefits, since the cash gives them more flexibility in their spending.

In general, an employee is willing to forgo a relatively large amount of salary in exchange for additional expenditures on fringe benefits, principally because of tax considerations. However, this willingness to substitute fringe benefits for cash declines as the employee receives more fringe benefits, because the employee begins to prefer the flexibility of cash. The compensation package should be designed so as to attract and retain employees at a reasonable cost in order to maximize shareholder value.

The Choice between Salary and Fringe Benefits

It is in management's interest to listen to employee preferences concerning fringe benefits. If employees prefer a dental policy to the same amount in cash, the firm should offer the dental policy instead of cash compensation. Offering the dental policy makes the employees better off and shareholder value no lower. Indeed, employees might value the dental policy so highly that the firm can lower total compensation, thereby increasing shareholder value. (The firm might do this by reducing raises in subsequent years.)

The willingness of firms to listen to the preferences of their employees suggests that employees effectively pay for their own fringe benefits. For instance, most companies would be willing to pay higher salaries if employees did not want health insurance. Lincoln Electric, a manufacturing company in Cleveland, makes this trade-off quite transparent to employees. Employees at Lincoln receive about half of their compensation in the form of annual bonus payments. The costs of fringe benefits are taken out of this bonus payment and are shown on the employees' pay stubs. On several occasions, Lincoln employees have voted against such benefits as dental plans because the majority of employees preferred cash.

While shareholder value is generally unaffected by the decision either to pay a given amount of cash to employees or to spend the same amount on fringe benefits, there are at least two complicating factors. First, taxes at the firm level can be important. For example, the firm generally has to pay Social Security taxes on wages but not on fringe benefits, making it more attractive from the firm's standpoint to offer higher fringe benefits and lower salaries. In designing compensation packages, however, management should consider the *total* tax bill for both the employee and the firm. Reducing the joint tax liabilities means that there is more money to split between the firm and its employees.

The level of tax rates obviously affects compensation design. For example, Sweden's extremely high tax rates have led to correspondingly high levels of fringe benefits, which are not taxed by the government. So when Ford purchased Volvo AB's car division in 1999, one of the many difficulties in integrating the two companies was the difference in the fringe benefits received by the two sets of employees. Although Ford plants have fitness centers, these centers do not have the amenities offered at the Volvo plants, such as Olympic-sized pools, badminton and tennis courts, tanning beds, and saunas. Ford worried that its employees in the United States might be tempted to argue for "perk parity."

Another complication is that fringe benefits can change employee behavior in ways that affect shareholder value. For example, sick leave can increase the number of days that an employee is not at work (people take their "sick days" for reasons other than actual illness). Similarly, liberal insurance coverage can reduce employee incentives to worry about prices for medical care, thereby raising medical expenses and increasing insurance premiums. These incentive effects can help determine the appropriate compensation package. Some firms have reduced the insurance coverage that they provide to employees, for the express purpose of giving employees stronger incentives to monitor their health care expenditures and even to negotiate with doctors over price. Presumably, employees do not like to bargain with doctors and must be offered higher wages to offset this increased cost, in addition to higher wages to offset the reduced insurance coverage in the fringe benefit package. However, the overall cost to the firm will be reduced if the increase in wages is less than the savings in insurance costs.

Using fringe benefits to attract particular types of employees. Employers often care about the personal characteristics of the individuals whom they hire. For example, firms for which turnover is more costly might favor hiring people with families, since such people are less likely to quit. Alternatively, firms with intense and demanding work environments, such as investment banks in New York City, might favor hiring single people because singles are generally more willing to work long hours and to spend more time on the road. While firms are likely to bump up against antidiscrimination laws if they simply offer more money to people with families than to people without families, they can attract different types of employees through changes to the mix of fringe benefits and salary. For example, people with families want health insurance for dependents; single people do not. If the benefits package includes health coverage for dependents, people with families are more likely to apply for the job. If the benefits package provides health coverage for the employee only and the employee must pay the cost of dependent coverage, relatively more single individuals are likely to apply.

The mix of fringe benefits. This same general reasoning also applies to the mix of fringe benefits. For example, it makes sense to provide employees with disability insurance rather than dental insurance if the employees prefer disability insurance—so long as the cost to the company is the same. In this spirit, some companies have adopted menu or *cafeteria-style* benefit plans, in which individual employees allocate a fixed fringe-benefit allowance among a variety of options. The advantage of these plans is that employees do not all value particular benefits equally. If they are allowed to make their own choices, they will be more willing to work for the firm at a lower overall cost. Note that a cafeteria plan is more likely to be valued by two-career families, since one spouse can acquire dental insurance, for example, while the other obtains health insurance.

Of course, cafeteria plans are more expensive to administer. Employees must be kept informed of all their options, and an administrative system must be maintained to record employees' choices, make the required payments to suppliers, allow for changes in choices, and complete the appropriate tax forms. In addition, cafeteria plans can increase the cost of benefits, particularly with regard to health, life, and disability insurance. Individuals know more about their health than an insurance company does, and when they are free to choose, the people who are most likely to buy coverage will be those who find the insurance a good deal at the quoted price (which will include relatively more people who plan to use health care services). Thus, at any given price, the insurance company is likely to attract a clientele that causes it to lose money. The insurance company can demand physical examinations and investigate past medical records before agreeing to insure an applicant, but this increases administrative costs. Allowing employees to opt out of health insurance only if they can document that they have alternative coverage (through a spouse's plan, for example) helps to ensure that the insurance company will have both low and high health risks in the pool.

Part-Time and Temporary Employees

Firms are attempting to reduce their expenditures on benefits by relying more heavily on part-time and temporary employees. For example, part-time personnel make up a growing proportion of the workforce at United Parcel Service. Because UPS has a peak load in the morning and then again in the afternoon, hiring part-time employees gives UPS more flexibility than does taking on more full-time employees. And many part-time employees like working a part-time schedule. Such employees can frequently obtain health insurance and other benefits through a full-time spouse's package.

In contrast to part-time jobs, temporary jobs can be full time (forty hours per week), but are not necessarily considered permanent. Many companies hire temps through employment agencies to fill in when permanent employees are on extended leave or when the job is expected to be temporary. These positions usually provide fewer fringe benefits. However, some firms have run into trouble when either a "permatemp" or the government files a lawsuit. Microsoft and Time Warner have been in court over whether temps who have been in the same position for several years are entitled to the same benefits as permanent employees. Who is the real employer—the employment agency or the company employing the temp? If it is the company, the temp should be receiving pension benefits. An IRS complaint against Microsoft states that many of Microsoft's 6000 temps are really common-law employees and entitled to company pension benefits.

In summary, then, managers approach basic compensation and promotion decisions in a variety of ways, with the objective of not only attracting and retaining qualified employees but also creating incentives for employees to work productively in value-adding ways. A balance must be struck between low wages and benefits (which might appear to save money, but can lead to excessive turnover) and high wages and benefits (which limit turnover but also adversely affect the firm's ability to compete). In the next chapter, we explore incentive compensation in more detail.

CHAPTER 9

Incentive Compensation

*T*he term incentive pay *conjures up images of piece rates, commissions, and cash bonus plans, with the employee being paid on the basis of some measure of output. Broadly speaking, however, any compensation plan, either explicit or implicit, that rewards employees for good performance (or punishes them for poor performance) can appropriately be considered incentive compensation. Rewards do not have to be monetary—they can consist of anything that employees value. The fundamental purpose of incentive pay is to increase shareholder value by motivating value-adding effort on the part of the employees. A closely related purpose is to reinforce the firm's value-creation formulas and strategic objectives. In this chapter, we provide insights into how companies can design compensation plans that effectively address incentive problems. One simple approach is to give employees an ownership stake in the firm through grants of stock or stock options, although stock ownership is unlikely to provide high-powered incentives to rank-and-file employees of large organizations. The important question is how to design an incentive plan whose benefits outweigh its potential disadvantages.*

Not All Incentive Plans Work

In October 1988, DuPont's fibers division announced "one of the most ambitious pay-incentive programs in America." Its plan, adopted initially for a three-year trial period, covered nearly all of the division's 20,000 employees, including management as well as rank-and-file employees. Under the plan, a portion of the employees' pay would be placed into an "at-risk pool." If the division exceeded its profit goals for the year, the employees would receive a multiple of the at-risk monies as a bonus. If it did not, the employees stood to lose the money in the pool. The intent was to eventually place as much as 6 percent of employees' annual pay at risk. Many companies were watching this experiment carefully to see what they could learn about incentive pay. "The attention that the American business community has given to the DuPont program is tremendous," said Robert C. Gore, a vice president at Towers Perrin Company, a major compensation consulting firm.

The fibers division, which was the largest of DuPont's chemical businesses, included departments making products that ranged from automobile seat covers to apparel. In 1990, the division target was 4 percent inflation-adjusted earnings growth in order for the employees to recover their at-risk pay. But earnings for the first nine months were off 26 percent, largely because of an economic downturn and unexpectedly high input prices. Demand for the division's products had declined substantially as a result of weak housing and automobile markets, and oil prices had risen because of the Gulf War. By the fall of 1990, it was obvious that the employees, largely because of factors beyond their control, were likely to lose all the monies that had been placed in the bonus pool. Employee discontent was high. In October 1990, DuPont precipitously canceled the incentive program with more than a full year left in the trial period. In the words of the fibers division chief, "I have to conclude it was an experiment that didn't work."

Is incentive pay, as some critics claim, simply a bad idea? If so, any firm adopting a large-scale incentive plan is making a mistake and is likely to experience a fate similar to that of DuPont. We argue, however, that the failure of DuPont's scheme can be traced to basic design problems that could have been avoided by more careful planning.

Forms of Incentive Pay

More than a quarter of the employees in the U.S. manufacturing sector receive at least part of their income through incentive plans such as piece rates, commissions, and cash bonus plans based on measurable output. And many other companies use other forms of incentive compensation, such as tying promotions and salary adjustments to performance. Any compensation plan that rewards employees for good performance or punishes employees for bad performance can be considered incentive pay. Under this definition, all the following rewards or sanctions become forms of incentive compensation *when they are based on performance:*

- Piece rates and commissions
- Bonuses and profit-sharing plans
- Prizes such as vacations
- Salary revisions
- Promotions and titles
- Preferred office assignments
- Stock ownership and stock options
- Firings, demotions, and other penalties
- Deferred compensation and unvested pensions that are forfeited upon separation

It is important to remember that rewards *do not have to be monetary*. As we discuss in Chapter 3, people are motivated by many things other than money, including the intrinsic appeal of a job well done. As a general rule, of course, an individual becomes better off as his or her total pay increases, at least over some range of pay, which suggests that money can be an important means of motivation. But rewards can consist of anything employees value. When managers have little flexibility in how much money they can pay their employees, as when pay scales are rigidly defined, they can still provide incentives by rewarding more productive employees with desirable job assignments, better offices, preferred parking spaces, special honors, and trips to training sessions in attractive locations.

To combat absenteeism, for instance, an automobile company adopted a plan wherein employees were awarded points for each day that they were present at the factory. The points could be redeemed for prizes, such as tickets to popular vacation attractions. The interesting feature of the plan was that the points were given not to the employee but to the employee's spouse. Reports indicate that with the spouse helping to monitor employee attendance, the absenteeism rate declined significantly. And in another example of nonmonetary incentives, Dawson Personnel Systems attributed a double-digit increase in sales to its practice of giving employees time off for exceeding their targets. Any salesperson could leave work at 2:00 P.M. each day for the rest of the month after hitting that month's sales targets.

Incentive compensation can also include penalties for poor performance. Take the case of Stephen Wiggins, former CEO of Oxford Health Plans. Oxford, the once high-flying managed-care company, suffered a loss of $291 million in 1997. The stock price fell 80 percent from its high a year earlier. Wiggins, who had founded the company and still owned about 5 percent of the stock in the firm, took a 61 percent pay cut. All but one of the six other highest-paid executives took pay cuts, and only two of the seven executives at Oxford in 1997 were still there in 1998. And Wiggins, although still chairman of the board, was replaced as CEO. In 1998, he resigned as chairman.

The Benefits of Incentive Pay

Incentive pay serves to bring the objectives of shareholders and employees into close alignment. If the objectives of shareholders and employees were in complete accord, there would be no need to worry about incentives. Incentive problems exist within firms because shareholders and employees have different objectives. For example, shareholders of a research company want its scientists to develop marketable products, whereas the scientists might prefer to work on more interesting but less marketable ideas. Owners in general would like employees to work diligently at increasing shareholder value, but the employees might prefer a more leisurely pace and longer coffee breaks. Shareholders benefit directly from any undertaking that creates value, but employees do not, or at least not to the same degree.

In fact, an employee's well-being generally declines as his or her level of effort increases, particularly at higher levels of effort (there is such a thing as working too hard). Of course, the firm's shareholders benefit from the employees' efforts, and they benefit more as the employees work harder. Yet any firm would acknowledge that it is not sensible to have its employees work absolutely as hard as is physically possible. At some point it is more cost-effective to hire another employee than to pay what an employee would demand to work at full capacity all the time.

By directly rewarding employees for their incremental productivity, incentive pay helps to bridge the gap between the benefits to the shareholders of the employees' efforts and the drawbacks to those employees of working hard. It allows the employee to share in the results of his or her efforts. An employee who is paid a straight salary based on an expected level of productivity, with no possibility for a salary increase, will have an incentive to work only to roughly that expected level of productivity. Lower levels of productivity can result in termination, of course, but there is no particular reason to reach for higher levels of productivity. A fixed wage provides *no* incentives to work harder, since the incremental effort is not rewarded.

The Allen-Edmonds Shoe Company, a manufacturer of high-priced shoes, learned this principle the hard way. For years, Allen-Edmonds paid its factory employees on the basis of individual output through a piece-rate system. Some years ago, however, following the advice of quality experts, the company abandoned its piece-rate system and started paying employees fixed hourly wages. The intent was to encourage employees to focus on quality and teamwork, with the idea that they would work harder because they were happier on the job. But productivity plummeted as employees were observed taking more breaks and "fooling around." After the company lost $1 million, it reinstated piece-work payments. Productivity and profits immediately shot back up. An executive of the company stated, "Our people needed the discipline that the piecework system gives to them." We would suggest that the issue was one of incentives rather than of discipline.

Or consider the case of Howie Rubin. In 1983, his first year out of the Salomon Brothers training program, Rubin generated $25 million in profits in the new mortgage-backed securities business. In return, Salomon paid Rubin $90,000—the most permitted under the pay scale for a first-year trader. In 1984, his second year, Rubin made $30 million for the firm and was paid $175,000—again, the most permitted under Salomon's pay scale. This is not an insignificant level of pay, but it was clearly not commensurate with Rubin's contribution to shareholder value, nor was there any meaningful incentive mechanism. So in early 1985, Rubin moved to Merrill Lynch for a three-year package: a minimum of $1 million a year plus a percentage of his trading profits. Salomon subsequently lost much of its market share in mortgage-backed securities to other firms such as Merrill Lynch.

An interesting study of the earnings of employees in the U.S. footwear and clothing industries found that piece-rate employees on average earned 14 percent more than employees paid straight salaries, even after allowing for union status, gender, and other variables that might affect compensation. There are at least three possible reasons for this wage differential. First, people may work harder under piece rates than under fixed salaries, and so their compensation reflects the extra effort. Second, because output is affected by random factors such as equipment failures, employees who are earning piece-rate pay may require a higher *expected* level of pay to compensate for the variability in their earnings (a compensating differential for risk bearing, as we will discuss later in this chapter). A third reason is the self-selection effect discussed in the previous chapter—piece rates are likely to have greater appeal to more highly skilled and productive employees, who will earn more under piece rates than with fixed salaries.

Rewarding Multiple Tasks

Because most jobs involve a variety of tasks (see Chapter 4), it is important to tailor incentive plans to encourage productive effort across an assortment of activities. For instance, employees on an assembly line can spend time assembling parts, improving quality, performing preventive maintenance, or helping coworkers. Managers are concerned not only with how hard employees work but also with how they allocate their time among the assigned tasks.

Motivating employees to strike the appropriate balance among tasks is not easy. To complicate matters, effort is more easily monitored and output more easily measured for some tasks than for others. Compensating employees on the basis of what is measurable encourages them to devote their efforts to those tasks at the expense of other tasks. For example, paying an assembly-line employee on the basis of parts assembled will encourage the employee to assemble more parts but to ignore quality and to avoid helping coworkers or performing maintenance. If preventive maintenance is a priority, management can reward employees for reductions in downtime. Evaluating the overall performance of an employee usually requires personal judgments (see Chapter 6), and the manager must work at developing a reputation for impartiality and objectivity. Managers can eventually obtain fairly reliable information about an employee's overall efforts and can use this information to reward good performance.

Reinforcing Strategic Objectives

Appropriately designed incentive compensation serves to bolster the interplay between the firm's organizational architecture and its strategy. After the firm has identified certain strategic objectives, those objectives should be considered in designing the incentive plan—just as they should in the assignment of decision authority and the development of performance measures. If quality is an overriding objective, then incentive compensation might be based on quality measures such as customer satisfaction (based on surveys), the percentage of product returns, the percentage of warranty claims, and the like. If cost control is a priority, the incentive plan might incorporate measures of cost reduction. But the design of incentive compensation plans depends on several important factors. A primary objective of this chapter is to provide insights into how incentive compensation can be designed to help foster corporate objectives.

In fact, if a firm has settled on a strategic course and has assigned decision authority and established performance measurement systems that are consistent with its strategic objectives, incentive compensation should fall readily into place. Employees will already know what is expected of them, and the incentive plan will serve to reinforce what they already know and motivate them to work toward achieving those goals. An important aspect of any incentive plan is that it be administratively manageable and easy to explain to employees.

Incentives from Ownership

In many cases, the simplest way to address incentive problems, even when the productivity of employees cannot be easily measured, is to make each employee an owner. This gives the employees a stake in the value they create, and they will thus make more productive choices. In the early 1980s in China, for example, each peasant family was given a long-term lease on a plot of land. The family was required to deliver a quota of produce to the government each year, but it could keep or sell any production above the quota. Over the period of these reforms, agricultural output increased by nearly 50 percent, because the families were part owners of their production.

In fact, ownership is already widespread as an incentive mechanism. A majority of the businesses in the United States are privately owned. Furthermore, about one-third of all retail sales in the United States are through franchised outlets. In franchising, the future profits of each unit are sold to franchisees, who as owners have strong incentives to maximize value. Most large companies have employee stock ownership plans, which serve not only to make the employees part owners (albeit with limited ownership stakes) but also to make them feel that they are part of the corporate team. Many companies provide grants of stock or stock options to employees at various levels of the organization, and there is evidence from the stock market that stock prices react favorably to the announcement of a new equity-based management compensation plan. Finally, the last two decades witnessed a large number of leveraged buyouts of both public firms and divisions of public firms, in which the managers became owners instead of merely employees. While some aspects of these buyouts might be controversial, the evidence nonetheless indicates that the managers operated the units more efficiently after they became owners.

But few employee or management groups have access to sufficient capital to finance the purchase of most large U.S. corporations, making significant ownership stakes infeasible in many cases. Moreover, because the separate contributions of each employee cannot be measured, joint stock ownership by employees creates an incentive for individual employees to free-ride on the productivity of other employees; the individual employee bears only a small fraction of the adverse effects of his or her lack of effort. Joint ownership also means that an individual employee is not always rewarded in full for his or her efforts, as the benefits of these efforts are spread over a large number of "owners." Finally, and perhaps most important, ownership exposes employees to random events that are beyond their control. For example, DuPont's profits were affected by changes in the oil, housing, and automobile markets. Employee ownership thus exposes employees to a greater level of risk; we discuss these effects next.

Optimal Risk Sharing

People differ in their attitudes toward risk. Some are willing to tolerate large financial risks, while others are not. Some investors are comfortable holding high-tech stocks, whereas others stick with government bonds. An efficient allocation of risk takes these different preferences into account. In addition, people are able to reduce risk to differing degrees. For example, the common stock of large corporations is typically owned by many investors, each of whom holds a well-diversified portfolio (perhaps in the form of a mutual fund). Because of this diversification, investors are not overly concerned about the fortunes of any one company. Events that are specific to individual firms tend to average out over a portfolio; that is, one firm's good luck offsets another firm's bad luck, thus dampening the overall price fluctuations of the portfolio.

Employees, in contrast, generally each have only one job and receive the bulk of their earnings from their employers; their financial well-being is thus tied quite closely to the fortunes of an individual firm. Therefore, the employees of a firm are less able to reduce firm-specific risk than are the firm's shareholders. It is not that employees' risk preferences are different from those of shareholders; rather, shareholders in large corporations are less concerned about firm-specific risk because of their ability to manage such risk through well-diversified portfolios.

Because the shareholders of the firm can diversify firm-specific risks more effectively than can employees, they are willing to bear these risks at a lower price. Thus, rather than spreading risks equally across employees and shareholders, it is more cost-effective from a risk-sharing standpoint to shift more of the risk to shareholders—and away from employees—by paying the employees fixed salaries and letting the shareholders bear the risk of random events. As we observed earlier, however, a fixed salary provides no incentive effects.

Of course, risk sharing can take an interesting twist. To return to the story of Howie Rubin, his new pay package at Merrill Lynch, which included a percentage of his trading profits, encouraged him to take highly risky positions. He benefited significantly from any trading profits, and the downside was limited—he was guaranteed his $1 million, and Merrill Lynch would absorb any trading losses. Rubin's trading positions ultimately moved against him (as they did against Enron, or Nick Leeson in the Barings case), and Merrill Lynch lost over $300 million. The design of the incentive payout was not necessarily at fault, but such a plan requires close supervision through the performance measurement system.

Effective Incentive Contracts

Our discussion up to this point suggests that compensation plans serve at least two important functions: First, they motivate employees, and, second, they spread risk more efficiently. But there is a trade-off between these two objectives. Efficient risk sharing suggests that it is better to pay employees fixed salaries. When the firm pays fixed salaries, shareholders absorb the effects of any random events and the firm avoids having to pay a compensating differential for risk to attract and retain the desired workforce. But incentive considerations suggest that it is better to tie pay to performance in order to coax more productive effort from the employees. A compensation contract must strike an appropriate balance between these two considerations. For this reason, many compensation plans consist of a fixed salary and one or more variable components based on performance. Of 735 publicly traded companies that responded to a 1998 survey, 73 percent offered performance-related variable pay in addition to a base salary for nonexecutive employees. In addition, 46 percent offered company stock options to nonexecutive employees.

In general, there are five factors that are likely to be important in weighing the trade-off between a fixed salary and incentive pay:

- The sensitivity of output to the employee's effort
- The employee's degree of risk aversion
- The level of risk that is beyond the employee's control
- The employee's response to increased incentives (the additional effort the employee will exert)
- The ability to measure the employee's output at low cost

The first factor is the sensitivity of output to additional effort from the employee, or the employee's incremental productivity. If additional effort on the part of the employee increases his or her output significantly, then more incentive pay (holding other factors constant) makes sense because the increase in value from motivating additional effort is high. A second factor is the risk profile of the employee. A highly risk averse employee will be uncomfortable with the variability in an incentive pay scheme and will probably require a higher fixed salary component to make up for the higher risk of the incentive component—although a higher fixed component increases the firm's expenses.

The third factor is the impact of events that are beyond the employee's control. When output is determined primarily by the employee's own effort, it makes sense to have higher levels of incentive compensation. But when outside forces can dramatically affect production or profits, as in the case of DuPont, incentive compensation can end up penalizing the employee unfairly. The fourth factor is how much additional effort the employee will exert as incentives are increased, or how receptive the employee is to exerting additional effort. If the employee is simply unresponsive to increased incentives, there is little reason to provide incentive pay. The final factor has to do with how easy it is to measure the employee's output. If this is very difficult, then incentive pay will not be very effective (see Chapter 6).

Performance Measurement Revisited

If an employee's contribution to shareholder value could be measured precisely, it would be relatively easy to design compensation programs that would motivate the appropriate level of effort. Some of the inefficiencies that result from incentive problems can thus be reduced by improvements in performance measurement. Although the standard indicator of an employee's effort is typically the employee's direct output, there are in reality many other ways to determine whether the employee has worked hard, as we saw in Chapter 6. For instance, by observing the increase in the price of oil and the performance of other companies and by gathering information on general business conditions, DuPont was able to determine that the employees were not responsible for the decline in profits in 1990. Appropriate use of this type of information increases the precision with which the employee's contribution to value can be measured and, when included in the compensation contract, increases the effectiveness of the incentive mechanism. In principle, the compensation plan should include a variety of indicators that provide additional information about the employee's effort—assuming that such measures are readily available.

In determining the year-end bonus for a salesperson on commission, for example, the sales manager should look at overall sales in addition to the salesperson's own results. If the salesperson's performance in a given year was poor but average sales in the company also declined substantially over the same time period, it is likely that the employee was simply affected by general market conditions. If other salespeople had great years, however, the salesperson is likely to have underperformed. Information about other employees' sales can thus be included in the compensation contract as a benchmark—that is, the contract can incorporate a *relative performance measure* (see Chapter 6).

DuPont's use of division profits in its incentive plan exposed the employees to factors beyond their control. The company could have reduced the risk imposed on its employees by incorporating other indicators into the incentive plan. For instance, rather than using an absolute performance standard (4 percent inflation-adjusted earnings growth), the target could have been set relative to the growth of other firms in the same industry. This type of contract would have avoided some of the problems that the company experienced in 1990, when employees were facing lowered compensation under the incentive plan because of circumstances beyond their control.

Alternatively, DuPont could have adjusted the earnings target to reflect external changes in market conditions. For example, the company could have adjusted division profits for the rise in oil prices due to the Gulf War. In fact, the firm might have entered financial contracts (such as futures, forwards, swaps, or options) to reduce the impact of such price fluctuations, thereby protecting both the company and the employees against price movements beyond their control.

Relative performance works both ways, however. Just as employees can be penalized for factors beyond their control, they can be rewarded for factors beyond their control as well. Many executives have profited enormously from stock options that increased in value largely because of the strength in the stock market during the 1990s. Some firms have experimented with industry stock indexes as benchmarks for their stock's performance, so that any increase in the firm's own stock is netted against the change in value of the industry index. But these plans often prove difficult to administer and hard to explain to plan participants. Current accounting rules also make index options undesirable to some firms.

Group Incentive Pay

Rather than trying to motivate employees by paying them on the basis of *their own output*, many firms base incentive pay on *group performance*. DuPont's incentive program is an example. There are at least three reasons why firms might favor group incentive plans over individual plans:

- Individual performance is often difficult to measure, whereas the performance of a group of employees can be ascertained fairly easily from the firm's internal accounting systems, which already measure the performance of business units for control purposes. Hence, these measures can also be used in administering group compensation plans at little additional cost.
- Group plans emphasize cooperation and teamwork, whereas individual incentive plans (depending on their design) motivate more self-serving actions.

- Group plans can motivate employees to monitor one another for poor performance. Mutual monitoring is beneficial because information about individual performance is often available only to coworkers.

Nonetheless, there are reasons to question whether group plans provide effective incentives—particularly when the group is quite large. In DuPont's fibers division, with its 20,000 employees, the efforts of individual employees have little discernible impact on the overall bottom line. By the same token, individual employees can slack off with no significant impairment to division profits. In this case, profit-sharing plans would appear to have limited incentive effects. Yet this is not surprising. Is it reasonable to expect that paying a janitor on the basis of overall company performance will motivate him or her to push the broom harder or to complain when other janitors slack off on their jobs? These arguments suggest that large-group incentive plans (like DuPont's) increase risk for employees but have limited benefits in terms of creating direct private incentives to exert effort.

In fact, the well-known Hawthorne experiments (see Chapter 3) illustrate how small-group incentive plans can be more effective than large-group plans. The experiments consisted of taking a small group of employees off the main assembly line, where individual employees had only minimal impact on overall productivity, and observing the effects of different working conditions on the performance of the smaller group. Changes were made to the number of hours in the work week, the number of hours in the work day, the number and duration of breaks, the time of the lunch hour, and the like. The members of the experimental group were paid on the basis of group output, as they had been on the main assembly line, only now their performance was measured by the output of a much smaller group. In such a setting, of course, individual members have a greater impact on output and so have an incentive to work harder. In fact, output increased with every change except one: It declined slightly when six five-minute breaks were introduced (the employees complained that the frequent breaks interrupted their rhythm). This finding has been naïvely attributed to the small group's willingness to cooperate whole-heartedly in the experiment because of group members' satisfaction at the attention being paid to them. We would suggest instead that it was the new high-powered financial incentives that brought about the increase in productivity.

Still, there are offsetting considerations that potentially help to explain the widespread popularity of large-group plans, particularly stock ownership plans. First, such plans increase employee awareness of the stock price performance and profitability of the company, and therefore foster a longer-term approach to value creation. By focusing on these measures, employees learn how their actions and the actions of managers affect the bottom line. For instance, employees might be less likely to complain about a corporate restructuring when they see that it increases the firm's stock price; similarly, they might feel more title to and be more enthusiastic about a new marketing campaign when the stock price increases upon its unveiling. Indeed, it probably requires quite limited stock ownership to motivate most employees to monitor the stock price on a frequent basis. Hence, these benefits can be obtained with minimal shifting of risk to the employees.

In addition, group plans may make employees less likely to take actions that will harm colleagues with whom they identify closely. Thus, when the group is eligible for incentive pay, employees may not want to lower their coworkers' pay by slacking off on the job. In this case, feelings like loyalty or guilt can motivate employees, even if they face only limited direct financial consequences from not pulling their own weight. Finally, paying employees on the basis of stock price performance and profits sends signals to employees about what is valued within the company. These signals serve to reinforce a performance-based corporate culture. To be most effective, however, stock ownership should be complemented by other features of organizational architecture that provide more direct incentives.

An Application: Telecommuting

Telecommuting, or employees working out of their homes, has been on the rise, and the trend has accelerated since the September 11, 2001, terrorist attacks on the World Trade Center and the Pentagon. Telecommuting is more prevalent in high-tech or knowledge-driven industries. The benefits of telecommuting are that (1) companies can reduce office expenses, because it is generally less expensive to reimburse an employee for a home office than to provide office space in an urban center, (2) employees avoid wasting time commuting to work, (3) firms can hire higher-quality employees at lower wages by offering them the flexibility of working out of their homes (enabling them to balance child care and career demands more easily), and (4) employees can be closer to customers (if salespeople tend to live in their sales territories). Companies are also realizing that, for business continuity reasons, it makes sense to operate out of multiple locations rather than out of one centralized facility.

At the ARO call center in Kansas City, where opportunities for telemarketers abound, employee turnover was high until ARO installed technology that permitted calls to its toll-free number to be transferred to employees working from their homes. Now, eighty-five of ARO's one hundred operators work at home—and ARO has reduced its turnover rate from as high as 60 percent to 4 percent. Cisco Systems, the computer-networking company, claims that telecommuting improves employees' productivity 25 percent and saves the company $1 million of overhead annually. In 1998, about 20 percent of IBM's 270,000 global employees spent at least two days a week working at home or visiting clients. However, not all companies enthusiastically endorse telecommuting programs. One consultant estimates that 20 percent of the programs fail; causes include resistant managers, isolated employees, and insufficient opportunities for teamwork. Telecommuters have fewer opportunities to talk shop, and informal communications ("water-cooler" chats) are reduced. IBM decided to schedule meetings and other social interactions to replace those that used to occur on an impromptu but regular basis before telecommuting took hold. Another solution used by some companies is to require telecommuters to spend at least a day or two per week at the office.

But our focus is on another potential concern with telecommuting—the problem of motivating employees to expend effort on their jobs. To analyze telecommuting, it is useful to envision the employee at home allocating time between home activities and work. The incentive to spend time on home activities is the personal satisfaction the employee obtains from playing with children, attending school functions, watching television, working in the garden, and so on. The incentive to spend extra time on work-related activities depends on the structure of the compensation plan.

Viewed in this context, there are at least two points related to telecommuting. First, it is probably even more important to provide incentive compensation to telecommuters than it is to provide it to employees who work at an office. Without sufficient incentives, employees will tend to devote more of their time to home activities in relation to work activities. Of course, the incentive compensation can take the form of a bonus plan or a promotion, rather than just commissions or piece rates. Second, the most viable jobs for telecommuting are those where output is easily measured, and thus lend themselves most readily to incentive compensation. For instance, sales jobs are often good candidates for telecommuting, since incentives can be provided by sales commissions. (In addition, synergies from having salespeople work out of a central location are likely to be relatively low.) If it is very difficult to measure employee output, it may make more sense to require the employee to come to work at a central location. This requirement has two effects. First, it makes it easier to monitor the employee's efforts. Second, it eliminates the incentive to spend time on home activities, since the employee is not physically present in the home. With fewer activities competing for their time, employees spend more time on work-related activities.

Do Incentives Work?

Throughout this chapter, we have argued that compensation plans motivate employees. While this argument is readily accepted by many people, it is not without controversy. Quality guru W. Edwards Deming has gone so far as to assert that "pay is not a motivator." In the same spirit, psychologist Alfie Kohn, in a controversial article on the merits of incentive pay, states, "Bribes in the workplace simply can't work."

But even Japanese firms, which have long been proponents of lifetime employment with relatively small differentials in pay among their employees, have moved toward merit pay systems in order to link individual performance more closely to compensation and promotions, and ultimately to shareholder value. In 1993, Honda became the first Japanese car company to adopt a plan that ties a manager's pay to achieving performance goals. In 1994, Toyota announced that it would depart from its seniority-based pay and promotion system. Mazda and Nissan announced that they were adopting merit pay systems in the summer of 1994. More recently, regulations have been changed to allow Japanese firms to pay executives with stock options.

Critics of incentive pay generally rely on two basic arguments. The first is that money does not motivate employees. As support for this view, they point out that when asked what makes a job attractive, employees usually assign a relatively low rank to money. Factors such as the nature of the work and the quality of colleagues appear to be more important. The second, more prominent criticism is that it is difficult (if not impossible) to design an effective incentive compensation plan. Support for this argument is provided by the many examples of flawed compensation plans that have produced undesirable results (including many of the plans cited in this book). Ironically, these two lines of criticism are fundamentally at odds. If money did not motivate people, incentive plans would not produce the adverse consequences that proponents of the second argument cite. In making a similar point, economist George Baker notes, "The problem is not that incentives can't work but that they work all too well."

Examples of incentives working too well can be found everywhere, even in the public sector, where money is not expected to be much of a motivating factor. To improve public education, a number of school districts have instituted cash bonuses to teachers if their school's test scores rise. However, such systems have spawned cheating among teachers to boost their ratings. In one incident, Kentucky created an annual test with a heavy emphasis on essay questions. Schools were rated on their students' test performance, along with attendance and dropout rates. But the essay questions were graded by the students' own teachers. Problems quickly surfaced. In 96 percent of the schools surveyed, independent auditors found that the grades assigned to the writing portion of the exam—which counted for 14 percent of each school's total score—were too generous by an average of 35 points on a 140-point scale. Teachers were found typing student essays. Students received tip sheets and advance copies of the test. Teachers explained questions to students during the exam. Students admitted to being coached by teachers during the test. Ed Reidy, state deputy commissioner for assessment, stated, "I operate under the assumption most people are ethical and what we need are procedures in place to catch folks when they're not." We would argue that what created the problems was a poorly designed, poorly implemented incentive program.

Certainly, it is easy to point to examples of compensation plans that have backfired in one way or another. We have done so throughout this book. Incentive plans also involve administrative costs for activities that range from measuring output to explaining the system to employees. The important question, however, is not whether incentive plans have costs—they certainly do. Rather, the question is whether it is possible to design incentive plans whose benefits exceed their costs. Examples like the Lincoln Electric Company (see Chapter 6) suggest that the answer is yes. Also, the fact that incentive plans—commissions, piece rates, bonus plans, and stock options—have survived for so long in a competitive marketplace suggests that there are net benefits to incentive pay plans (the economic Darwinism principle). The bottom line is that incentive compensation can be value enhancing if it is properly designed and implemented.

CHAPTER 10

Leadership: Initiating, Motivating, and Managing Change

*E*ffective leadership involves a great deal more than just developing an appropriate strategic vision for the company—
it is also critical to motivate people to implement that vision.
*The organizational architecture framework developed in this book can
provide insights into more effective leadership, insights that are important not only for those at the top of the organization but also for
any employee who has an opportunity to assume a leadership role or
who wants to have his or her ideas adopted within the organization.*

*A discussion of leadership must also address the question of cor-
porate ethics. Over the past decade, a great deal of public attention
has been devoted to business ethics and corporate responsibility.
Many U.S. corporations have responded by issuing formal codes of
conduct, appointing ethics officers, and instituting training programs
in ethics. But a key question is whether the desired behavior is consistent with the incentives established by the current organizational
architecture of the firm. Strategy, business ethics, and organizational
architecture are interdependent, and it is important that the firm be*

structured in such a way as to foster the behavior that the firm is espousing. To encourage employees to work toward implementation of the firm's vision with regard to both strategy and ethics, the three legs of the stool—decision authority, performance measurement systems, and reward systems—must be designed appropriately and in tandem.

Leadership is clearly important in the internal marketing of a strategic or ethical vision, but it plays an even bigger role in recognizing and then making the alterations to a firm's organizational architecture necessary to fulfill that vision—as well as in knowing when and how to work within the existing architecture rather than making too many changes at once.

Leading the Vision

When David Kearns was appointed CEO of Xerox Corporation in the early 1980s, the company faced serious problems. Between 1976 and 1982, Xerox's share of installations of new copiers in the United States had dropped from about 80 percent to 13 percent. Japanese companies—Canon, Minolta, Ricoh, and Sharp—had become major players in this market and were selling copiers at prices below Xerox's cost. A primary reason for Xerox's decline in market share was poor product quality. As Kearns put it:

> Our customer cancellations were rapidly on the rise, and our response to the problem was to try to outrun them by pushing hard to get enough new orders to offset the customers we had lost. Customers were fed up with our copiers breaking down and our service response.

Kearns reasoned that if something were not done, "Xerox was destined to have a fire sale and close down by 1990." The "only hope for survival was to urgently commit the company to vastly improving the quality of its products and services."

According to Kearns, most Xerox employees understood neither the extraordinary gravity of the problem nor the fundamental importance of improving product quality. Kearns also realized that he stood little chance of implementing his vision of increasing product quality simply by ordering thousands of employees to start focusing on quality. First, not all employees had the skills and training required to produce quality products. Second, unless the employees could be convinced that it was in their self-interest to focus on quality, it would be difficult to motivate them to alter their behavior. Certainly, Kearns did not have time to monitor each employee to see if his strategic vision was being implemented. And he faced a difficult balancing act: He feared that painting too dismal a picture would cause key people to leave the company.

Kearns initiated a plan to shift Xerox's corporate direction. He realized that many employees would oppose the kind of dramatic change that he envisioned. They might fear losing their jobs, being reassigned, or having to relocate. So Kearns first targeted a select group of key executives and convinced them of the need to improve product quality. These individuals helped to refine the quality vision and convinced other employees of the potential benefits of the change in focus. Employees throughout the company received substantial training in quality-improvement techniques. The importance of quality was emphasized at every opportunity—media releases, management speeches, signs on bulletin boards, and so forth. In addition, management stressed the potential crisis posed by Japanese competition.

Yet despite the additional training and internal publicity, the desired change in culture simply was not occurring. Kearns realized that to change employee behavior, senior management had to do more than just exhort, cajole, and plead—they had to make changes to the performance measurement and compensation systems. As Kearns says,

> Unless people get rewarded and punished for how they behave, no one will really believe that this is anything more than lip service. A widespread problem that was singled out was that people said we were still promoting and rewarding employees who weren't true believers and users of the quality process. This was creating noise in the system and sending mixed signals. It had to stop.

Kearns "put teeth in the program" by changing the criteria for promotions and compensation decisions to place a heavy weight on the employee's level of commitment to and efforts toward implementing the new focus on customer satisfaction and quality. These changes finally brought about the necessary shift in culture at Xerox.

Leadership and Decision Making

Webster's defines *leadership* as "leading others along a way, guiding." This definition suggests that there are at least two important characteristics of good leadership. First, the leader must help the organization choose the right path by developing a vision, goal, or plan. Second, the leader must help motivate people to follow that path. The popular literature on leadership stresses these two characteristics. To quote John Gardner, author of *On Leadership*, "The two tasks at the heart of the popular notion of leadership are goal setting and motivating." Since these tasks are performed by people throughout the organization, leadership is in no sense the exclusive domain of top management. Many employees assume important leadership roles in one way or another.

Vision Setting

By vision, we simply mean a strategic course of action for the firm. Sometimes leaders independently conceive a corporate vision. According to Kearns, he was among the first to envision Xerox as a quality-based organization. But senior executives do not always have all the relevant knowledge to single-handedly develop important strategic visions. In many cases, a vision emanates from the wetware of a lower-level employee or even from a person outside the firm, such as a consultant. The wetware for formulating a vision often comes from the experience of more than one individual, and firms typically try to involve many employees in the development of strategic mission statements. An important aspect of effective leadership is establishing an organizational architecture that motivates employees who have the relevant knowledge to offer value-adding proposals—to take part in vision setting. It is this view that has prompted much of the current literature on the role of managers in empowering employees to "unleash their untapped creativity."

Motivation

While an appropriate vision is important, it cannot increase shareholder value unless it is implemented. *It is often better to successfully implement a pretty good plan than to identify yet fail to implement the perfect plan.* Thus, the task of motivation is at least as important as the task of goal setting. Literature on leadership often emphasizes these motivation skills:

- "Leadership is the *process of persuasion* or example by which an individual induces a group to pursue objectives held by the leader or his or her followers."
- "I define leadership as leaders *inducing* followers to act for certain goals that represent the values and the motivations—the

wants and needs, the aspirations and expectations—of both leaders and followers."

- "The one who knows the right thing but cannot achieve it fails because he is ineffectual. The great leader *needs . . . the capacity to achieve.*"

Vision Setting: Lessons from the Enterprise

Well-run companies have a basic strategy that employees know and understand. This strategy is typically formalized in a mission statement. An exceptional mission statement is the following:

> These are the voyages of the Starship *Enterprise*. Her five-year mission: To explore strange new worlds, to seek out new life and new civilizations, to boldly go where no man has gone before.

Crew members of the *Enterprise* know exactly what they are supposed to do. If any team on the ship encountered a strange new world, what would it do? Explore it. The mission statement also tells them how to go about exploring it—boldly.

Suppose your company faces a new opportunity. Without a basic strategy, even your smartest employees will have to improvise when they encounter a new opportunity or a challenging situation. Companies could do worse than rewriting the *Star Trek* mission statement. Make the language exact, the goal specific, and your employees will make you proud.

Some argue that leaders motivate people through personal charisma, style, and inspiration. Certainly, strong emotional ties can motivate individuals to follow a leader's call to action. But while business managers may glean valuable lessons by studying the styles of inspirational leaders, charisma is a difficult quality for most people to learn.

Our framework suggests that there are other attributes of effective leadership that *can* be learned. People make choices that are in their own self-interest—they are generally more concerned about their own welfare (which can include concerns about family, colleagues, community, and so on) than they are about the welfare of the owners or shareholders of the company. From this perspective, the problem of motivating employees to follow a proposed direction or course of action is just the standard incentive problem. And our organizational architecture framework provides techniques to address it.

Decision making is often regarded as a purely intellectual exercise: Relevant alternatives are identified, analysis is conducted, and the best alternative is chosen. Implementation is treated as an afterthought. In this view, good leadership is equivalent to conducting careful analysis and initiating good proposals. Within most firms, however, conducting careful analysis and developing good proposals are important, but they are far from sufficient for effective leadership. Just because a proposal would create value is no guarantee that it will be either adopted or implemented. Good analysis alone does not motivate the implementation of new ideas in an organization. Managers often must make a concerted effort to gain the support of other employees in order for their proposals to succeed.

As we mentioned in Chapter 2, Xerox's Palo Alto Research Center (PARC) invented the first personal computer, the first graphics-oriented monitor, an early version of a hand-held computer mouse, the first word processing program for nonexpert users, the first local area communications network, the first object-oriented programming language, and the first laser printer. However, Xerox failed to capitalize commercially on any of this innovative technology. One reason was that PARC was physically removed from the rest of Xerox and apparently did not understand the importance of motivating other units in the firm (such as the marketing division) to support its technological vision. Employees at PARC were characterized as arrogant and suffering from a "we/they attitude toward the rest of Xerox." In the words of Jeffrey Pfeffer, author of *Managing with Power:*

By not appreciating the interdependence involved in a new product launch and the skills required to manage that interdependence, PARC researchers lost out on their ambition to change the world of computing, and Xerox missed some important economic opportunities. Organizations, particularly large ones, are like governments in that they are fundamentally political entities. To understand them, one needs to understand organizational politics, just as to understand governments, one needs to understand government politics.

In a similar vein, former Secretary of State Henry Kissinger offered the following observation about decision making:

> Before I served as a consultant to Kennedy, I had believed, like most academics, that the process of decision-making was largely intellectual and all one had to do was to walk into the President's office and convince him of the correctness of one's view. This perspective I soon realized is as dangerously immature as it is widely held.

Understanding Attitudes toward Change

Some people are more receptive to change than others. But it is the rare employee who will support a proposal that reduces his or her well-being. Nor is an employee likely to support a proposal enthusiastically simply because it increases shareholder value—it must also be perceived as somehow increasing the employee's well-being. For instance, if employees think that a proposal will increase the likelihood of layoffs, they will oppose the change. But they will not necessarily come right out and express their concerns about the consequences of the proposal. Instead, they might question the underlying analysis—even if they think the analysis is correct. Or they might waste time developing spurious evidence to convince others that the proposed program is unworkable. They might try to block the program by failing to do their part during its implementation. If a large number of employees in the firm engage in actions like these, the proposal is doomed.

It is not always possible to accurately gauge the personal preferences of a group of employees. But senior management can analyze how a change is likely to affect employees and make an educated guess as to how they will react. This can be done within the context of the existing organizational architecture. For instance, what decision authority do various employees currently have, and how will it be affected by the proposal? Will the performance measurement system be changed to reflect the new proposal, so that everyone is focusing on the right goals? How are employees compensated, and how will the determination of rewards change under the new proposal? If employees are paid bonuses based on divisional sales and the proposal is likely to reduce those sales (perhaps by deemphasizing certain product lines), it is reasonable to assume there will be opposition to the proposal.

Managing the Process of Change

Gaining employee support can be accomplished in several ways. First, senior management can change elements of the organizational architecture to strengthen the employees' interest in supporting a proposal. However, it is often necessary to exercise leadership within the existing architecture—not all managers are empowered to make changes in the allocation of decision authority or in the performance measurement or reward system. It may also be preferable to work within the existing organizational architecture because too-frequent changes in measurement and reward systems can discourage employees from making long-range decisions and developing effective relationships with colleagues. There are methods that managers can use to implement their proposals within the existing organizational architecture, including modifying the proposal in ways that will increase employee buy-in and marketing the proposal by communicating its benefits. Of course, these techniques can also be used in conjunction with changes in the architecture. We discuss each of these general tactics in turn.

Changing Organizational Architecture

There are two general types of changes in a firm's organizational architecture that can help gain employee support for a proposal. The first involves identifying individuals who are likely to support the proposal and giving them increased decision authority—and correspondingly reducing the decision authority of individuals who are likely to oppose the proposal. The second involves modifying the performance evaluation and reward systems so that it is in the self-interest of many employees to support the new program. David Kearns realized that he was proposing a dramatic change in the culture at Xerox, and he ultimately implemented the appropriate changes in architecture. Key managers were made responsible for improvements in quality, and the performance measurement and compensation systems were changed so as to make it in the employees' interest to work toward improving quality.

Proposal Design

Flexibility. Employees are likely to support a new proposal if its risk can be lowered. One way to reduce the risk of a proposal is to design the proposal in such a way that it can be modified easily after it is underway. A manager might suggest starting with a limited pilot program, involving only one region or a single product. If the pilot is successful, the program can be expanded. If not, it can be discontinued at low cost. A small-scale test does not commit the firm to adopting the program throughout the company—it merely gives it the option of doing so. Experiments of this type commit only limited resources while providing good estimates of the costs and benefits of a proposed action. This information is available both to the senior executives who must approve an expanded program and to the employees in other areas of the firm where the program might eventually be implemented.

Commitment. While flexibility has its benefits, it also has its disadvantages. If employees think that senior management is not committed to a particular proposal, they may be less inclined to take the proposal seriously. In addition, those employees who are against a change are more likely to try to convince senior management that the change is a bad idea. Managers can demonstrate their commitment in a variety of ways—speeches, meetings, and devoting resources to the idea. David Kearns made it quite clear that he was committed to the quality program at Xerox and that employees should take the change seriously.

Interestingly, managers in firms that are financed primarily by equity may feel less pressure to make changes that increase cash flows, since they have more flexibility to decrease cash payouts to security holders in the event of a downturn. Taking on additional debt can thus serve as a signal of management's commitment to making changes in the firm that will increase cash flows (for example, through cutting costs) so as to be able to meet the debt payments. Managers in more highly leveraged firms thus have their feet to the fire, since they risk losing their jobs if the firm becomes insolvent. This suggests that one determinant of the optimal amount of debt financing can be the desire of senior managers to indicate to employees and outside stakeholders a commitment to a course of action that will increase or maintain high cash flows.

Easing the pain. In most proposals for change, some employees gain and others lose. For instance, a plan to eliminate a tier of middle managers will make some middle managers worse off but will benefit certain line employees. Managers can incorporate provisions that offset these effects and promote support among key decision makers. For example, reassigning middle managers to report to other key managers may increase support for the proposal.

Marketing a Proposal

Employees' attitudes toward a proposed change will depend on their assessment of the expected payoffs and risk under the new proposal. The sponsor of the proposal can affect this assessment by marketing the proposal.

Careful analysis and groundwork. Because people are generally risk-averse, they are likely to oppose a new idea when they are unsure of the consequences of the proposal relative to the status quo. It is therefore important to thoroughly explain the analysis underlying the proposal and to convince key employees that the analysis is correct. Senior managers might meet with these employees to discuss the proposal and answer questions. They can give speeches on the topic, write an article for the company paper, and so on. Carefully communicating the reasons for supporting the plan can help to reduce uncertainty and thereby increase support for the proposal. Unless the proper groundwork is laid, a proposal is likely to be tabled for further study or simply rejected.

Relying on reputation. People are inclined to listen to a person with an established reputation for offering sound proposals. Past success is an indicator of analytical and organizational skills and thus portends future success. Decision makers often rely on the advice of people with established reputations. This tendency is emphasized by management scholar Henry Mintzberg:

> I found that chief executives faced complex choices. They had to consider the impact of each decision on other decisions and on the organization's strategy. They had to ensure that the decision

would be acceptable to those who influence the organization as well as ensuring that resources would not be overextended. They had to understand the various costs and benefits as well as the feasibility of the proposal. They also had to consider questions of timing. All this was necessary for the simple approval of someone else's proposal. At the same time, however, delay could cost time, while quick approval could be ill considered and quick rejection might discourage the subordinate who had spent months developing a pet project. One common solution to approving projects is to pick the man instead of the proposal. That is, the manager authorizes those projects presented to him by people whose judgment he trusts.

Successful people have strong incentives to conduct a careful analysis in order to avoid damaging their established reputations. If other employees are confident that a manager usually makes good decisions, they will view that manager's proposals as less risky and hence are more likely to offer support for those proposals. A manager with an established reputation can garner support for a proposal merely by asserting that it is a worthwhile undertaking. A proposal's sponsor can also increase support for his or her proposal by obtaining the endorsement of other managers with good reputations. If, after detailed discussions, these managers agree with the analysis, the validity of the analysis is more securely established. Moreover, their endorsement will increase support and forestall opposition throughout the organization.

Emphasizing a crisis. Another strategy for overcoming the normal preference for the status quo is to create an awareness that the current situation is worse than people realize. Employees are most likely to favor change when an organization faces a crisis—when a failure to change will put the organization in peril. Managers can promote a receptiveness to change by convincing employees that the firm's situation is grave. Kearns gained support for his quality program at Xerox by repeatedly highlighting the threat from Japanese competition. Of course, individuals are aware that a proposal's sponsor has an incentive to declare that there is a crisis, and they will not accept this argument unless it is credible. In Xerox's case, it was easy to document the decline in market share. Also, it was easy to point to other industries, such as steel and automobiles, with similar problems. The idea is to make employees less optimistic about the status quo and hence more open to change. However, this is a tactic that must be employed judiciously. If each attempt at change is justified as a response to a crisis, there is the danger of the manager being seen as crying wolf.

Organizational Power

The sponsors of some proposals have more personal power than others do to determine how a proposal affects various employees. An effective manager understands the sources of this power and how to acquire it.

Sources of Power

What are the sources of power within organizations? Corporate power does not come from the ability to force others to follow one's commands; there are no laws that require people to obey or support the wishes of others within the firm. Ultimately, power comes from the ability to make others voluntarily agree to comply with one's wishes or proposals by persuading them that it is in their interest to do so. This section discusses potential sources of power and influence.

Formal authority.   Some power comes from a person's formal position within the organization. If a manager has the right to fire, promote, and compensate an employee, then the employee obviously has an economic incentive to comply with the manager's wishes. In 1914,

Ford Motor Company paid a wage rate of $2.20 per day to factory workers, which was in line with the prevailing market rate in the Detroit area. Annual turnover at Ford was over 300 percent, with employees leaving to take jobs at different companies for slightly higher wages. Management thus had little power over its employees. If a supervisor was too demanding or too difficult, an employee would simply quit and go to work for a different firm. To combat this problem, Henry Ford increased the daily wage to $5 per day. This wage rate gave Ford tremendous power over the employees, who now wanted to keep their jobs rather than work for someone else at $2.20 per day. To quote Henry Ford:

> I have a thousand men who if I say "Be at the northeast corner of the building at four a.m." will be there at four a.m. That is what we want: Obedience.

However, the power attached to a formal position has its limits. Employees have the usual incentives to ignore their manager's wishes. Also, disgruntled employees might form a coalition to complain to the CEO that a manager is incompetent and should be replaced (a "palace revolt").

Control over budgets and resources.   Control over resources is another source of power within an organization. Some individuals have budget authority, while others decide on the allocation of office space or the priority for using copy machines. Individuals are reluctant to challenge a person who controls an important resource because they fear that doing so will affect their access to that resource. It is thus possible to increase one's organizational power by gaining control over key resources. This concept is important in deciding whether to apply for a particular job or assignment within the firm—jobs and tasks are more attractive if they provide decision authority over resources that others value. Also, an individual can create power by developing a service or product that becomes important to other people within the organization. For example, the information technology manager in a company might increase his or her personal power by offering a repair service for computers within the organization, particularly if the firm limits access to external vendors.

Control of information. Information is a particularly important resource in most organizations. The information held by any one employee depends on such factors as the employee's position, office location, social network, and specialized skills, and such information can be a source of power because of its value to others. Individuals can attempt to increase their access to information (and power) by lobbying for centrally located office space (for example, at the corporate headquarters), by developing a social network within the organization, by applying for jobs that are "in the information loop," or by volunteering for key committee assignments.

Information can give a person substantial power. For example, it would be quite difficult to fire an employee who has been the primary contact for a key customer for twenty years. That employee possesses specific information on issues ranging from company promises to customer requirements, and turnover in this position would be costly for the firm. In fact, managers sometimes get involved in projects that give them an informational advantage and thereby make themselves less replaceable.

An interesting example of the power of information comes from a French cigarette plant in the 1960s. The equipment in the plant was highly automated and subject to mechanical failures. The manuals that explained how to repair the equipment had been destroyed in a fire, and the only people who knew how to fix the machines were the maintenance engineers at the factory. This information monopoly gave the engineers enormous power. The plant could not run without the engineers, and it was impossible to replace them. Indeed, the engineers had sufficient pull to have a managing director of the company removed from his job. When new engineers were trained in the plant, they were given hands-on and verbal instruction only and instructed to destroy any notes they might have made once they mastered the techniques, so that the engineers could maintain their power.

Friends and allies. Having close personal ties with decision makers increases the likelihood that the decision makers will act on your behalf. A manager will tend to hire friends or promote them into key positions over equally qualified candidates because friends will be more supportive and more enjoyable to work with. It is not unusual for employees to do favors for other individuals within the firm (for example, providing assistance on difficult projects or filling in for them when they are on vacation) in the hope of being similarly supported in the future. Or managers will "horse trade"—the marketing manager will agree to support the manufacturing manager's new plant proposal in exchange for support for the new ad campaign. And sometimes it is possible to piggyback on the power of other people in the firm to gain support for a proposal. Claiming that a proposal is an integral part of the CEO's vision for the company makes it less likely that other employees will raise objections; they will hesitate to argue against an important initiative sponsored by the CEO.

Is Organizational Power Bad?

We have argued that managers and employees often use their personal power and political skills to motivate change within organizations. Yet words like *power* and *politics* have negative connotations for many people. Firms that survive are likely to have found ways to limit unproductive power grabs. But power and political skills have important benefits. Organizations involve people working together. Without political skills and power, leaders will be unable to implement value-adding plans, and the organization will suffer. Power and political skills are thus neither good nor bad in and of themselves. They are important attributes that can be used for either productive or unproductive purposes. Managers would be naive to think that they can be effective without these attributes. According to author and Stanford Business School professor Jeffrey Pfeffer,

> The development and exercise of power in organizations is about getting things accomplished. The very nature of organizations— interdependent, complex systems with many actors and many points of view—means that taking actions is often problematic. Failures in implementations are almost invariably failures to build successful coalitions. Although networks of allies can obviously be misused, they are nevertheless essential in order to get things done.

The Use of Symbols

Popular business literature often stresses the idea that effective leadership requires the clever use of symbols, such as role modeling, formal creeds, stories, legends, and logos. A CEO who is interested in improving customer service might take the time to talk to customers directly—and then broadcast these talks to employees through media releases and videotapes. He or she might also publicize stories about employees who have gone out of their way to serve customers. For example, Nordstrom's department stores are famous for stressing customer service and satisfaction. The vision of the Nordstrom family (who manages the firm) is to offer the customer the best in service, selection, quality, and value. The importance of customer service is impressed upon employees by frequently relating stories about sales clerks who went so far as to change a customer's flat tire in a store parking lot, pay a customer's parking ticket, or lend money to a customer who was short on cash to make a purchase. But Nordstrom's does not rely exclusively on stories of this type to motivate employees to provide customer service—it also has a comprehensive incentive system that stresses sales and customer service.

A company may also adopt formal creeds and statements to emphasize senior management's basic vision for the company. Symbols of this type are an important aspect of corporate culture in that they remind employees of what is valued in the company. A slogan like "At Ford, Quality Is Job 1" emphasizes that employees are expected to focus on quality and customer service. Given this slogan, along with other reinforcing signals from top management, Ford employees have a pretty clear idea of what is expected of them, even without formal instructions. Similarly, the slogan "Merrill Lynch: Still Bullish on America" served to reassure and inspire employees and customers alike in the wake of the terrorist attack on the World Trade Center. But again, symbols are unlikely to be effective unless they are reinforced by the firm's performance evaluation and reward systems. David Kearns came to realize this and ultimately had to change the reward system at Xerox before he could successfully implement his quality program.

Continental Airlines has also demonstrated how a change in corporate culture can be accomplished by implementing changes in all three legs of the stool and instituting effective employee communications programs. For years, morale at Continental was low as a result of layoffs, financial difficulties, and wage cuts. Colleagues bickered with one another as planes departed half full. Employees had ceased to trust management. A turnaround occurred when Continental hired a new CEO, Gordon Bethune, who initiated a four-part Go Forward plan. Since then, the airline has ranked first or second in measures such as on-time performance, baggage handling, and customer satisfaction. Bethune eliminated twenty of sixty vice presidents. He got employees involved in downsizing decisions, established a phone line to handle employee complaints, and invited employees to call his personal voice mail.

Bethune also began to measure every department on the basis of things that mattered to customers. He paid every employee an extra

$65 every month that Continental finished in the top half of the federal rankings of on-time flights and $100 if it finished first. And these checks were sent to the employee's home—they were not part of the employee's regular pay. Instead of arguing over whose job it was to deliver wheelchairs to the gate, ramp workers and gate agents began to cooperate and help customers. Mechanics began fabricating their own noncritical parts. One employee remarked, "Getting the plane off the gate isn't my job or your job, we act like it's everybody's job." *Fortune* magazine continues to rank Continental among the one hundred best companies to work for, and Continental was again named "Airline of the Year" in 2001 by the aviation industry's leading monthly trade publication, *Air Transport World*. Bethune used organizational architecture in a cohesive way to implement his strategic vision.

Ethics and Organizational Architecture

People generally have a pretty good idea of what they mean when they describe a person as "ethical." Most of us feel an emotional allegiance to the Golden Rule that urges us to treat others as we would have them treat us, and we value such qualities as honesty, integrity, fairness, and commitment to the task at hand. But should the strategy of the corporation involve ethics? And what does it mean for a corporation to behave ethically? First, we have to understand what the term *ethical* means, and then we need to see how it relates to the firm's strategy.

Ethics is an enormous subject area that has engaged some of history's best minds; moral philosophers have been debating ethics since ancient times. Yet there is no universally accepted philosophical consensus as to which behaviors are ethical and which are not. Lying, cheating, and stealing are almost universally viewed as wrong, but other behaviors or activities that are viewed by some as wrong are viewed by others as right—witness the debates over abortion, affirmative action, animal testing, the death penalty, genetically engineered crops, stem cell research, sweatshops, and the right to die, to name but a few. In these cases, there is simply no universally accepted code of ethics by which one can readily assess right and wrong.

Furthermore, when it comes to defining the ethics of public corporations, there is bound to be confusion. A corporation, after all, is simply a collection of individuals. In this sense, corporations do not behave ethically—only individuals do. Nonetheless, business ethics defines those behaviors in which employees should not engage, such as giving or taking extravagant gifts, bribing government officials, misrepresenting data, and discriminatory hiring practices. Many of these behaviors are illegal, yet legality alone is not always sufficient to frame policy. For example, using child labor in a textile mill may be legal in Pakistan, but American or European customers might object because the practice is illegal in the United States and Europe. Business norms help to codify ethics, and yet these norms can vary in different countries. A useful guide might be to think about the potential reaction if a particular business practice were reported on the front page of the newspaper.

Social Responsibility

One source of confusion is the concept of "corporate social responsibility," which is often used interchangeably with corporate ethics. In 1969, Ralph Nader and several other lawyers launched their Project on Corporate Responsibility with the following statement:

> Today we announce an effort to develop a new kind of citizenship around an old kind of private government—the large corporation. It is an effort which rises from the shared concern of many citizens over the role of the corporation in American society and the uses of its complex powers. It is an effort which is dedicated toward developing a new constituency for the corporation that will

harness these powers for the fulfillment of a broader spectrum of democratic values.

As Nader's statement suggests, the goal of some advocates of corporate social responsibility is nothing less than to change the purpose of the corporation. In Nader's view, the corporation is to be transformed from a means of maximizing investor wealth into a vehicle for using private wealth to redress social ills. The corporate social responsibility movement seeks to make business managers responsible for upholding "a broader spectrum of democratic values." Corporate support for such values could take the form of philanthropic activities, the provision of subsidized goods and services to certain segments of the community, or the expenditure of corporate resources on public projects such as education, environmental improvement, and neighborhood reclamation projects.

In contrast, many managers are inclined to endorse Nobel laureate Milton Friedman's prescription that the social mission of the corporation is "to make as much money for its owners as possible while conforming to the basic rules of society." In this view, it is more efficient for the corporation to focus on creating wealth and to let shareholders, employees, and customers undertake their own charitable efforts. By maximizing their shareholders' (or owners') wealth, corporations effectively enlarge the pool of individual (noncorporate) resources available for charity.

And yet the fundamental goal of making money is itself viewed as immoral by many advocates of corporate social responsibility. Still, the contrast between these two views is not as pronounced as it might appear. Corporations that wish to maximize shareholder value generally find that it is in their interest to devote corporate resources to constituencies such as employees, customers, suppliers, and local communities. For example, a company with a large plant in an inner city might decide that investing corporate resources and personnel to improve area schools would lead to better-trained job applicants, more productive employees, and lower-cost products. Giving money to the local university might benefit the firm by improving its research and development, increasing its access to top graduates, or enhancing cultural and educational opportunities for its employees (thereby reducing turnover). Improving the environment lowers the company's legal exposure to environmental damage claims. Maximizing shareholder value thus requires expending some of the firm's resources on important corporate constituencies in order to improve the terms of their dealings with the firm. As a result, companies will find it in their shareholders' interest to invest in social causes of various kinds. Creating shareholder value accordingly entails allocating corporate resources to all constituencies that affect the process of shareholder value creation—but only to the point at which the benefits from such expenditures do not exceed their additional costs. If the corporation maximizes the size of the pie, each constituency—including shareholders, bondholders, managers, employees, customers, suppliers, charities, and local communities—receives a larger slice.

In short, ethical behavior can help to create shareholder value. We focus on those facets of the corporate ethics problem that involve the issue of incentives, which can be resolved within the context of our organizational architecture framework. In our earlier examples of Enron, Barings Bank, and Sears Auto Centers, ethical problems arose from a lack of balance among the three legs of the stool. People may be honest in general, but the promptings of conscience and the desire to maintain a good reputation are neither universal nor constant, and they can certainly be influenced by the firm's performance measurement and reward systems.

Encouraging Ethical Behavior

Are codes of ethics effective in deterring unethical behavior? If so, how and why are they effective? The most cynical view is that a corporate code of ethics is nothing more than a document that helps the firm defend itself against charges of illegal behavior. For example, when an individual is found guilty of wrongdoing, his or her employer is also vulnerable to federal sanctions such as fines. The organization can obtain a reduction in these penalties of as much as 50 percent simply by demonstrating that it has a compliance program in place that meets the U.S. Sentencing Commission's standards. (A compliance program minimally consists of a code of ethics and a training program.)

And yet ethical codes can certainly alter employee behavior. In the first place, they clearly set out acceptable and unacceptable actions. Such codes typically emphasize the following:

- Employees must obey the law and observe statutory regulations.
- The reputation and integrity of the company in its relations with customers are of great importance.
- Employees must support the company's policies toward customers.
- Conflicts of interest between the company and the employee must be avoided.
- Confidential information gained in the course of business must not be used improperly.
- It is improper to conceal dishonesty and to protect others who are dishonest.
- Employees' dealings with other employees must be professional in all respects.
- Advice to customers should be restricted to statements about which the employee is confident.

Specifying behaviors in this way informs employees that certain behaviors can damage the reputation of the firm and that the firm will impose severe penalties on employees found engaging in such actions.

Ethical guidelines can also highlight behaviors that create value and hence will be rewarded by the firm. Corporate codes of ethics help to eliminate uncertainty about ethical standards and how to live up to them. Employees may be well versed in production techniques, but ethical behavior is generally less well defined. For example, what might have been acceptable behavior ten or twenty years ago may not be acceptable today. Social changes such as those brought about by movements as disparate as civil rights and women's rights on the one hand, and corporate restructuring on the other, have clearly altered conceptions of socially accepted behavior.

But simply having a code of ethics in place is not sufficient. To create the value-based or customer-focused organization that many companies seek to become, intangible aspects of corporate culture such as codes of ethics must be reinforced by more tangible structures. That is, the formal organizational systems that assign decision authority and measure and reward performance must all be internally consistent and designed to encourage value-adding behavior.

For example, consider the transfer pricing problem faced by a corporation with multiple divisions that buy from and sell to one another. The efforts of division managers to increase their respective divisions' profits may be at the expense of the other divisions' profits and possibly also at the expense of firmwide profits (see Chapter 7). Top management may hope that instituting a code of ethics will encourage division managers to adopt a less provincial attitude and look beyond their own self-interest. But as long as the division managers are *paid* on the basis of the profits of their own divisions, they are unlikely to drastically alter their behavior. The firm's organizational architecture will have to be redesigned to change the division managers' incentives. A common solution to the transfer pricing problem is to give divisional managers stock options with payoffs tied to the overall value of the company, in addition to bonuses for divisional performance.

It is unlikely that Sears would have experienced consumer indignation, financial penalties, and unfavorable publicity if it had anticipated the (quite predictable) incentives for dishonesty that its compensation plan would create (see Chapter 3). If the compensation plan rewards unethical behavior, then unethical behavior is exactly what the company will get. Corporations develop ethics programs in an effort to persuade employees to put the interests of the organization or its customers ahead of their own. Leadership can be equally important in this effort. But consistency in the organizational design of the firm is crucial.

Our approach accepts people's self-interest as given and rests on the principle that incentives work. It is the organizational architecture of the firm that will ultimately drive ethical behavior as well as shareholder value. Whatever the firm's objectives—strategic, ethical, or other—the organizational architecture framework provides a solid foundation for success.

CHAPTER 11

The Process of Management Innovation

*I*f history offers any guide to the future, management techniques will continue to come and go, and innovations—many of them reviving elements of older techniques—will no doubt appear. *The process of management innovation raises a number of important questions:*

- *What explains the popularity of various management techniques?*
- *Why do they often fail to produce their touted benefits?*
- *How can managers tell if a particular technique is appropriate for their firm?*
- *What can managers do to increase the likelihood that a technique will be successful?*

These questions can be addressed within our organizational architecture framework. Thinking in terms of organizational architecture can help managers evaluate the expected costs and benefits of management innovations for their own companies. The fundamental issue is that virtually all management techniques focus on a specific prob-

*lem confronting the organization and ignore the effects of the pro-
posed solution on other aspects of the firm. In terms of our
organizational architecture framework, such programs typically apply
to only one or two legs of the stool and thus leave the stool unbal-
anced. As an obvious example, a too-rigid insistence on just-in-time
principles can lead to big customer service problems; thus, managers
who adopt JIT should consider increases in staffing (and perhaps
incentive pay) in their customer service departments to accompany
the change. Our framework can help managers who are considering
a potentially valuable set of organizational changes to identify other
facets of the organization that will also require attention and corresponding adjustment. This chapter examines the general topic of management innovations—why they are popular, why some work while
others fail, and how managers can successfully change their organizational architecture.*

Management Innovations

The titles in the business section of any good bookstore these days
present an astonishing array of management prescriptions: total quality management, reengineering, benchmarking, activity-based costing,
just-in-time production, quality circles, outsourcing, Economic Value
Added, balanced scorecards, empowerment, self-directed teams, venturing, incentive compensation, cycle-time reduction, strategic alli-
ances, management by objectives, 360-degree performance reviews,
matrix organizations, downsizing, learning organizations, market-
based management, core competencies, groupware, and so on. Judging from book sales, consulting fees, and the proliferation of seminars,
the corporate thirst for managerial innovations is unquenchable.

Consider reengineering and total quality management, two of the
more popular management techniques of the 1990s. One survey of
500 U.S. managers from large companies reported that 76 percent of

the companies represented in the survey had tried TQM and 69 percent had employed some form of reengineering. These remarkable adoption rates have spawned legions of management consultants, many of whom can be counted on to claim that TQM or reengineering is essential for the success of most if not all companies. There is even a highly coveted national prize, the Malcolm Baldrige National Quality Award, which is presented each year to the most successful organizations applying the principles of TQM.

But for all their successes, a substantial number of TQM and reengineering programs have failed to live up to expectations. Press stories have described growing dissatisfaction with reengineering programs, and reports of discontent with TQM surfaced in the early 1990s. A Gallup poll of over 1200 corporate employees reported that while over half said that quality was the top priority, only one-third considered their companies' programs to be effective. A survey of 300 large companies conducted by *The Wall Street Journal* found that only 40 percent of executives were satisfied with TQM. Some companies, such as McDonnell-Douglas Aircraft and Florida Power & Light, have abandoned their TQM programs. After winning the Baldrige Award in 1990, Wallace Company filed for bankruptcy in 1992. And a study of 584 U.S., Canadian, German, and Japanese firms concluded, "Many businesses may waste millions of dollars a year on quality-improvement strategies that don't improve their performance and may even hamper it."

These mixed reviews are not confined to TQM and reengineering. Figure 11.1 shows the rise and fall of other management innovations as reflected in the percentage of published business articles mentioning a particular management technique in a given year. For example, as shown in the first graph in Figure 11.1, almost 1.5 percent of all business articles published in 1993 contained the words *total quality management* or *TQM*. The graph also shows that, after reaching a peak in 1993, mentions of TQM fell sharply. A similar pattern can

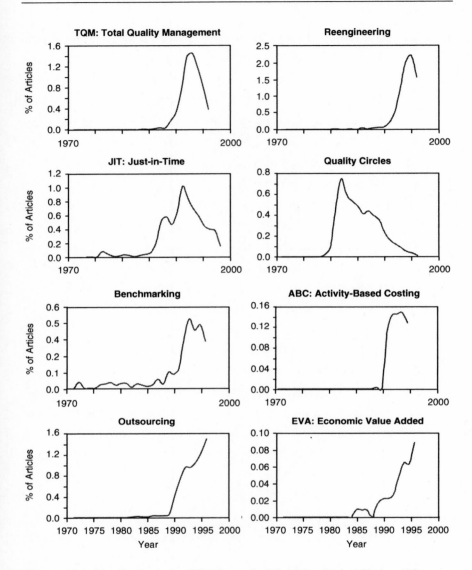

Figure 11.1 The Percentage of Business Articles Mentioning Various Management Techniques by Year

be observed for *reengineering*, which achieved peak prominence in 1995. And two management preoccupations of the 1980s, *just-in-time production* and *quality circles*, have virtually ceased to receive any press coverage. The last four graphs—*benchmarking, activity-based costing, outsourcing*, and *Economic Value Added*—cover more recent innovations. Benchmarking and ABC are starting to fade, although EVA and outsourcing continue to rise.

In reviewing the business literature of the past thirty years, we find an essentially continuous stream of articles decrying various management fads. Here are two samples from the 1970s:

> Companies have developed many special devices to meet specific needs in their executive compensation plans. But other companies, wishing to be up to date, have indiscriminately put these devices in their own plans. The results have been—to say the least— embarrassing. The fads include: see-saw options, split-dollar insurance, . . .

> Perhaps the greatest time waste of all is the casting about after fads in Organizational Development, such as constantly jumping on the bandwagons and mindlessly switching from T Group to Team Building, Transactional Analysis, Gestalt Approaches, etc.

Or consider a more recent example:

> If a manager achieves success, the world comes asking for the key to that success. Organization after organization embraces the latest management fads, of which there certainly is no shortage. . . . Total Quality Management (TQM), like so many other elixirs, did not fail for companies because the idea was bad. TQM failed because managers dealt with it superficially.

These articles all argue in one way or another that the uncritical adoption of the managerial innovation *du jour* is a prescription for disaster. Yet new management tools are being introduced and adopted continually. We believe it is helpful to understand the market for management innovations in order to make reasoned decisions about whether your organization might benefit from the newest management technique.

The Demand for Management Innovation

With the dramatic shifts in the business environment that have resulted from deregulation, rapid technological change, and more intense global competition, whole classes of firms now face new challenges. For many companies, what might once have been an appropriate architecture is beginning to show signs of wear. As a growing number of large, once-successful companies lose ground to smaller, more flexible (and in some cases overseas) competitors, the problems with poorly structured organizations are reflected in declining shareholder returns. This, in turn, increases the demand for management prescriptions that will help companies more effectively respond to a changed environment. The demand for management innovations can thus be viewed as a rational response by managers to changes that have caused aspects of their organizational architectures to become obsolete. But a successful firm in a stable business environment should be extremely cautious about undertaking radical changes in corporate strategy or organizational architecture. And not all firms will benefit from a particular management innovation.

The Rise of TQM and Other Innovations

Take the case of the broad-based adoption of TQM principles in the 1990s. Before TQM, the standard approach to ensuring product quality was to inspect it in. Inspection stations and quality-assurance inspectors were placed along the production line to weed out inferior products. Statistical sampling methods were used to analyze a random sample drawn from each batch; if an unacceptable number of bad units were detected, the entire batch would be rejected. Sections of the factory were used to store defective units that were waiting to be reworked or scrapped. In some cases, if customer demand exceeded production for some period, slightly defective products might be released under special warranty arrangements.

By the mid-1980s, two factors working together had changed this traditional approach to quality in many industries. The first was a change in technology. Improved computerized instrumentation allowed the identification and correction of problems while the product was in process. At the same time, increases in the cost of labor (including fringe benefits) made manual identification of errors considerably more expensive than doing it electronically. A second key factor in the rise of TQM was the expansion of worldwide competition. Not only were there price wars, but competition also took the form of a push for higher-quality products. Customers shifted to more reliable products—many of whose producers were based overseas. Perhaps the most dramatic case of such quality-driven competition was the auto industry in the early 1980s. Once Japanese companies gained price competitiveness against American automakers, they focused their attention on achieving quality advantages.

Thus, the total quality movement was spurred by both the lower costs of detecting defects and the increase in global competition. To reduce defects, companies redesigned their products to require fewer parts, making it easier to maintain tighter control over the quality of their suppliers. Product designers redesigned parts that failed. Production processes were changed to reduce defects. Robots and additional instrumentation were built into manufacturing to ensure more uniform production. Thus, the original insights that were reflected in a firm's (or its consultants') wetware were translated into both software and hardware in the development and implementation of TQM programs (see Chapter 3).

While many firms initiated TQM programs to improve the tangible aspects of product and service quality for external customers, these programs were eventually expanded to include efforts to improve both the quality and the efficiency of processes and services for internal customers as well. In this sense, the boundaries between TQM and other popular innovations, such as reengineering, have been somewhat blurred, as we discuss next.

Reengineering

Its proponents describe reengineering as "the fundamental rethinking and radical redesign of business processes to achieve dramatic improvements in critical, contemporary measures of performance, such as cost, quality, service, and speed." One way of distinguishing reengineering from TQM is to view reengineering as a set of major, one-time changes, as opposed to TQM's widely heralded emphasis on continuous improvement. Like that for TQM, the demand for reengineering stems from both technological changes and heightened competition in the 1980s and 1990s. We have experienced what some have called a "Third Industrial Revolution" over the past decade or two. One major by-product of this wave of technological change has been more rapid product obsolescence and, as a consequence, overcapacity in certain global industries. Many of the major restructurings, consolidations, and downsizings associated with reengineering can be seen as value-adding managerial responses to excess capacity.

JIT

Technological advances in instrumentation, computers, and telecommunications have also been a key element in the rise of just-in-time production. These advances have allowed factories to be redesigned along the continuous-flow lines required by JIT. Suppliers' computers are linked electronically to their customers' computers, and electronic order processing is commonplace. But if JIT has been made possible by technological change, its popularity also reflects a major change in market conditions. Large corporate customers increasingly are demanding that their suppliers deliver products in continuous, small-order lot sizes—in part to reduce inventories and hence to improve efficiency.

Outsourcing

As part of the process of shedding excess assets and capital in order to increase operating efficiency and shareholder value, many U.S. companies also pursued a refocusing strategy during the 1980s and 1990s. Along with selling or spinning off unrelated businesses, outsourcing of functions that were previously performed internally became a widely practiced method for sharpening corporate focus. Outsourcing involves a fundamental change in organizational architecture. It reassigns assets, decision authority, and even employees from inside the company to another firm. In 1989, Eastman Kodak sold its mainframe computers to IBM and contracted with IBM to do much of Kodak's data processing for the next ten years. Such partnerships have been prompted in part by changes in information technology that have made it easier to identify and communicate with partners outside the firm. Besides allowing management to focus more of its attention on internal activities in which it has a comparative advantage, outsourcing also enables companies to acquire goods and services from other firms at lower prices by allowing the latter to specialize and achieve economies of scale.

Why Management Innovations Often Fail

Many companies that have adopted new management techniques have been dissatisfied with the outcomes. We now explore potential explanations for this dissatisfaction—and more generally, for the tendency of successful new techniques to rise sharply in popularity and then, often just as abruptly, to fall out of favor, thus prompting skeptics to brand them as fads.

Marketing

The demand for management solutions is met by consulting firms, academics, and management gurus (and these groups are not mutually exclusive). A consultant who is working with a client firm will identify a specific set of problems and recommend a package of changes. This requires that the consultant's insights, intuition, and solutions be transformed from wetware to software that can be communicated and transferred to the client firm. If the changes appear to improve the operations of the client firm, the consultant will quite naturally try to identify and market to other potential clients who are in similar circumstances and who might benefit from similar changes.

Setting Inappropriate Expectations

One reason for the lack of success of many management techniques is that in their marketing of these management innovations, consultants create inappropriate expectations. They will claim that a particular technique can increase productivity and raise profits. However, if competing firms in the industry also adopt the technique, competition will lower prices and any abnormal profits will be eliminated by competition. As we argue in Chapter 2, an asset that competitors can replicate is not a basis for sustainable profits. Thus, while a particular management approach may be effective and productive, its adoption will not necessarily be followed by higher profits. The appropriate comparison here is not future profits versus past profits, but future profits under the new approach versus future profits with the old architecture. Thus, even a highly successful technique might result in a firm's simply avoiding losses rather than actually generating profits.

Another reason for the relative lack of success of a management innovation is the tendency of the consultants marketing it to emphasize its expected benefits while downplaying its costs. This is not to suggest that management consultants are less honest or forthright than the rest of us. But because they are proponents as well as beneficiaries of change, consultants are likely to provide detailed information on companies for which their techniques appeared to work and be somewhat less forthcoming about those whose experiences were not as favorable. And having acquired knowledge and experience in addressing a specific set of corporate issues and problems, consultants are understandably less well informed about other aspects and concerns of the organization. As we will argue later, it is the potential interdependencies among these sets of problems that frequently lead to unintended and undesired consequences when organizational changes are made.

Of course, managers recognize that consultants have incentives to present an optimistic view of their services. And most managers attempt to adjust for this bias when deciding whether, or to what extent, to implement a consultant's recommendations. But even so, the corporate failure rate in adopting management innovations would be lower if managers had a more accurate source of low-cost information at their disposal.

Quality is not free. In some instances, management consultants offer advice that simply defies logic. Perhaps the most egregious example is noted quality expert Phillip Crosby's assertion in the title of his book that *Quality Is Free*. Crosby writes,

> If you concentrate on making quality certain, you can probably increase your profit by an amount equal to 5 to 10 percent of your sales. That is a lot of money for free. . . . What costs money are the unquality things—all the actions that involve not doing jobs right the first time.

Included in Crosby's list of the costs of "not doing jobs right the first time" are unnecessary or excessive costs associated with the prevention of defects (design reviews, supplier evaluations, tool control, preventive maintenance), quality monitoring (prototype tests, receiving inspections and tests, packaging inspections), and preventable failures (including the costs of redesign, engineering change orders, rework, scrap, product warranties, and product liability).

But what does Crosby really mean when he says that quality is free? Taken literally, the statement suggests that managers can achieve substantial reductions in product failures at no cost to the organization. But this can't be the intended meaning, for, as Crosby surely knows, improving product quality clearly requires a major commitment of both management time and other corporate resources. Defects must be discovered and their causes investigated and corrected, employees must be trained in quality methods, and products must be redesigned. In fact, improving quality can be quite costly.

Rather than thinking of quality in Crosby's terms, it makes economic sense to view a TQM initiative as an investment of corporate resources with a potential future return in the form of lower costs, higher revenues, or both. Improving product quality usually lowers the cost of reworking defects, inspection costs, warranty costs, and customer complaints. And to the extent that the value of the firm's brand name is higher when product quality is improved, demand for the product and hence revenues will increase. But given the commitment of resources necessary to achieve such improvements in quality, the critical question for senior management becomes: *Does the expected rate of return justify the initial and ongoing investment, including the management effort and other costs associated with changing the organization?* Crosby asserts that the answer to this question—for all companies and for arbitrarily large commitments, as far as we can tell—is yes. We are unconvinced.

The assertion that quality is free also obscures the fact that it typically requires relatively larger investments of corporate resources to attain ever-higher levels of quality—and that at some point, the enhancements to quality will be small in comparison to the additional investment required to achieve those enhancements. This is turn implies that there is generally an "optimal," or value-maximizing, level of quality.

At relatively low levels of quality, improvements in quality lead to increases in shareholder value in two ways: by reducing production, inspection, and warranty costs and by increasing consumer demand for, and the prices commanded by, the products. But at some point, the returns on further investment in quality-increasing measures fall below acceptable levels. Ultimately, it is the company's customers who must pay for enhanced quality. The costs of additional improvements in quality will eventually exceed the premium that customers are willing to pay—as well as any further production cost savings. Value-maximizing managers will want to undertake only those quality improvements for which the incremental benefits from enhanced quality exceed the incremental costs of the quality improvement.

Perhaps one way to make sense of Crosby's statement might be to argue that managers systematically underestimate the total costs of poor quality. For example, companies that place too much emphasis on short-term financial measures might not pursue quality improvements. Or if managers are about to retire, they might be reluctant to spend money today on quality programs that will not yield benefits until after they retire. But this is just the standard horizon problem that is a factor in all decisions where expected benefits span several periods. In this sense, quality programs are no different from capital investments, R&D, or advertising. Successful firms find ways to control these horizon problems.

An alternative interpretation is that some managers fail to appreciate the costs of reduced consumer confidence in their products. They underestimate the benefits of reducing defects and thus underinvest in programs to improve quality. When this sort of myopic behavior exists, companies might benefit from educational programs focused on the importance of quality.

But regardless of whether an underemphasis on quality is attributed to ignorance or to distorted incentives, quality is still not free. Decisions to improve quality, like all corporate investment decisions, require accurate estimates of all expected costs and benefits. It is just as dangerous to underestimate the costs of quality programs by arguing that quality is free as it is to underestimate their benefits. Overinvestment in quality-improvement programs can end up destroying just as much value as can underinvestment. Management's job is to find the value-maximizing level of quality—neither too much nor too little—based on the firm's markets and internal capabilities.

Underestimating the Costs of Change

Another important reason that TQM and other management innovations can prove ineffective is that some managers underestimate the costs of change. As we have observed, changes in market conditions, technology, or government regulations can affect the firm's optimal architecture. But organizational change is by no means a costless process. In evaluating the merits of an organizational restructuring, it is important to assess its costs in addition to its benefits.

First, there are the direct costs. The new architecture has to be designed and communicated. Changes in reporting structures and performance measurement systems frequently require costly changes to the firm's accounting and information systems; what might appear to be a minor change in the performance evaluation system sometimes becomes quite a costly project for the firm's data processing and accounting departments. (Just look at the estimated costs of identifying and correcting Y2K problems.)

Second, and at times more important, there are the indirect costs. Most changes in architecture will affect some employees positively and others negatively. Thus, attitudes toward change can be expected to vary among employees, thus creating incentive problems that are costly to control. And frequent changes in architecture can have un-desirable effects on incentive. Increasing the likelihood of change re-duces employees' incentives to invest in learning their current assignments, devising more efficient production processes, or devel-oping relationships with teammates. Constant restructuring leads to a greater focus on shorter-run payoffs and less of a focus on longer-run investments. This is not a new phenomenon; the following quote has been attributed to first-century Roman author and satirist Petronius Arbiter:

> We trained hard, but it seemed that every time we were beginning to form into teams we would be reorganized. I was to learn later in life that we tend to meet any new situation by reorganizing, and what a wonderful method it can be for creating the illusion of progress while producing confusion, inefficiency, and demor-alization.

Failure to Consider Other Legs of the Stool

Perhaps the most important reason that management innovations do not succeed, however, is their failure to focus on all three components of a firm's organizational architecture. In Table 11.1 we list a set of popular management techniques along with their primary focus.

TQM.   For example, let's go back to the case of TQM. As shown in Table 11.1, TQM programs typically change both decision authority and performance measures, but leave the reward system largely un-changed. And this appears to be by design. Echoing quality guru W. Edward Deming's well-known disdain for financial incentives, Crosby argues, "People really don't work for money. They go to work for it, but once the salary has been established, their concern is ap-preciation. Recognize their contribution publicly and noisily, but don't demean them by applying a price tag to everything."

Table 11.1 Focus of Management Techniques*

Technique	Assignment of decision authority	Performance evaluation	Reward system
Total quality management	X	X	
Reengineering	X		
Outsourcing	X		
Just-in-time production	X	X	
Balanced scorecard	X	X	
Quality circles	X	X	
Benchmarking†	X	X	X
Activity-based costing		X	
Economic Value Added		X	X
Empowerment	X		
Self-directed teams	X	X	
Venturing	X		
Incentive compensation			X
Cycle-time reduction	X		
Strategic alliances	X		
Management by objectives		X	
360-degree performance reviews		X	
Matrix organizations	X		

*For each management technique, we indicate whether it focuses on decision authority, performance evaluation, or the reward system.

† Any corporate policy can be benchmarked; thus benchmarking can be applied to all parts of the organization's architecture. However, in practice firms often benchmark only one facet of the organization.

Apparently, this notion has been widely embraced. For instance, a study by the American Quality Foundation and Ernst & Young found that performance measures involving quality were not important variables in determining senior manager's compensation in 80 percent of the firms surveyed. But when decision authority is pushed down to the people with the knowledge about processes and customer preferences, it is important that companies use their reward systems to reinforce their new performance measurement systems.

Critics of incentive compensation argue that pay for performance does not work because it ends up rewarding people for doing the wrong things. And such criticism is undoubtedly correct in the sense that an ill-designed compensation system can indeed elicit undesirable behavior (remember the Sears auto centers). But this argument alone is not sufficient reason to conclude that incentive pay should be abandoned. Monetary and nonmonetary incentives are not mutually exclusive—employees clearly value both types of rewards. Appropriately linking financial incentives to the new performance measures reinforces the desired changes in behavior.

Reengineering. A similar criticism can be directed at many reengineering programs. As suggested in Table 11.1, reengineering focuses almost exclusively on a single leg of our three-legged stool: the reassignment of decision authority. Most advocates of reengineering pay lip service to the importance of the performance evaluation and reward systems, but they offer little guidance—and even in some cases inappropriate advice—on how the evaluation and reward systems must change. For example, in *Reengineering the Corporation,* Michael Hammer and James Champy are content to provide only the following advice: "Substantial rewards for outstanding performance take the form of bonuses, not pay raises." But clearly, the compensation decision is far more critical to the outcome of the change than this superficial treatment suggests.

For example, one important part of corporate performance/reward systems is promotions. By creating smaller, flatter organizations, reengineering reduces advancement opportunities. But most reengineering articles are silent about how to create new career paths and promotion systems to motivate individuals within a flatter, process-oriented organization. To increase the chances that reengineering efforts will succeed, significant managerial thought and effort must be devoted to reengineering the performance measurement and reward systems.

EVA. On the other hand, too strong a focus on performance measurement and rewards can also cause problems. Take the case of *Economic Value Added*, which attempts to make the economist's concept of residual income the basis for incentive compensation, not only for corporate executives and senior divisional managers but "all the way down to the shop floor." Such a prescription can backfire because of its failure to take into account the limited decision authority (and risk tolerance) of lower-level employees. Employees with little control over the factors that drive their business unit's EVA may find little motivation in—and in fact may be subjected to excessive risk by— such an evaluation and reward system.

ABC. As one final example, let's use our organizational architecture framework to explore why the practical achievements of another innovation listed in Table 11.1 have fallen well short of some managers' expectations. In the late 1980s and early 1990s, a new accounting system, *activity-based costing (ABC)*, appeared on the scene to great acclaim. An article in *Fortune* magazine declared, "Trim waste! Improve service! Increase productivity! But it does all that—and more."

How does ABC work? In traditional accounting systems, overhead costs are allocated to products or lines of business using very simple formulas, such as the percentage of direct labor or the percentage of total revenue. For example, suppose both riding and push lawn mowers are produced in the same plant and both types of mowers use common resources. In calculating the accounting costs of the mowers, the plant's overhead costs are allocated to the two types of mowers on the basis of the percentage of direct labor charged to each type of mower. But since direct labor may well be an unreliable indicator of the level of manufacturing overhead a given operation really generates, the traditional system may misrepresent costs. For example, the costs of more complicated products involving little direct labor but a great deal of specialized overhead resources will be understated; managers using these costs to guide pricing decisions might charge too little for such products.

Under ABC, different categories of overhead, such as purchasing, engineering, and inspection, are assigned to products on the basis of the underlying cost drivers of that overhead department. For example, purchasing department costs are allocated to different products on the basis of the quantity of purchase orders issued or the number of different parts purchased for each product. As a result, ABC is said to provide a more accurate estimate of a product's real costs and, hence, a more reliable basis for decision making than traditional overhead allocations.

But for all its theoretical appeal, the promise of ABC has largely failed to materialize. While many companies have investigated ABC systems and some have conducted pilot studies, few have abandoned their older, simpler cost allocation methods. Although some firms employ ABC-based numbers for special studies, they continue to rely on their traditional accounting systems for performance measurement. One important reason that ABC is not replacing traditional accounting systems for purposes of performance evaluation goes back to the separation of decision management and decision control (see Chapter 4). ABC systems are typically designed by operating managers, who have the greatest knowledge about the overhead cost drivers. Yet these are precisely the people whose performance is being evaluated by the ABC measures.

But it's not just the opportunity for managerial self-enrichment that makes most companies reluctant to adopt ABC for performance evaluation. It's the internal turmoil that such changes potentially unleash. Altering accounting cost allocations creates both winners and losers, and people can be counted on to struggle mightily to ensure that they are among the winners. The fact that a good deal of subjective judgment goes into determining these ABC measures means that the internal battles are likely to be long, hard-fought, and costly.

One firm implemented activity-based costing and then abandoned it after only a year. The controller explained that with the old system, which had just a few cost drivers, everyone understood the weaknesses of the system and accepted its faults. With the new system, managers were constantly arguing over the appropriate cost drivers because switching cost drivers changed product costs and thus affected managers' performance measures. Valuable management and employee time was consumed in debating the merits of particular cost drivers. To put an end to the bickering, the controller abandoned ABC.

Because ABC changes product costs and hence product-line profits, successful implementation of ABC throughout the firm requires that new profit targets be established for managers with profit responsibility. The new profit targets should attempt to eliminate any windfall gains and losses for these managers arising from the change to ABC. This requires detailed changes in compensation plans.

And while the goal of ABC is to produce more accurate product costs, doing so could actually work against the firm's business strategy. For example, suppose a firm is unionized, and reducing labor content is part of its business strategy. Changing the overhead allocation base from direct labor to, say, the number of different parts in the product will weaken managers' incentives to reduce labor content because overhead is no longer allocated on the basis on direct labor.

Take the case of a VCR manufacturing plant owned by Hitachi, the Japanese electronics producer. Even though this plant is highly automated and the managers know that direct labor is not an adequate overhead cost driver, Hitachi continues to allocate overhead on the basis of direct labor to reinforce the managers' commitment to further automation. The "tax" on direct labor via cost allocations is one way to accomplish this aim, thereby lowering production costs.

In sum, one of the main reasons ABC has failed to achieve widespread adoption is that it changes only one of the three legs of the firm's organizational architecture—the performance evaluation system. Without complementary changes in decision authority and performance rewards (such as establishing new profit targets in compensation plans), there is no reason to believe that firm performance will be enhanced.

Managing Changes in Architecture

Our point in insisting that changes in architecture be coordinated is not that all facets of the firm's architecture must be changed simultaneously. Rather, we suggest that it is important to understand the entire set of policies that must be changed and to develop a plan for implementing that set of changes. An effective plan for implementing a major reorganization will often call for changes to be accomplished sequentially—perhaps in stages—rather than all at once.

To use an analogy, a good golf pro knows that there are about thirty different factors that have to come together for him or her to be able to hit a perfect shot—factors such as grip, stance, take-away, position at top, swing plane, release, tempo, and follow-through. After watching a new pupil hit only a few balls, the pro will observe at least a dozen things that are not quite right. But rather than tell the pupil to think about a dozen things at once, a good teacher will identify the major problem and focus the pupil's attention on fixing that one aspect of the game. In future lessons, the other problems will be addressed in turn. The pro knows that asking someone to think about too many things at once will make it virtually impossible for that person to hit the ball. Thus, to produce better shots, the pro plans a sequence of lessons that, over time, will correct the problems and improve the student's game.

Fostering major change within an organization frequently requires the same approach. Telling employees that everything is going to be changed at once can create uncertainty, anxiety, and confusion—with the result that productivity suffers. Moreover, most senior managers simply do not have the resources to oversee a massive organizational overhaul. Identifying the organization's major problem and focusing employees' attention on changing that one facet of the organization is difficult enough. After that change is digested, additional changes can be instituted.

Sequencing Organizational Changes at GM

Choosing the appropriate sequence for implementing organizational changes can be quite important. Consider the case of General Motors's attempts to implement additional outsourcing after it had previously adopted just-in-time inventory policies. When GM announced that it was planning to outsource more of its activities, workers at the Dayton brake plant went out on strike. Because of the recently adopted JIT program, which had sharply reduced brake inventories, it took only a week for GM's auto production throughout North America to be severely curtailed. The walkout by this local union's 3000 members idled over 43,000 GM workers and closed twelve assembly plants.

In effect, the JIT program had substantially increased the local union's bargaining power. Under its old policy, GM would have had an inventory of brakes sufficient to meet production demands for several months, thus giving the company more time to negotiate without affecting overall auto production.

This view of the process of organizational change suggests that corporate executives should understand their basic business environment and have a good sense of the kinds of organizational changes that are required in order to enhance performance. To help them get a better sense of the entire set of changes, they might retain a consulting firm for assistance. But again, it is important to recognize that consulting firms naturally specialize in certain problems and techniques. And while management might benefit from this expertise, costly problems can arise from the consulting firms' lack of experience in dealing with issues involving changes in facets of the organization that are outside their area of expertise.

Organizational Change Checklist

When analyzing business problems and challenges, managers often find it useful to ask themselves the following set of questions:

- Does our existing business strategy fit the business environment (technology, market conditions, and regulation) and the capabilities of our firm?
- What are the key features of our current architecture? And does our architecture fit our business environment and strategy?
- Are the three legs of the stool mutually consistent? Given the decision authority system, do the control and reward systems fit, and vice versa?
- If the answers to any of the previous questions suggest a problem, what changes in strategy and architecture should our firm consider?
- What problems will our firm face in implementing these changes? What can be done to increase the probability of success?

These policy choices represent fundamentally difficult organizational decisions. There are limited public data on internal organizational policies across firms—in part because this information is not easy to gather and summarize and in part because management considers it proprietary. The various dimensions of the problem suggest that these policy choices are inherently complex. When making such decisions, information costs are high and errors are potentially substantial. Thus, it is useful to recall Yogi Berra's observation: "You've got to be careful if you don't know where you're going, because you might not get there." We believe that our organizational architecture framework can provide a more detailed understanding of "where you're going"—it focuses your attention and thus helps you frame better questions. The answers are not always easy. But by asking better, more focused questions and structuring a more complete, coherent analysis, our framework helps to ensure that you will in fact "get there."

Sources

Chapter 1

Portions of this chapter were published in J. Brickley, C. Smith, and J. Zimmerman, "The Economics of Organizational Architecture," *Journal of Applied Corporate Finance*, 8(2): 19–31, 1995. The importance of the three organizational features that we collectively call organizational architecture has been recognized by a number of authors in economics and management. For instance, see M. Jensen and W. Meckling, "Specific and General Knowledge, and Organizational Structure," *Journal of Applied Corporate Finance*, 8(2): 4–18, 1995; P. Milgrom and J. Roberts, *Economics, Organization and Management* (Englewood Cliffs, N.J.: Prentice-Hall, 1992); and D. Robey, *Designing Organizations* (Burr Ridge, Ill.: Richard D. Irwin, 1991). Enron material is from *Business Week*, "At Enron, 'The Environment Was Ripe for Abuse,'" February 25, 2002. Barings quotes are from *The Wall Street Journal*, Mar. 6, 1995, p. A1; and *Financial Times*, Feb. 28, 1995, p. 17. The Daiwa Bank case was written up in *The Wall Street Journal*, Sept. 22, 1995, p. A2. The grounded airplane example is from M. Hammer and J. Champy, *Reengineering the Corporation: A Manifesto for Business Revolution* (New York: Harper Business, 1993). The section on economic Darwinism draws on the analysis in A. Alchian, "Uncertainty, Evolution, and Economic Theory," *Journal of Political Economy*, 58: 211–221, 1950; G. Stigler, "The Economics of Scale," *Journal of Law and Economics*, 1: 54–71, 1951; and E. Fama and M. Jensen, "Separation of Ownership and Control," *Journal of Law and Economics*, 26: 301–325, 1983. The Coke and Pepsi example is from *Business Week*, Nov. 17, 1997, p. 50. The Just for Feet example is from *Business Week*, July 20, 1998, pp. 70–71. The Tianjin Optical example is from *The Wall Street Journal*, Sept.

15, 1999, p. A26. The fads quote is from *The Wall Street Journal*, July 6, 1993, p. A1.

Chapter 2

Details of the ITT/O. M. Scott example are from G. Baker and K. Wruck, "Organizational Changes and Value in Leveraged Buyouts: The Case of the O. M. Scott & Sons Company," *Journal of Financial Economics*, 25(2): 163–190, 1989. The Keidanren quote comes from a report on its Web site—http://www.Keidanren.or.jp/—while the quote from the German beer executive comes from *The Wall Street Journal*, June 21, 2001, p. A1. The evidence on the valuation effects of LIFO versus FIFO is from S. Sunder, "Optimal Choice between LIFO and FIFO," *Journal of Accounting Research*, 14(2): 277–300, 1976. The example of Dell computers designed for First Union Capital Markets Group is from *Fortune*, May 11, 1998, pp. 58–70. Some of the Wal-Mart details are from *The Wall Street Journal*, Sept. 6, 1998, p. B1. The Kraft Lunchables example is from the *Democrat and Chronicle* (Rochester, N.Y.), July 19, 1999, p. 1F. The McDonald's example is from *The Wall Street Journal*, Sept. 30, 1999, p. B1. P. Romer's analysis and quote was published in "Roundtable on the Soft Revolution: Achieving Growth by Managing Intangibles," *Journal of Applied Corporate Finance*, 11(2): 9, 1998. Xerox's Palo Alto Research Center was written up in J. Pfeffer, *Managing with Power* (Boston: Harvard Business School, 1992). The Sharp example is from D. Collis and C. Montgomery, *Corporate Strategy* (Chicago: Irwin, 1997). The Polaroid example is from *Fortune*, Nov. 12, 2001, p. 44. The paper industry example is from a Stern Stewart EVA roundtable in *Journal of Applied Corporate Finance*, 7(2): 46–70, 1994. The Kodak CD-ROM example is from the *Democrat and Chronicle* (Rochester, N.Y.), Nov. 2, 1997. The JC Penney example is from *The Wall Street Journal*, May 8, 1986, p. A1.

Chapter 3

The section on converting knowledge into value builds upon the discussion by P. Romer in "Roundtable on the Soft Revolution: Achieving

Growth by Managing Intangibles," *Journal of Applied Corporate Finance*, 11(2): 9, 1998. The Cholach Chariot example is from S. Frangos with S. Bennett, *Team Zebra* (Essex Junction, Vt.: Oliver Wight Publications, 1993). The section on general versus specific knowledge draws on F. Hayek, "The Use of Knowledge in Society," *American Economic Review*, 35: 519–530, 1945; and M. Jensen and W. Meckling, "Specific and General Knowledge, and Organizational Structure," *Journal of Applied Corporate Finance*, 8(2): 4–18, 1995. The number of résumés on the Internet is from the *Democrat and Chronicle* (Rochester, N.Y.), July 19, 1999, p. 1F. The General Electric example is from *Business Week*, Sept. 17, 1984, p. 62. The Sears example is from *Financial Times*, "Customers on Target," Aug. 18, 1995. The Apple Computer example is from *Business Week*, June 7, 1993, pp. 54–57. The Trilogy Software example is from *The Wall Street Journal*, Sept. 21, 1998, p. A1. The Lincoln Electric example is from a 1975 Harvard Business School Case 376-028 by N. Fast and N. Berg, "The Lincoln Electric Company." The software bug example is from *The Wall Street Journal*, May 22, 1995, p. A12. The section on alternative models of behavior draws on material in W. Meckling, "Values and the Choice of the Model of the Individual in the Social Sciences," *Schweizerische Zeitschrift für Volkswirtschaft und Statistik*, 112: 545–560, 1976. The Hawthorne example is from H. Parsons, "What Happened at Hawthorne?" *Science*, 183: 922–932, 1974. The example of the workers in Siberia is from *The Wall Street Journal*, July 1, 1998, p. A1. The MasterCard example is from *The Wall Street Journal*, Aug. 20, 1997, p. B6. The Bank of Credit & Commerce International example is from *The Wall Street Journal*, Mar. 1, 1999, p. A1. The quote regarding RJR Nabisco is from B. Burrough and J. Helyar, *Barbarians at the Gate: The Fall of RJR Nabisco* (New York: Harper & Row, 1990).

Chapter 4

Details of the Honda example are from C. Chandler and P. Ingrassia, "Just as U.S. Firms Try Japanese Management, Honda Is Centralizing," *The Wall Street Journal*, Apr. 11, 1991; M. Williams, "Redesign of

Honda's Management Faces First Test with Unveiling of New Accord," *The Wall Street Journal*, Sept. 1, 1993; and E. Thornton, L. Armstrong, and D. Woodruff, "Honda: A Heckuva Time to Switch Drivers," *Business Week*, Aug. 31, 1998. The source for the information on Kodak's Zebra Team is S. Frangos with S. Bennett, *Team Zebra* (Essex Junction, Vt.: Oliver Wight Publications, 1993). The quote from Alfred Sloan is from A. Sloan, "The Most Important Thing I Ever Learned about Management," *System*, p. 124, 1924. The source for Häagen-Dazs is *Business Week*, Sept. 7, 1998, pp. 56–57. The source for Bombardier is *The Wall Street Journal*, June 30, 1998, p. A15. Our discussion of how decentralization varies by type of firm draws on A. Christie, M. Joye, and R. Watts, "Decentralization of the Firm: Theory and Evidence," *Journal of Corporate Finance* (forthcoming). Sources for McKinsey are J. Katzenbach and D. Smith, *The Wisdom of Teams* (Boston: Harvard Business School, 1993) and McKinsey.com (1999). The source for Cypress Semiconductors is *Fortune*, June 17, 1991, p. 46. The source for Hallmark is *Fortune*, Sept. 22, 1992, pp. 92–98. The source for Eaton is *The Wall Street Journal*, Sept. 8, 1997, p. A1. The source for Monsanto is *The Wall Street Journal*, Feb. 23, 1998, p. B1. The source for Compuware is *Business Week*, July 5, 1999, pp. 74–84. The source on English guild auditors is E. Boyd, "History of Auditing," in R. Brown (ed.), *History of Accounting and Accountants* (New York: A. M. Kelley, 1968), p. 79; and R. Watts and J. Zimmerman, "Agency Problems, Auditing, and the Theory of the Firm: Some Evidence," *Journal of Law & Economics,* 26: 613–633, 1983. The source for Reynolds Tobacco is B. Burrough and J. Helyar, *Barbarians at the Gate: The Fall of RJR Nabisco* (New York: Harper & Row, 1990), p. 58. The case on joint CEO and board chair is from *USA Today*, Apr. 22, 1993; and J. Brickley, J. Coles, and G. Jarrell, "Leadership Structure: Separating the CEO and Chairman of the Board," *Journal of Corporate Finance,* 3: 189–220, 1997. The material on influence costs draws on the analysis in P. Milgrom, "Employment Contracts, Influence Activities and Efficient Organization Design," *Journal of Political Economy,* 96: 42–60, 1988. The section on decision management and control draws on the analysis in E. Fama and M. Jensen, "Separation of Ownership and Control," *Journal of Law & Economics,* 26: 301–326, 1983. As an example of the standard treatment of the topic of centralization versus decentralization, see R. Kaplan and A. Atkinson, *Advanced*

Management Accounting (Englewood Cliffs, N.J.: Prentice-Hall, 1989). Also see M. Jensen and W. Meckling, "Specific and General Knowledge, and Organizational Structure," *Journal of Applied Corporate Finance,* 8(2): 4–18, 1995; and A. Christie, M. Joye, and R. Watts, "Decentralization of the Firm: Theory and Evidence," *Journal of Corporate Finance* (forthcoming). For a more technical discussion of these issues, see S. Athey, J. Gans, S. Schaefer, and S. Stern, "The Allocation of Decisions in Organizations," working paper, Stanford University, Palo Alto, Calif., 1994; M. Aoki, "Horizontal vs. Vertical Information Structure of the Firm," *American Economic Review,* 76: 971–983, 1986; J. Cramer, "A Partial Theory of the Optimal Organization of Bureaucracy," *Bell Journal of Economics,* 11: 683–693, 1980; J. Marshak and R. Radner, *The Economic Theory of Teams* (New Haven, Conn.: Yale University Press, 1972); and R. Sah and J. Stiglitz, "Committees, Hierarchies and Polyarchies," *Economic Journal,* 98: 451–470, 1988.

Chapter 5

Details of the IBM Credit example are from M. Hammer and J. Champy, *Reengineering the Corporation: A Manifesto for Business Revolution* (New York: Harper Business, 1993); and M. Hammer and J. Champy, "The Promise of Reengineering," *Fortune*, May 3, 1993, pp. 94–97. The Adam Smith discussion is from A. Smith, *The Wealth of Nations* (1776; reprint, New York: Modern Library, 1937), p. 4. The source for the Cadillac example is W. Davidow and M. Malone, *The Virtual Corporation* (New York: Harper Business, 1993). The discussion of the development of the railroad industry is from A. Chandler, Jr., *The Visible Hand: The Managerial Revolution in American Business* (Cambridge, Mass.: Belknap Press, 1977). The source for the oil company example is H. Armour and D. Teece, "Organizational Structure and Economic Performance," *Bell Journal of Economics,* 9: 106–122, 1978. The source for the Intel case is A. Dhebar, "Intel Corporation: Going into Over Drive," Harvard Business School Case 9-593-096, 1993. The source for the Xerox case is D. Kearns and D. Nadler, *Prophets in the Dark* (New York: Harper Business, 1992), pp. xv–xvi. The source for the GTE example is T. Stewart, "Reengineering: The Hot New Management Tool," *Fortune*,

Aug. 23, 1993, pp. 40–48. The quote from Alfred Chandler is from A. Chandler, Jr., *Strategy and Structure* (Garden City, N.Y.: Doubleday, 1966), pp. 382–383. For a more detailed discussion of matrix organizations, see W. Baber, *Organizing for the Future* (Tuscaloosa: The University of Alabama Press, 1983). For a discussion of network organizations, see W. Baker, "The Network Organization in Theory and Practice," in N. Nohria and R. Eccles (eds.), *Networks and Organizations* (Boston: Harvard Business School, 1992), pp. 397–429. The study of organizational communication is from N. Andreeva, "Do the Math—It *Is* a Small World," *Business Week*, Aug. 17, 1998, pp. 54–55.

Chapter 6

Details of the Lincoln Electric example are from N. Fast and N. Berg, "The Lincoln Electric Company," Harvard Business School Case 376-028, 1975; and Lincoln Electric's financial reports. The source for the information on Japanese car makers is R. Johnson, "Advance or Perish, Honda Tells Managers," *Automotive News*, Mar. 18, 1994. The automobile engine assembly plant example is from R. Kaplan and A. Sweeney, "Peoria Engine Plant (A)," Harvard Business School Case 9-193-082, 1993. The source for the information on laundromats is R. Ho, "Is There a Place for the Blockbuster of Coin Laundries?" *The Wall Street Journal*, July 7, 1998. The source for the information on mining is E. Lawler and J. Rhode, *Information and Control in Organizations* (Santa Monica, Calif.: Goodyear Publishing, 1976), pp. 87–88. The source for the information about Prudential is L. Scism and S. Paltrow, "Prudential's Auditors Gave Early Warnings about Sales Abuses," *The Wall Street Journal*, July 7, 1998, p. A1. Evidence on multibank holding company turnover is from D. Blackwell, J. Brickley, and M. Weisbach, "Accounting Information and Internal Performance Evaluation: Evidence from Texas Banks," *Journal of Accounting and Economics,* 17: 331–358, 1994. Information on CEO pay is from R. Gibbons and K. Murphy, "Relative Performance Evaluation for Chief Executive Officers," *Industrial and Labor Relations Review,* 43: 30S–51S, 1990; and "The New Age of Villainy," *PC Magazine*, Sept. 27, 1988. The Hawthorne experiments are written up in H. Parsons, "What Happened at Hawthorne?"

Science, 183: 927, 1974. The information on W. L. Gore & Associates is from J. Lopez, "A Better Way?" *The Wall Street Journal Supplement,* Apr. 13, 1994, p. R6. Information on the Society for Human Resource Management survey is from T. Schellhardt, "It's Time to Evaluate Your Work, and All Involved Are Groaning," *The Wall Street Journal,* Nov. 19, 1996. The Merck survey is from K. Murphy, "Performance Measurement and Appraisal: Motivating Managers to Identify and Reward Performance," in W. Bruns (ed.), *Performance Measurement, Evaluation, and Incentives* (Boston: Harvard Business School, 1992), pp. 37–62. The Fiat example is from K. Merchant and A. Riccaboni, "Evolution of Performance-Based Management Incentives at the Fiat Group," in W. Bruns (ed.), *Performance Measurement, Evaluation, and Incentives* (Boston: Harvard Business School, 1992), pp. 63–96. The information on Levi Strauss is from R. Mitchell, "Managing by Values," *Business Week,* Aug. 1, 1994, p. 50; and R. King, "Levi's Factory Workers Are Assigned to Teams and Morale Takes a Hit," *The Wall Street Journal,* May 20, 1998, p. A1. The Mercer Management survey and following are from E. Neuborne, "Companies Save, but Workers Pay," *USA Today,* Feb. 25, 1997, p. 1B. The ratchet effect is discussed in A. Leone and S. Rock, "Empirical Tests of Budget Ratcheting and Its Effect on Managers' Discretionary Accrual Choices," *Journal of Accounting and Economics,* 33(1): 43–67, 2002. For a more formal treatment of the principle of measuring output more precisely when incentive compensation is involved, see P. Milgrom and J. Roberts, *Economics, Organizations, and Management* (Englewood Cliffs, N.J.: Prentice-Hall, 1992), p. 226. The section on problems with subjective performance evaluation draws on material in C. Prendergast and R. Topel, "Discretion and Bias in Performance Appraisals," *European Economic Review,* June 1993, pp. 355–365; C. Prendergast and R. Topel, "Favoritism in Organizations," *Journal of Political Economy,* 104: 958–978 (1996); and J. Medoff and K. Abraham, "Experience, Performance, and Earnings," *Quarterly Journal of Economics,* 95: 703–736 (1980). The Japanese performance evaluation example is from N. Hatvany and V. Pucik, "Japanese Managerial Practices and Productivity," *Organizational Dynamics,* 13, 1981. Also, M. Aoki, *Information, Incentives and Bargaining in the Japanese Economy* (Cambridge: Cambridge University Press, 1988).

Chapter 7

Details of the CSX example are from S. Tully, "The Real Key to Creating Wealth," *Fortune*, Sept. 20, 1993, pp. 38–50. EVA is a registered trademark of Stern Stewart & Co., Inc. Material in the section on measuring divisional performance draws on the analysis in M. Jensen and W. Meckling, "Divisional Performance Measurement," in M. Jensen, *Foundations of Organizational Strategy* (Cambridge, Mass.: Harvard University Press, 1998), pp. 345–361. The information on transfer pricing and taxes is from S. Wrappe, K. Milani, and J. Joy, "The Transfer Price Is Right," *Strategic Finance*, July 1999, pp. 39–43; M. Scholes, M. Wolfson, M. Erickson, E. Maydew, and T. Shevlin, *Taxes and Business Strategy* (Upper Saddle River, N.J.: Prentice-Hall, 2002). Dual transfer pricing systems and Hewlett-Packard are both discussed in I. Springsteel, "Separate but Unequal," *CFO,* August 1999, pp. 89–91. The discussion of Eastman Gelatine is from A. Klein, "Who Knew Kodak Would Keep So Many Skeletons in Its Closet?" *The Wall Street Journal*, Jan. 18, 1999, p. A1. For a more detailed discussion of residual income, see D. Solomons, *Divisional Performance: Measurement and Control* (Burr Ridge, Ill.: Richard D. Irwin, 1968). Material in the section on transfer pricing draws on J. Brickley, C. Smith, and J. Zimmerman, "Transfer Pricing and the Control of Internal Corporate Transactions," *Journal of Applied Corporate Finance,* 8: 60–67, 1995. Material in the section on accounting and performance measurement draws on the analysis in J. Zimmerman, *Accounting for Decision Making and Control* (Burr Ridge, Ill.: McGraw-Hill, 2002). For a more complete discussion of the Nirvana fallacy, see H. Demsetz, "Information and Efficiency: Another Viewpoint," *Journal of Law & Economics,* 12: 1–22, 1969. The management survey is given in S. McKinnon and W. Bruns, *The Information Mosaic* (Boston: Harvard Business School, 1992).

Chapter 8

Details of the RKO example are from S. Shimer, under the supervision of G. Baker, "RKO Video, Inc.: Incentive Compensation Plan," Harvard Business School Case 9-190-067, 1993. Material in the section on human capital draws on the analysis in G. Becker, *Human Capital* (Chicago:

University of Chicago Press, 1983). The source for the Pratt & Whitney case is J. White, "How a Creaky Factory Got Off the Hit List, Won Respect at Last," *The Wall Street Journal*, Dec. 26, 1996, p. A1. For an expanded discussion of compensating differentials, see R. Ehrenberg and R. Smith, *Modern Labor Economics,* 3d ed. (Glenview, Ill.: Scott Foresman, 1988), chapter 8. The source for the information on compensating differentials for working at night is S. King and H. Williams, "Shift Work Pay Differentials and Practices in Manufacturing," *Monthly Labor Review,* 108: 26–33, 1985. The source for the Bridgestone Tire case is A. Nomani, "Muffed Mission: Labor Secretary's Bid to Push Safety Runs into Skepticism," *The Wall Street Journal*, Aug. 19, 1994, p. A1. Sources for examples of company efforts to retain employees are A. Bernstein, "We Want You to Stay. Really," *Business Week*, June 22, 1988, pp. 67–72; and B. Wysocki, "Retaining Employees Turns into a Hot Topic," *The Wall Street Journal*, Sept. 8, 1997. The source for professionals becoming personal trainers is K. Helliker, "They Left Professions for a True Calling as Personal Trainers," *The Wall Street Journal*, Feb. 25, 1999, p. A1. The source for the Nucor case is N. Perry, "Here Come Richer, Riskier Pay Plans," *Fortune*, Dec. 19, 1988, p. 58. For further reading on implicit employment contracts, see S. Rosen, "Implicit Contracts," *Journal of Economic Literature,* 23: 1144–1175, 1985. The source of the information on Japanese internal labor markets is M. Aoki and R. Dore (eds.), *The Japanese Firm* (Oxford: Oxford University Press, 1994). For further reading on which types of firms use internal labor markets, see P. Doeringer and M. Piore, *Internal Labor Markets and Manpower Analysis* (Lexington, Mass.: D. C. Heath, 1971). The source for the Mitsubishi case is B. Bremner and E. Thornton, "Mitsubishi: Fall of a Keiretsu," *Business Week*, Mar. 15, 1999, pp. 86–92. For a more detailed analysis of paying premium wages, see G. Akerlof, "Gift Exchange and Efficiency Wages: Four Views," *American Economic Review,* 74: 78–83, 1984; C. Shapiro and J. Stiglitz, "Equilibrium Unemployment as a Worker Discipline Device," *American Economic Review,* 74: 433–444, 1984; and J. Yellen, "Efficiency Wages Models and Unemployment," *American Economic Review,* 74: 200–208, 1984. Material in the section on job seniority draws on the analysis in E. Lazear, "Why Is There Mandatory Retirement?" *Journal of Political Economy,* 87: 1261–1284, 1984. The source for the Price Waterhouse case is T. Schellhardt, "Rookie Gains in Pay Wars Rile Veterans," *The Wall Street Journal*, June 4, 1998. Material in the section on promotions draws on the analysis in E. Lazear and S. Rosen, "Rank Order Tournaments as Optimal Labor Contracts," *Journal of Political Economy*, 89: 841–864, 1981. For more information on the drawbacks of promotion-based schemes, see G. Baker, K. Murphy, and M. Jensen, "Compensation and Incentives: Practice and Theory," *Journal of Finance*, 43: 593–616, 1988. The source for the GE CEO case is R. Vancil, *Passing the Baton* (Boston: Harvard Business School, 1987). For a more detailed discussion of the Hay system, see G. Milkovich and J. Newman, *Compensation* (Burr Ridge, Ill.: Richard D. Irwin, 1993), chapter 4. Material in the section on the salary–fringe benefit mix draws on the analysis in R. Ehrenberg and R. Smith, *Modern Labor Economics*, 3d ed. (Glenview, Ill.: Scott Foresman, 1988), chapter 11. The survey ranking job benefits was reported in *The Wall Street Journal*, May 5, 1998, p. A1. The source for the WRQ case is "Rooms with a View and Flexible Hours Draw Talent to WRQ," *The Wall Street Journal*, Aug. 13, 1997. The source for the Volvo case is A. Latour, "Detroit Meets a 'Worker Paradise,'" *The Wall Street Journal*, Mar. 3, 1999. Sources for examples on part-time and temporary workers are M. Phillips, "Part-Time Work Issue Is Greatly Overworked," *The Wall Street Journal*, Aug. 11, 1997; and A. Bernstein, "When Is a Temp Not a Temp?" *Business Week*, Dec. 21, 1998, pp. 67–72. The American Productivity and Quality Center data are from N. Perry, "Here Come Richer, Riskier Pay Plans," *Fortune*, Dec. 19, 1988, pp. 50–58. The study on length of service with one employer was reported in J. Aley, "The Myth of the Job Hopper," *Fortune*, Sept. 19, 1994, p. 32.

Chapter 9

The information on DuPont is from L. Hays, "All Eyes on Du Pont's Incentive Program," *The Wall Street Journal*, Dec. 5, 1988, p. B1; and R. Koening, "Du Pont Plan Linking Pay to Fibers Profit Unravels," *The Wall Street Journal*, Oct. 25, 1990, p. B1. The information on Allen Edmonds Shoe is from B. Marsh, "Allen-Edmonds Shoe Tries 'Just-in-Time' Production," *The Wall Street Journal*, Mar. 4, 1993, p. B2. The survey on piece rates comes from E. Seiler, "Piece Rate vs. Time Rate: The Effect of Incentives on Earnings," *Review of Economics and Statistics*, 66: 363–376, 1984. The information on Oxford Health Plans comes from R. Winslow, "Wiggins, Ex-CEO of Oxford Health, Took 61% Cut in Total Pay Last Year," *The Wall Street Journal*, May 4, 1998. The information on the automobile attendance plan and Dawson Personnel Systems comes from R. Ehrenberg and R. Smith, *Modern Labor Economics* (Glenview, Ill.: Scott Foresman, 1988), p. 417; and S. Shellenbarger, "Work and Family," *The Wall Street Journal*, Dec. 29, 1999, p. B1. Information on CEO bonuses based on achieving individual performance targets is from R. Bushman, R. Indejejikian, and A. Smith, "CEO Compensation: The Role of Individual Performance Evaluation," *Journal of Accounting and Economics*, 21: 161–193, 1996. The information on Chinese agriculture is from J. McMillan, *Games, Strategies, and Managers* (New York: Oxford University Press, 1992), pp. 96–98. The information on Kentucky school testing is from B. Stecklow, "Kentucky's Teachers Get Bonuses, but Some Are Caught Cheating," *The Wall Street Journal*, Sept. 2, 1997, p. A1. The information on Cisco Systems is from A. Tergesen, "Making Stay-at-Homes Feel Welcome," *Business Week*, Oct. 12, 1998, pp. 155–156. The ARO example is from "Since Attacks, Big Offices Lose Appeal," *International Herald Tribune*, Oct. 30, 2001, p. 1. Data on incentive pay in the manufacturing sector are from J. McMillan, *Games, Strategies, and Managers* (New York: Oxford University Press, 1992), p. 93. The forms of incentive compensation emanate in part from G. Baker, M. Jensen, and K. Murphy, "Compensation and Incentives: Practice versus Theory," *Journal of Finance*, 43: 593–616, 1988. Material in the section on measuring multiple tasks draws on B. Holmstrom and P. Milgrom, "Multitask Principal-Agent Analysis: Incentive Contracts, Asset Ownership, and Job Design," *Journal of Law, Economics and Organization*, 7: 24–52, 1991. Evidence on managerial performance in buyouts is from S. Kaplan, "The Effects of Management Buyouts on Operating Performance and Value," *Journal of Financial Economics*, 24: 217–254, 1989. Material in the section on performance measurement draws on B. Holmstrom, "Moral Hazard in Teams," *Bell Journal of Economics*, 13: 324–340, 1982. The percentages of firms offering performance-related pay and company stock options were provided by Kevin J. Murphy based on his analysis of the American

Compensation Association data. The Kohn quote is from A. Kohn, "Why Incentive Plans Cannot Work," *Harvard Business Review,* September–October 1993, pp. 54–63. The Baker quote is from G. Baker, "Rethinking Rewards," *Harvard Business Review,* November–December 1993, pp. 44–45. Evidence on stock price reactions to equity-based compensation plans is from J. Brickley, S. Bhagat, and R. Lease, "The Impact of Long-Range Compensation Plans on Shareholder Wealth," *Journal of Accounting and Economics,* 7: 115–129, 1985.

Chapter 10

The Xerox example is from D. Kearns and D. Nadler, *Prophets in the Dark* (New York: Harper Business, 1992). The Gardner quote is from J. Gardner, *On Leadership* (New York: Free Press, 1990), p. 11. The quotes on motivation are taken, respectively, from J. Gardner, *On Leadership* (New York: Free Press, 1990), p. 1; J. Burns, *Leadership* (New York: Harper & Row, 1978), p. 19; and R. Nixon, *Leaders* (New York: Warner Books, 1982), p. 5. The information on vision setting is from D. Marinaccio, *All I Really Need to Know I Learned from Watching Star Trek* (New York: Crown Publishers, 1994). The Pfeffer quote is from J. Pfeffer, *Managing with Power* (Boston: Harvard Business School, 1992), p. 8. The Kissinger quote is from H. Kissinger, *The White House Years* (Boston: Little, Brown, 1979), p. 39. The Mintzberg quote is from H. Mintzberg, "The Manager's Job: Folklore and Fact," *Harvard Business Review*, July–August 1975, pp. 49–61. The Ford example is from D. Halberstam, *The Reckoning* (New York: Avon Books, 1986); and S. Meyer, *The Five Dollar Day: Labor, Management, and Social Control in the Ford Motor Company, 1908–1921* (Albany: State University of New York Press, 1981). Information on management entrenchment is from A. Shleifer and R. Vishny, "Management Entrenchment: The Case of Manager-Specific Investment," *Journal of Financial Economics,* 25: 123–139, 1989. The information on the French tobacco company is from M. Crozier, *The Bureaucratic Phenomenon* (Chicago: University of Chicago Press, 1964). The Pfeffer quotation on power is from J. Pfeffer, *Managing with Power* (Boston: Harvard Business School, 1992), p. 8.

The information on Nordstrom is from H. Weston, *Nordstrom: Dissension in the Ranks*, Harvard Business School Case 9-191-002, 1991. The Xerox Palo Alto Research Center example is from J. Pfeffer, *Managing with Power* (Boston: Harvard Business School, 1992), pp. 38–39. The disciplinary effect of debt financing is discussed in M. Jensen, "Agency Costs of Free Cash Flow, Corporate Finance, and Takeovers," *American Economic Review*, 76: 323–329, 1986. Portions of the material on ethics were published in C. Smith, "Economics and Ethics: The Case of Salomon Brothers," *Journal of Applied Corporate Finance*, 5(2): 23–28, 1992; and J. Brickley, C. Smith, and J. Zimmerman, "Ethics, Incentives, and Organizational Design," *Journal of Applied Corporate Finance*, 7(2): 20–30, 1994. Some of the Continental Airlines details are from *The Wall Street Journal*, May 15, 1996, p. A1. The quote on the Project for Social Responsibility is from J. Collins, "Case Study—Campaign to Make General Motors Responsible," reprinted in T. Donaldson and P. Werhane (eds.), *Ethical Issues in Business: A Philosophical Approach*, 6th ed. (Englewood Cliffs, N.J.: Prentice-Hall, 1979), p. 90. The material on social responsibility draws on M. Jensen and W. Meckling, "Can the Corporation Survive?" *Financial Analysts Journal*, 34: 31–37, 1978; and J. Brickley, "Managerial Goals and the Court System: Some Economic Insights," *Canada-United States Law Journal*, 13: 79, 1988. Material in the section on sources of power draws on the analysis in J. Pfeffer, *Managing with Power* (Boston: Harvard Business School, 1992). The Ralph Nader quote is reprinted in T. Donaldson and P. Werhane (eds.), *Ethical Issues in Business: A Philosophical Approach*, 6th ed (Englewood Cliffs, N.J.: Prentice-Hall, 1979), p. 90. The quote on organizational power is from J. Pfeffer, *Managing with Power* (Boston: Harvard Business School, 1992), p. 108.

Chapter 11

The quotes on management fads are from *Financial Executive*, August 1973, pp. 58–66; *Personnel*, March/April 1977, pp. 26–33; and *Business Quarterly*, Summer 1996, pp. 11–13. The Crosby quote is from P. Crosby, *Quality Is Free* (New York: Mentor, 1980), p. 1. The information on Hitachi is from T. Hiromoto, "Another Hidden Edge—Japanese Management Accounting," *Harvard Business Review,* 66: 22, 1988. For firms' use of ABC systems, see A. Sullivan and K. Smith, "What Is Really Happening to Cost Management Systems in U.S. Manufacturing," *Review of Business Studies,* 2: 51–68, 1993; R. Cooper, R. Kaplan, L. Maisel, E. Morrissey, and R. Oehm, "From ABC to ABM," *Management Accounting,* November 1992, pp. 54–57; and *Cost Management Update,* a newsletter published by the Cost Management Group of the National Association of Accountants, Inc., January 1991. The survey results on the number of companies trying TQM or reengineering were reported in "Missions Possible," *The Globe and Mail* (Toronto, Canada), Sept. 13, 1994, p. B22. The Gallup poll findings were reported in *The Wall Street Journal,* Oct. 4, 1990, p. B1. The survey results on levels of satisfaction with TQM were reported in *The Wall Street Journal,* July 6, 1993, p. A1. The study of U.S., Canadian, German, and Japanese firms was reported in *The Wall Street Journal,* Oct. 10, 1992, p. B7. The reengineering quote is from M. Hammer and J. Champy, *Reengineering the Corporation: A Manifesto for Business Revolution* (New York: Harper Business, 1993), p. 32. Michael Jensen refers to the "Third Industrial Revolution" in his 1993 paper entitled "The Modern Industrial Revolution, Exit, and the Failure of Internal Control Systems," *Journal of Finance,* 48: 831–880. The study by the American Quality Foundation and Ernst & Young was reported in *Fortune,* Oct. 8, 1993, p. 68. Our discussion of reengineering draws on M. Hammer and J. Champy, *Reengineering the Corporation: A Manifesto for Business Revolution* (New York: Harper Business, 1993). Our discussion of EVA draws on J. Stern and J. Shiely with I. Ross, *The EVA Challenge* (New York: J. S. Wiley, 2001). The ABC quote is from *Fortune,* June 14, 1993, pp. 124–129. The Yogi Berra quote is from Y. Berra, *The Yogi Book* (New York: Workmen Publishing Co., 1998), p. 102.

We refer the reader who would like additional, more technical material on any of the topics in this book to our textbook, *Managerial Economics and Organizational Architecture*, 2d ed. (New York: McGraw-Hill/Irwin, 2001).

For Further Reading

Chapter 1

Alchian, A. "Uncertainty, Evolution, and Economic Theory." *Journal of Political Economy,* 58: 211–221, 1950.

Jensen, M. "Organization Theory and Methodology." *The Accounting Review,* 58: 319–339, 1983.

Jensen, M., and W. Meckling. "Specific and General Knowledge, and Organizational Structure." *Journal of Applied Corporate Finance,* 8(2): 4–18, 1992.

Chapter 2

Baker, G., and K. Wruck. "Organizational Changes and Value in Leveraged Buyouts: The Case of the O. M. Scott & Sons Company," *Journal of Financial Economics,* 25(2): 163–190, 1989.

Besanko, D., D. Dranove, and M. Shanley. *Economics of Strategy.* New York: Wiley, 2000.

Brandenburger, A., and B. Nalebuff. *Co-opetition.* New York: Doubleday, 1996.

Collis, D., and C. Montgomery. "Competing on Resources: Strategy in the 1990s," *Harvard Business Review,* July-August 1995, pp. 118–128.

Romer, P. "Bank of America Roundtable on the Soft Revolution: Achieving Growth by Managing Intangibles." *Journal of Applied Corporate Finance,* 11(2): 8–27, 1998.

Chapter 3

Hayek, F. "The Use of Knowledge in Society." *American Economic Review,* 35: 519–530, 1945.

Herzberg, F., B. Mausner, and B. Snyderman. *The Motivation to Work.* New York: John Wiley & Sons, 1959.

Maslow, A. *Motivation and Personality.* New York: Harper & Row, 1970.

Chapter 4

Fama, E., and M. Jensen. "Separation of Ownership and Control." *Journal of Law & Economics,* 26: 301–326, 1993.

Jensen, M., and W. Meckling. "Specific and General Knowledge, and Organizational Structure." *Journal of Applied Corporate Finance,* 8(2): 4–18, 1995.

Kaplan, R., and A. Atkinson. *Advanced Management Accounting.* Englewood Cliffs, N.J.: Prentice-Hall, 1989, chapter 13.

Miller, G. *Managerial Dilemmas: The Political Economy of Hierarchy.* Cambridge: Cambridge University Press, 1993.

Chapter 5

Hammer, M., and J. Champy. *Reengineering the Corporation: A Manifesto for Business Revolution.* New York: Harper Business, 1993.

Williamson, O. *Markets and Hierarchies.* New York: Free Press, 1975.

Chapter 6

Alchian, A., and H. Demsetz. "Production, Information Costs and Economic Organization." *American Economic Review,* 62: 777–795, 1972.

Baker, G. "Incentive Contracts and Performance Measurement." *Journal of Political Economy,* 100: 598–614, 1992.

Baker, G., R. Gibbons, and K. Murphy. "Subjective Performance Measures in Optimal Incentive Contracts." *Quarterly Journal of Economics,* 109: 1125–1156, 1994.

Barzel, Y. "Measurement Cost and the Organization of Markets." *Journal of Law & Economics,* 25: 27–48, 1982.

Lazear, E., and S. Rosen. "Rank Order Tournaments as Optimal Labor Contracts." *Journal of Political Economy,* 89: 841–864, 1981.

Milkovich, G., and J. Newman. *Compensation.* Burr Ridge, Ill.: Richard D. Irwin, 1993.

Milkovich, G., and A. Wigdor. *Pay for Performance.* Washington, D.C.: National Academy Press, 1991.

Prendergast, C. "The Provision of Incentives in Firms." *Journal of Economic Literature,* 37: 7–63, 1999.

Chapter 7

Eccles, R. *The Transfer Pricing Problem: A Theory for Practice.* Lexington, Mass.: Lexington Books, 1985.

Scholes, M., M. Wolfson, M. Erickson, E. Maydew, and T. Shevlin. *Taxes and Business Strategy.* Upper Saddle River, N.J.: Prentice-Hall, 2002.

Solomons, D. *Divisional Performance: Measurement and Control.* Burr Ridge, Ill.: Richard D. Irwin, 1968.

Stern, J., and J. Shiely with R. Ross. *The EVA Challenge.* New York: John Wiley & Sons, 2001.

Zimmerman, J. *Accounting for Decision Making and Control,* 4th ed. Burr Ridge, Ill.: McGraw-Hill/Irwin, 2002.

Chapter 8

Aoki, M. *Information, Incentives, and Bargaining in the Japanese Economy.* Cambridge: Cambridge University Press, 1988.

Becker, G. *Human Capital.* Chicago: University of Chicago Press, 1983.

Ehrenberg, R., and R. Smith. *Modern Labor Economics: Theory and Public Policy,* 7th ed. Reading, Mass.: Addison-Wesley, 1999, chapters 8, 9, and 11.

Chapter 9

Baker, G., M. Jensen, and K. Murphy. "Compensation and Incentives: Practice versus Theory." *Journal of Finance,* 43: 593–616, 1988.

McMillan, J. *Games, Strategies, and Managers.* New York: Oxford University Press, 1992, pp. 91–129.

Milgrom, P., and J. Roberts. *Economics, Organization, and Management.* Englewood Cliffs, N.J.: Prentice-Hall, 1992, pp. 206–247.

Chapter 10

Donaldson, T., and P. Werhane (eds.). *Ethical Issues in Business: A Philosophical Approach,* 6th ed. Englewood Cliffs, N.J.: Prentice-Hall, 1979.

Gardner, J. *On Leadership.* New York: Free Press, 1990.

Jensen, M., and W. Meckling. "Can the Corporation Survive?" *Financial Analysts Journal,* 34: 31–37, 1978.

Kearns, D., and D. Nadler. *Prophets in the Dark.* New York: Harper Business, 1992.

Nash, L. "Ethics without the Sermon." *Harvard Business Review,* November–December 1991.

Newton, L., and M. Ford. *Taking Sides: Clashing Views on Controversial Issues in Business Ethics,* 5th ed. Guilford, Conn.: Dushkin/McGraw-Hill, 1998.

Shaw, W. *Business Ethics,* 3d ed. Belmont, Calif.: Wadsworth Publishing, 1999.

Chapter 11

Baker, G., M. Jensen, and K. Murphy. "Compensation and Incentives: Practice vs. Theory." *Journal of Finance,* 43: 593–616, 1988.

Crosby, P. *Quality Is Free.* New York: Mentor, 1980.

Hammer, M., and J. Champy. *Reengineering the Corporation: A Manifesto for Business Revolution.* New York: Harper Business, 1993.

Juran, J. *Juran on Leadership for Quality.* New York: Free Press, 1989.

Juran, J., and Gryna, F. *Quality Planning and Analysis*. New York: McGraw-Hill, 1993.

Keating, S., and K. Wruck. "Sterling Chemicals Inc.: Quality and Process Improvement Program." Harvard Business School Case 9-493-026, 1994.

Lederer, P., and S. Rhee. "Economics of Total Quality Management." *Journal of Operations Management,* 12: 353–367, 1995.

Wruck, K., and M. Jensen. "Science, Specific Knowledge and Total Quality Management." *Journal of Accounting and Economics,* 18: 247–287, 1994.

INDEX

About the Authors

James A. Brickley, Ph.D., is the Gleason Professor of Business Administration at the University of Rochester's Simon Graduate School of Business. He has coauthored a number of influential books, and his work has appeared in numerous professional journals, including *The Journal of Business* and *The Journal of Finance*.

Clifford W. Smith, Jr., Ph.D., is the Louise and Henry Epstein Professor of Business Administration at the Simon Graduate School of Business. He is the author or coauthor of more than a dozen books and numerous journal articles and has served as an economist with the Securities and Exchange Commission.

Jerold L. Zimmerman, Ph.D., is the Ronald L. Bittner Professor of Business Administration at the Simon Graduate School of Business. The author or coauthor of several books, he is a founding editor of the *Journal of Accounting and Economics* and has (along with coauthors Brickley and Smith) extensive corporate consulting experience.

Janice Willett is a senior manuscript editor with the *Journal of Financial Economics* and associate editor of the *Journal of Applied Corporate Finance*.